THE PEOPLE'S ENGLISH

THE PEOPLE'S ENGLISH

a guide to the six great social classes in the United States—and, more particularly, to their speech and writing standards

James E. Hamilton

KENDALL/HUNT PUBLISHING COMPANY
Dubuque, Iowa

Grateful acknowledgment is made for permission to reprint the following selections (listed alphabetically):

From "The ACLU: What Are We Talking About?" Seattle *Argus*, Feb. 15, 1963.

From Peter Barnes, "How Wealth Is Distributed: The GNP Machine," *The New Republic*, Sept. 30, 1973, and (anon.) "Rich and Poor," *The New Republic*, Aug. 11, 1973. Reprinted by permission of *The New Republic*, © 1973, The New Republic, Inc.

From John Kenneth Galbraith, *The Affluent Society*, copyright 1958, Houghton Mifflin Co.

From Suzanne Keller, *Beyond the Ruling Class*, copyright 1963, Random House, Inc.

From Fabian Linden, "The Characteristics of Class," *The Conference Board Record*, Oct. 1973.

From Ferdinand Lundberg, *The Rich and the Super-Rich*, copyright 1968, Lyle Stuart Publishing Co.

From Russell Lynes, *A Surfeit of Honey*, copyright 1954, 1957 by Russell Lynes. By permission of Harper & Row, Publishers, Inc.

From Charles Merrill Smith, *Instant Status, or How to Become a Pillar of the Upper Middle Class*, copyright 1972, Doubleday & Company, Inc.

From W. Lloyd Warner, Marchia Meeker, and Kenneth Eells, *Social Class in America*, copyright 1963. By permission of Harper & Row, Publishers, Inc.

From John M. Wasson, *Subject and Structure: An Anthology for Writers*, 5th ed., pp. 383, 385. Copyright © 1975 by Little, Brown and Company, Inc.

From Thorstein Veblen, *The Theory of the Leisure Class*, copyright 1973, Houghton Mifflin Co.

Copyright © 1975 by James E. Hamilton

Library of Congress Catalog Card Number: 75—18075

ISBN 0—8403—1239—3

All rights reserved. No part of this publication may be reproduced, stored in a retrieval system, or transmitted, in any form or by any means, electronic, mechanical, photocopying, recording, or otherwise, without the prior written permission of the copyright owner.

Printed in the United States of America

CONTENTS

Preface vii
1. Class Structure in America 1
2. A Closer Look at the Class Structure 13
3. Lower-Lower Language 21
    Speech Patterns 24
    Grammar (sentence types, basic sentence elements, fragments, comma faults, fused sentences, mixed constructions) 25
    Usage 44
    Punctuation (question mark, exclamation point, period) 46
    Spelling 47
    Mechanics (use of numbers) 48
4. Upper-Lower Language 51
    Grammar (verbs, agreement with subject, pronoun agreement, pronoun reference and case) 53
    Usage 74
    Punctuation (semicolon) 77
    Spelling 78
    Mechanics (abbreviation, manuscript form) 79
    Composition (the paragraph) 82
5. Lower-Middle Language 89
    Grammar (adjectives and adverbs, sentence modifiers and conjunctive adverbs, misplaced elements, dangling modifiers, shifts in point of view, incomplete constructions, comparability) 90
    Usage 100
    Punctuation (comma) 104
    Spelling (rules) 110
    Mechanics (apostrophe) 114
    Composition (narration and description) 115

v

6. Upper-Middle Language 123
    Grammar (*shall, will*) 127
    Usage 129
    Punctuation (colon, dash, parentheses, brackets, quotation
       marks) 134
    Spelling 139
    Mechanics (italics, hyphen, ellipsis, capitalization) 140
    Composition (exposition, logic, argument, informal documenting) 146

7. Lower-Upper Language 167
    Grammar (*for, yet*) 169
    Style (parallelism, subordination, variety, emphasis) 170
    Usage 176
    Spelling 178
    Mechanics (the documented paper) 179
    Propaganda Analysis 202
    Composition (persuasion) 210

8. Upper-Upper Language 213
    Grammar (*that, which*) 217
    Usage (idioms, history of the language, Latin and Greek
       roots and affixes, foreign words) 217
    Style (appropriate diction, precision, economy, sounds) 224
    Spelling 231
    Composition (the literary critique, other essay types) 232

9. Some Recommendations 237

Appendix A: Business letters—including the job-application
       letter 244
Appendix B: The personal data form 248

Notes 251

Index 259

> *Full opportunity for full development is the unalienable right of all. He who denies it is a tyrant; he who does not demand it is a coward; he who is indifferent to it is a slave; he who does not desire it is dead.*
> —Eugene Debs, 1904

PREFACE

This book is far more composed than its author, who has spent twenty frustrating years trying, often clumsily and ineffectually, to improve college students' written composition and widen their understanding of English grammar, usage, and mechanics. I have decided the concepts herein have been tested long enough; these latter days occasionally bring gratifying results. My notions, moreover, seem to have acquired some solidity. This volume feels *right* to me, the way a good poker hand does. Of course, like most books, this is simply a reshuffled deck of borrowed ideas. And like most authors I must now try justifying the rearrangement.

The foundations, the deck's chief cards, are the beliefs (1) that, as many respected sociologists and economists have taught us, society is clearly class-structured; (2) that, driven by ambition, or something, representatives of all classes find their way these days to various kinds of colleges; (3) that society has a certain responsibility for each of these new students, despite the difficulties caused by their heterogeneity; (4) that this obligation requires multiple teaching and learning techniques in perhaps all fields, and (5) that this is certainly true in English composition classrooms, where there should be greatly expanded opportunities for individualized instruction and independent study.

The Table of Contents will give a hint of what's to come. About one-third, you'll find, is a sociological argument, a set of attempted solutions to rhetorical problems; about two-thirds is English handbook, with material arranged in order of increasing difficulty. The student is encouraged to go as far up the ladder as his ambition and talents will permit. The book is designed to help.

For the help I received in the idea-shuffling process, I wish to commend, first, my wife and sons, for their patience and understanding. To them the book is dedicated. Whenever I use "I" in these pages I'm forgetting their support; when I use "we" I'm remembering them.

But I also wish to thank Dr. Phyllis Harris and Ms. Orabelle Connally, colleagues at Everett Community College, for their generous assistance in reading the manuscript. (Its remaining flaws are due chiefly to my obstinacy.) The proofreading of my wife, Anne, also caught many errors. For all of this aid I am very grateful.

J.E.H.
Everett, Wash.
1975

> *Experience declares that man is the only animal which devours his own kind, for I can apply no milder term . . . to the general prey of the rich on the poor.*
> —Thomas Jefferson, 1787

CHAPTER 1
CLASS STRUCTURE IN AMERICA

The United States, some say, is virtually a classless society; it has escaped the fate of ancient cultures with entrenched hereditary aristocracies. According to this view, the nation was born democratic and class-free, and our yeasty social mobility has kept it that way—that is, much too fluid for classifications.

Now, it's possible that this squares with your thinking, too. Perhaps you've never thought of yourself as, say, middle class, or indeed a tenant of any class. For the purposes of this book, however, it's time to think it through.

Let's begin with some basic economic facts. If you'll recall your U.S. history, you'll perhaps remember that indentured or bonded servants, some of them blacks and Indians and felons, were common in America from the earliest colonial days.[1] Maybe, as Crèvecoeur thought, the "rich and poor are not so far removed from each other as they are in Europe,"[2] but it wasn't really very difficult to tell an apprentice shoemaker from a prospering Boston tobacco merchant, and both from a well-to-do Maryland planter. Distinct socioeconomic classes did exist—topped by many of the Founding Fathers in their powdered wigs, silken breeches, and silver-buckled shoes. We can be grateful that not all of the Revolution's statesmen were rich and arrogant. Indeed, some, like James Madison of Virginia, had a sane suspicion of the aristocracy: "the most common and durable source of factions has been the various and unequal distribution of property. Those who hold and those who are without property have ever formed distinct interests in society. . . . A landed interest, a manufacturing interest, a mercantile interest, a moneyed interest, with many lesser interests" —all of them needing, said Madison drily, "regulation."[3]

But fortunately or unfortunately, depending upon your view, the rich and powerful have never been really regulated at all. The piling of wealth in the hands of a few Federalist plutocrats continued with, to them, gratifying speed during the early years of our nation. By 1810, according to economist Robert Gallman, the top one per cent of American families owned 21 per cent of its wealth.[4] The expropriation of Indians, the horrors of cotton and sugar-cane Negro slavery, the degradations of the Industrial Revolution's factories and sweatshops, and the financial obscenities of the Robber Baron days—all of these 19th C. phenomena are too well known to require more than mention here. Suffice it to say that, by 1915, ownership of U.S. wealth was "concentrated to a degree which is difficult to grasp. The 'Rich,' two percent of the people, own 35 per cent of the wealth. . . . The largest private fortune in the United States, estimated at one billion dollars, is equivalent to the aggregate wealth of 2,500,000 of those who are classed as 'poor' . . ."[5]

1

Today's top one per cent owns perhaps an even greater share: an estimated 25 per cent of all personal assets, which is several times the wealth possessed by the bottom *half* of the populace.[6] And if we focus only upon the juiciest goodies, income-producing wealth, the figures become really dramatic. According to one source, that top *one* per cent owns more than half of the nation's corporate stock, 47 per cent of its outstanding bonds (many of them tax-exempt), 24 per cent of its notes and mortgages, and 16 per cent of its real estate.[7] This despite antitrust legislation, an (inefficient) income tax, the Great Depression of the 1930's, and various recessions—some of them, it is known, triggered by princes of finance. (See Figure 1.)

If we swing from imagined pools of accumulated *wealth* to the streams of annual *income*, we find the disparities of fortune still astonishing. "Studies back to the 1920s show that the richest fifth of the population has consistently received at least seven times as much annual income as the bottom fifth"; a 1972 Joint Economic Committee study revealed that the lowest stratum "took

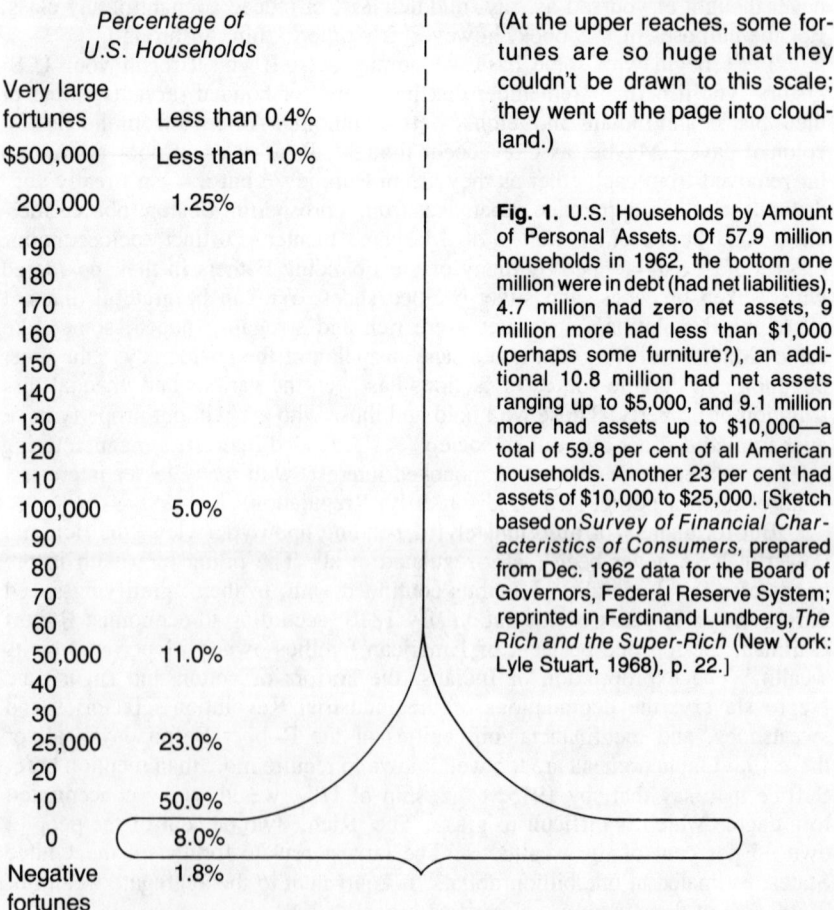

Fig. 1. U.S. Households by Amount of Personal Assets. Of 57.9 million households in 1962, the bottom one million were in debt (had net liabilities), 4.7 million had zero net assets, 9 million more had less than $1,000 (perhaps some furniture?), an additional 10.8 million had net assets ranging up to $5,000, and 9.1 million more had assets up to $10,000—a total of 59.8 per cent of all American households. Another 23 per cent had assets of $10,000 to $25,000. [Sketch based on *Survey of Financial Characteristics of Consumers,* prepared from Dec. 1962 data for the Board of Governors, Federal Reserve System; reprinted in Ferdinand Lundberg, *The Rich and the Super-Rich* (New York: Lyle Stuart, 1968), p. 22.]

home 5.6 per cent of America's before-tax earnings in 1969, while the top fifth garnered 41 per cent."[8] In 1973, the Census Bureau reported, the rich and poor seemed to be growing even farther apart.[9]

How, you ask, can such a thing be in an ostensibly civilized nation? The fault lies in our tax procedures, chiefly. Peter Barnes, a *New Republic* editor, did an apparently careful analysis of our lopsided 1972 incomes situation. Like many professional economists, he concluded that our tax policy is mistaken. It "does virtually nothing to improve the American before-tax distribution, primarily because the mild progressivity of federal income taxation is all but cancelled by the regressivity of payroll, sales and property taxes."[10] (A "progressive" tax system is one in which the rate increases as the taxable amount increases. "Regressivity" here refers to a flat or constant rate, or nearly so, which obviously hurts the poor man much more than the rich man. Many state legislatures, and many voters, for some reason seem fond of the flat rate.[11]) Our income-tax deduction and exclusion policies are rigged to benefit the wealthy, as was revealed in, for example, Pres. Richard Nixon's tax returns. Indeed, some millionaires have in the past paid *no* income tax; since 1970 most have supposedly made token payments. Our regressive Social Security tax, from its inception, has penalized the poor. And, of course, there are currently several ways of evading inheritance taxes; all one needs is a competent attorney or accountant.

The 19th Century cynically understood it: "The rich get richer and the poor get poorer." In the 20th Century we seem to have slowed these tendencies, at least in some cases, but we have not yet learned to reverse them. The rich families stay rich, and the poor stay poor. See Figure 2.

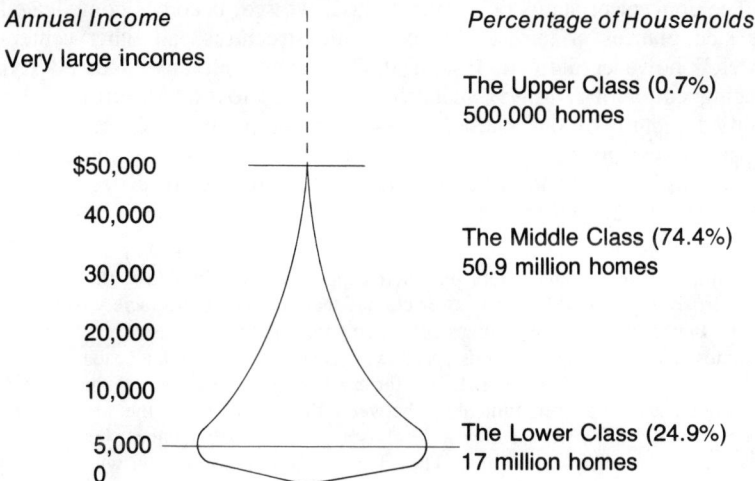

Fig. 2. shows in a crude way how our society might be pictured—somewhat like a tall, skinny Christmas tree—if we were to accept a simple three-class model based entirely on household *income* distribution. As in Fig. 1, the upper reaches are so high that they cannot even be drawn to this scale. (1972-73 data from Fabian Linden, "The Characteristics of Class," *The Conference Board Record,* Oct. 1973, p. 63.)

So much for "basic economic facts"; the United States was a class society from its earliest days, and remains one today. Indeed, Americans admit it when they (most of them) say they are "middle class." But what exactly do we mean by these notions? Do we estimate our social level solely in terms of wealth and income? I think not—or at least not quite.

It seems to me "social class" is an extraordinarily slippery concept to work with. How *do* we define it? Almost entirely in economic dimensions, with Karl Marx and Friedrich Engels? And like them do we focus upon only two classes, the propertied bourgeoisie and the bereft proletariat? Or do we set up models of many different groups, with shifting interrelationships—with, for example, the 19th C. sociologist Max Weber? Weber's pluralism is echoed in the work of many American sociologists, including for instance Joel B. Montague, Jr., who did a post-World War II study of "the working class." He announced later that it became "a problem in analyzing the existing relationships and interaction between *economic factors* (amount of real income in money and services, source of income, and patterns of consumption), *power factors,* and *status factors* (prestige, social honor, style of life, etc.)."[12] That "power factor" term "refers to the latent or actual ability to introduce force into social situations. Social classes may be power groups in this sense."[13] As to the third concept: "Social status tends to rise with increased economic well-being and with the acquisition of power, but there is no one-to-one relationship... Status and prestige tend to lag behind economic and power changes." The reason, he says, is that prestige is always linked to a person's support, or denial, of society's values.[14] The renegade is usually an outcast. Countless others must patiently "prove themselves."

The concept of status or of social class, we see, becomes complicated by these side glances at interlocking economic structures and other centers of "power," however defined. But in 1957 a noted journalist, Russell Lynes, managing editor of *Harper's* magazine, managed to sketch out a somewhat simplified picture of our national life—a set of pyramids containing major occupational categories. "In America," he noted, "we are far more likely to judge a man by the position he occupies... than by the social level he thinks of himself as belonging to."[15] And again:

> Instead of being divided horizontally into levels and strata, as we are used to thinking of it, our society has increasingly become divided vertically. Instead of broad upper, middle, and lower classes that cut across the society of the nation like the clear but uneven slices on a geological model, we now have a series of almost free-standing pyramids, each with its several levels and each one topped by an aristocracy of its own. It is a far cry from the top of one of these pyramids to the next, and communication between the members of the aristocracies is occasionally difficult, for they not only speak different languages, but their minds are on quite different things. They have different notions of what constitutes success (though they all like money, of course), and their "status symbols," to use a sociologist's term, are as unlike as, say, a swimming pool and an academic hood.[16]

There are, said Lynes, pyramids for big businessmen (and for small), for the communications field, for entertainers, for the underworld, for intellectuals, labor, politics, and sports. Each has its own tycoons and moguls, beaming contentedly atop the scramble.

A refined and more sophisticated statement of this concept came in 1963 in Suzanne Keller's *Beyond the Ruling Class*. She pointed to the tips of a handful of giant pyramids ("strategic elites") but also to a swarm of lesser ones ("segmental elites").

> Whereas all elites are important in some social and psychological contexts, only some are important for society as a whole.... There is, in effect, a hierarchy among elites; some elites are more elite than others. Beauty queens, criminal masterminds, champion bridge players, and master chefs all hold top rank in certain pyramids of talent or power, but not all are equally significant in the life of society. Certain elites may arouse momentary attention, but only certain leadership groups have a general and sustained social impact.... We refer to these groups as strategic elites, distinguishing them from segmental elites.

Her "strategic" elites included leaders in six broad fields—the political, economic, military, moral, cultural, and scientific aspects of our societal life.[17]

Whereas Lynes had apparently assigned equal elevations to his pyramids, creating a mountain range of uniform heights, Dr. Keller's panorama is different. Not only does she distinguish between mountains and mere hills, but she can accommodate different measurement scales. Marx, for instance, argued that those who control the means of production bulk largest on the horizon, since they really control all major institutions. Others have had their own villains, or heroes; "a single elite has frequently been elevated to permanent stardom— be it the technological elite of Veblen, the managerial elite of Burnham, or the moral elite of Toynbee..."[18] But circumstances, Dr. Keller says, alter cases, and societies have had different, shifting, transient criteria in distributing power and prestige.[19]

A further refinement: the social topography should clearly show, I think, that not all peaks rise directly from the plains. Some large social pyramids, to be sure, do contain representatives of all skill levels, all prestige strata, all income positions, even the very lowest in society. In the sports world, for example, there are no doubt hundreds of underemployed bush-league baseball players—many for each nationally known star. In politics, the same. But I doubt seriously that Professor Keller, in surveying her segmental elites, would find a "champion bridge player" or "master chef" below what we call the middle class. Perhaps some unfortunate person who has come upon evil times and is now, as the French say, *déclassé*. But surely he is only a *former* bridge champion; his current bout with alcoholism disqualifies him, at least for the present, from his earlier honors and perquisites.

Point No. 1 here is that in their models Mr. Lynes and Ms. Keller err, I believe, in ignoring or obliterating the familiar lines of economic strata. Lynes boldly announces, "Now we have only a middle class,"[20] but soon recognizes that he has to hedge a bit. Ms. Keller also has to testify, here and there in her work, to "the tenacity of privilege."[21] Point No. 2 is that if one circumscribes and limits a pyramid very narrowly, as Ms. Keller herself has done, that status ladder has a tendency to float to its natural class level, rather than being anchored

5

at the society's bottom. Unless, of course, its class is already at society's bottom. We can think of criminal hierarchies—pickpockets, muggers, and some others—that operate chiefly or entirely below the middle class, no matter how that term is defined. We can also conceive of upper-class pyramids: university presidents? federal judges? It is relatively easy to create tiny pyramids which are very tightly class-oriented. It is also a simple matter to create some which span two classes but not the third. Bridge players and skiers, for instance, are in the middle and upper classes but not lower class. Bowlers, though, are middle and lower class but not, ordinarily, upper class.

To accommodate these "mini-pyramids" I should like you to consider a new conceptual model, one that combines horizontal with "vertical" stratification. Figure 3 shows one version of it. The society retains roughly the tree shape given it in Figure 2, along with the bands indicating three classes. Superimposed thereon is a representation of a few of society's many status heaps, some large and anchored, some smaller and "floating" at their appropriate class level or levels.

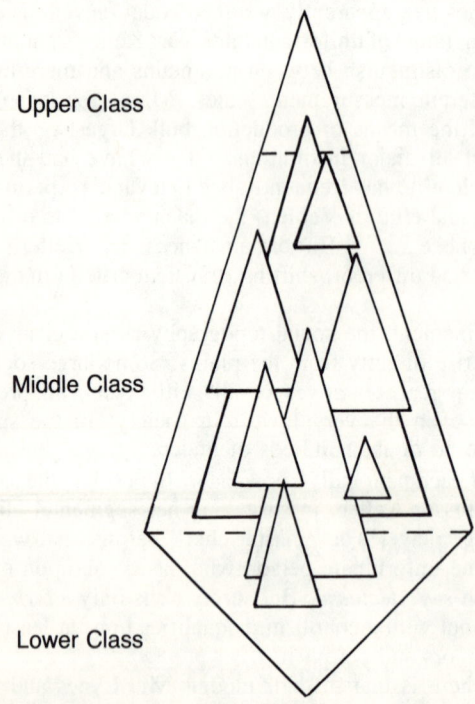

Fig. 3. A Crude Conception of Socioeconomic Relationships in American Society.

What I am arguing, you see, is that we need both concepts. We should try to fuse our folk understandings of social and economic "classes" with this useful model of occupational "pyramids." Each concept modifies and helps to explain the other. Neither alone provides enough sociological answers; taken together they may be of real help.[22]

There is one matter more, however; our model needs more stripes. In much of the sociological "literature" there is agreement that the folk concept of *three* classes is much too crude. It just won't discriminate properly among the various status strata of a complex industrial society. Some say there are five socio-economic levels now; some say ten. For the sake of an elegant simplicity, let's work with a set that is quite well known, a six-class model used by W. Lloyd Warner and others.[23]

In his "Yankee City" studies Warner and his co-workers simply divided each of the three classes into an upper and lower level. Or, rather, the town's populace made that the logical choice. Here's the picture, somewhat updated for our purposes:

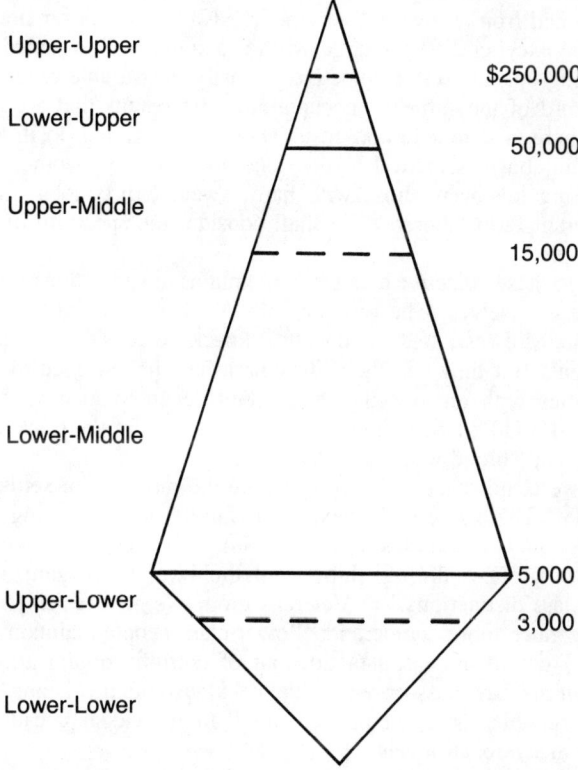

Fig. 4. A Conception of Socioeconomic Classes in American Society (based on approximate 1972 household income, but subject to various modifying factors—among them language skills).

How did Warner *et al.* distribute their status labels among the citizenry? Did money talk, again? Well, yes, it *shouted*—but the investigators were ordinarily more interested in the *source* of the income than in the raw amount. A much better indicator of social prestige, they said. As a yardstick they created a multi-layer scale, recording income derived from (1) inherited wealth, (2) "earned" wealth, (3) profits and fees, (4) salaries, (5) wages, (6) private relief and, at the bottom of the ladder, (7) public relief and such unrespectable income as that from gambling, prostitution, and bootlegging. (It is unrespectable, we might observe, unless it is made in very great sums.) People on pensions, incidentally, were given the rank they held during their active years.

Most prestigious, let's note, is that kind of good fortune which allows the recipient to escape altogether the rigors of honest labor. The masses may hold the "idle rich" in occasional contempt—but they more often suffer, quietly or no, from a gnawing envy.

Also weighted heavily by the Warner group were the things money can buy—in particular an impressive residence at an impressive address, where, amid park-like surroundings, every prospect pleases. The house types, for instance, ranged from a low of "very poor" dwellings (not repairable) upward to a high of "excellent" (very large, with spacious, well-groomed lawns).

Rounding out this set of objective or easily measurable criteria was, once again, a record of the subject's occupation, with results that are perhaps predictable. (There is a notable consensus about status-giving positions.) Scoring high were big businessmen, lawyers, doctors, and some other professional people; scoring low were those with hard, sweaty, dirty jobs—scrubwomen, miners, migrant farm laborers. We shall consider the spectrum of jobs further in later chapters.

Added to these objective data were mountains of subjective reports from the townspeople themselves. The residents of "Yankee City" and, later, "Jonesville" in the Midwest, had an uncanny knack for assigning status to their fellow citizens. But they had their idiosyncrasies; they seemed to regard well-placed families with an awe that gave status even to many a black sheep. Conversely, if a lad's family lived on the wrong side of the tracks, that stigma had persistence; "blood will tell."

There were, however, ways of escaping the mold, or of settling in it ever more deeply. "The clique ranks next to the family in contributing to the placement of individuals in the class order."[24] Similarly, certain associations "such as discussion groups, dining clubs, and the like, are organizations which emphasize class distinctions."[25] Veterans groups (*e.g.*, the American Legion) tended to be much more democratic; "lower-class people maintain membership because they derive more satisfaction out of patriotic organizations."[26] And although churches are class-oriented, they lack absolute precision: "The church is not very reliable for exact placement of an individual because it spreads through too many social levels."[27]

In any event, in one way or another the community managed to assign prestige-ranking to all its members, and the Warner group recorded it painstakingly. These data were matched with the wealth-and-position findings and, with great regularity, the correlations were remarkable. Out of it all came a picture of six more or less distinct social classes.

This six-class system will do, I think. We are ready now to draw our conceptual model in its final form.

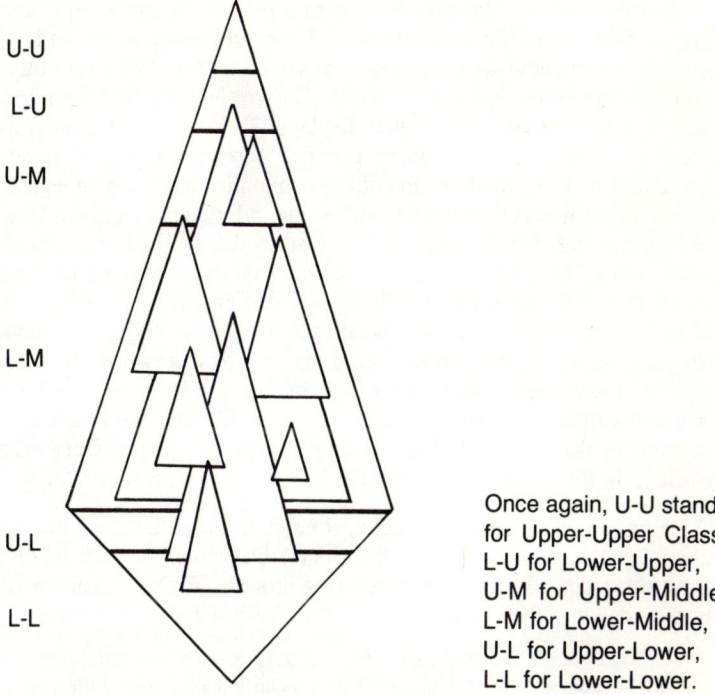

Once again, U-U stands for Upper-Upper Class, L-U for Lower-Upper, U-M for Upper-Middle, L-M for Lower-Middle, U-L for Upper-Lower, L-L for Lower-Lower.

Fig. 5. A Revised Conception of Socioeconomic Relationships in American Society.

To those unfamiliar with sociological jargon, rattling off that set of terms, out loud, will seem not just awkward and embarrassing; it will sound ludicrous. But, with a little practice, you will get better at it, and even come to take the whole matter seriously.

For, in fact, it *is* a serious matter. A man of more sober mien than Marx (or, indeed, his disciples and followers) would be hard to imagine, and *he* regarded the problem of social inequality with the utmost gravity and earnestness. Marx, you will recall, saw in 19th C. capitalism some few virtues, but mainly boom-and-bust, the capitulation of governments to the richer bourgeoisie, and the increasing misery of the poor. He was suspicious of capitalist "progress"—as in the advance of technology and the accumulation of capital—because in a capitalistic society "all means for the development of production transform themselves into means of domination over, and exploitation of, the producers; they mutilate the labourer into a fragment of a man, degrade him to the level of an appendage of a machine, destroy every remnant of charm in his work and turn it into a hated toil...." Worse still, such advances all "drag his wife and children beneath the wheels of the Juggernaut of capital." Bourgeois accumulation of wealth, he concluded, is "accumulation of misery, agony of toil, slavery, ignorance, brutality, mental degradation."[28]

But the 19th C. capitalistic system also had its supporters, and they too were earnest men. Some of them had recently been impressed—nay, mesmerized—by the new doctrine of natural selection (the "survival of the fittest"), as enunciated by evolutionists Charles Darwin and Herbert Spencer in one of history's most dazzling intellectual displays. To American business it was clear almost immediately: evolutionary progress for man depended upon a rugged individualism in all matters, including economic ones. "Although the natural law of competition is sometimes hard on the individual, wrote Andrew Carnegie in 1889, it is best for the race, since it insures the survival of the fittest in every department. The laws of economic individualism and of competition, he argued, bring wealth to those with the superior energy and ability to produce it, and keep it from the drones, the weak, the incompetent."[29] The economic life, with its bustling temples, was "an arena in which men met to compete. The terms of the struggle were established by the market. Those who won were rewarded with survival and, if they survived brilliantly, with riches. Those who lost went to the lions."[30] This wisdom, known as Social Darwinism, is still enshrined in the hearts of conservatives more than a century later.

Now, as we have already seen, it came to pass that great heaps of wealth were indeed created—although the Social Darwinists tended to overlook the role of inheritance in the whole glittering process. Russell Lynes wrote a wryly amused account of upper-class life at the close of the 19th Century:

> They built tremendous marble "cottages" at Newport or Lenox which they ornamented with furnishings from European palaces; they built vast greenhouses in which tropical trees produced exotic fruits and flowers for their tables. Terraced lawns stepped down to artificial lakes where swans floated.... Streams of water splashed from the bronze mouths of satyrs into wide marble basins ... men with rakes smoothed the pebbled driveways after each visiting carriage.[31]

And he told a little story about the depression of the 1890's, amid which the Bradley Martins of New York decided to give a costume ball "to give impetus to trade." Mrs. Bradley Martin was "the wife of a man of leisure. Her husband had inherited a more than considerable fortune from his father, a self-made lawyer and shrewd investor." They were socially acceptable "even in Mrs. Astor's circle of 'four hundred.'" Thus they were in a position to stage a ball which cost them and their guests $369,200 (about a million "if equated with the current dollar") and which gave employment to "dressmakers, costumers, hairdressers, headwaiters, caterers" and others. The party was held in the ballroom of the Waldorf-Astoria Hotel, transformed for the night into a replica of a gleaming Versailles hall. One New York newspaper, the following day, devoted its first five pages to the affair.[32]

Meanwhile, back at the tenement and out on the prairie, the depression of the Nineties was dragging along through painful months and grim, dreary years. Depressions weren't uncommon in America; there had been severe ones as early as 1720 and 1730.[33] But this one was a lulu. The unemployed and their families existed, frequently, on one or two scanty meals a day. In 1897 Theodore Roosevelt sounded a gloomy note: "The rich have undoubtedly grown richer; . . . there has been a large absolute, though not relative, increase in poverty and . . . the very poor tend to huddle in immense masses in the cities."[34]

And, if you will take the time and trouble, you will discover these extremes of fortune, in the richest nation on earth, to this very day.

There appear to exist two distinct classes, the rich and the poor; the oppressed and the oppressor; those that live by their own labor and they that live by the labor of others...
—Working Men's Republican Political Association, Penn Township, Pa., *ca.* 1835

CHAPTER 2
A CLOSER LOOK AT
THE CLASS STRUCTURE

Perhaps you have been wondering, as you've threaded your way through statistics, diagrams, and footnotes, what all these figures are doing in an English handbook. Since you have been good enough to bear with me till now, it is only just and fit that I start making the book's purpose clear.

It seems to me self-evident that the American people have never been receptive to radical or even mildly socialistic movements, and indeed have looked upon them with stern suspicion. Except for occasional fits, Americans have quit struggling for "economic justice," that far-off goal—have given up striving for massive income and wealth redistribution. They have watched attentively, through New Deals, Fair Deals, Wars on Poverty, and the like, and have not failed to note that very, very little has been accomplished. Leftists who were not already given over to skepticism and cynicism have been filled with a galling sense of futility. Most people are inclined to hang on, doggedly, to what's theirs, and if those below them hurt, that's tough.

Illustrative of the decline of American political and economic idealism was the Presidential election of 1972. Sen. George Stanley McGovern of South Dakota, who had begun talking about the desirability of some welfare reforms, was immediately branded a radical—and many blue-collar (L-M, some U-L) voters decided then and there he wasn't their candidate. He also alarmed the three highest classes, who would be asked to pay the bills. Meanwhile the incumbent, Richard M. Nixon, was promising not reform but rather the *status quo*, stability, "law and order." As usual, about 80 per cent of the nation's newspapers supported the right-of-center position. The outcome of all this (and much more) on election day? Despite early evidence of Republican hanky-panky and even criminality at the Watergate, Nixon won more than 60 per cent of the national vote, carrying 49 states. Most commentators viewed it as a strongly conservative tide.

In *The Status Seekers,* one of his best-selling books, Vance Packard argues that "Class lines in several areas of our national life appear to be hardening. And status striving has intensified."[1] Now, whether we agree or not, we must at least admit our social stratification shows few signs of cracking and crumbling. Because of the ingrained conservatism of the American people, it would seem that we should expect the persistence of capitalistic forms in our "mixed" economy. It would seem that, as before, "the vast majority of people live and die within the boundaries and tastes of their own class."[2]

Continued acceptance of sharp social-class disparities must be taken as a central fact of American life. But what about the robust person who is unwilling to accept his or her lot? If he can expect little help from society—the electorate—can he still make it on his own? Can he jump the class barriers and find a better life?

The answer—indeed, the cheery message of this book—is that *of course* he can! What it takes is pluck, determination, good old American get-up-and-go! Oh, in centuries past, the great cultures were rigid in their stratification. A citizen was born into a caste or class, and he stayed in it until his death. But not so in the United States. The vigorous individual has always had a chance. Just recall the Horatio Alger stories. What it takes is ambitiousness and, just as importantly, the *appearance* of ambitiousness.

There is a great deal of anecdotal supporting evidence. In those moments when the goal seems far distant, when we are discouraged, when the world seems against us, it is heartening to remember the lustrous examples of those who have gone before us, blazing the various trails toward Success.

• Take, for instance, the young H. L. Hunt, who wandered around the West employed as a barber, cowhand, lumberjack, and gambler, until he became an Arkansas cotton farmer. In 1921 he turned instead to the oil business and was immediately "swept off his feet toward riches. According to the Hunt legend, he struck oil on the first try with a drilling rig he bought with a $50 loan. Another version is that he won the money, or the rig itself, in a card game."[3] At his death in 1974 he was worth an amount somewhere between $250 and $700 million,[4] although other estimates were even higher.

• Or take Clara Barton, a timid little girl on a Massachusetts farm, who through diligent studies became a teacher, then a famous nurse, and finally founder of the American Red Cross. A very solid citizen, revered by philanthropists and now ensconced in history books.

• Or consider the inventor Dr. Edwin Land, who developed (along with dozens of other discoveries in the field of optics) the Polaroid Land camera—and who, according to a 1965 *Saturday Evening Post,* suddenly became worth $185 million.[5]

• Or maybe the story of Marian Anderson, an immensely talented contralto who rose from humble beginnings to the stages of the greatest concert halls of the world.

• Or, instead, the skills of an Oakland Athletics outfielder named Reggie Jackson, who, upon being voted the Most Valuable Player in the American League, promptly announced that he would require $150,000 for his services during the 1974 season.

• Or Andrew Carnegie, who made a vast bundle in steel but became truly respectable only after giving millions to education and creating his many libraries.

• Take the case of—well, perhaps several successful Hollywood starlets. Some of them, no doubt, had real acting talent, but it was undeniably their physical charms that rocketed them to cinema-land prominence and swank Beverly Hills mansions.

- Finally, consider any one of a number of bright young people fortunate enough to marry into the Du Pont dynasty.

And there we have some recognized techniques by which people have been able to leap one, two, even three social classes with a single bound. According to Warner, these have been the chief avenues of upward social mobility: money, education, occupation, talent, skill, philanthropy, sex, and marriage.[6] All you need to do is choose, and then charge ahead. If the others can do it, so can you.

A word of caution, however: let's suppose you have set your sights on a class above you, and have industriously worked your way very near that goal. With your current status has come a higher income level—but the situation, please note, now demands a certain amount of finesse. It just won't do for you to play bull in the china shop. For example, mobility experts would surely frown on your attempting simply to buy your way into the class above. "Something more than a large income is necessary for high social position." Money must be transformed into what Warner calls "socially approved behavior and possessions." This is a sociologist's way of saying that the social-climbing party guest should usually refrain from making boozy passes at a very unamused hostess—and should be wearing exactly the appropriate clothing for the affair, garments that speak quietly and with dignity of his impeccable taste. Good taste, that is, as determined by the status group he hopes to join. The correct behavior and possessions "must be translated into intimate participation with, and acceptance by, members of a superior class."[7]

Here at last is an opportunity to introduce this book's chief topic: the good taste or "acceptability" of one's language. English teachers make the point that language, spoken or written, almost always occurs in a social context. It's a social activity, just like any other shared behavior. One of my arguments here, an extension of this idea, is that this language is always automatically typed as to class level. *Most* social behavior is.

The whole book, really, rests on that thesis. Now, if you agree, you will affirm something more, I think: that if a person sets out to learn the socially acceptable ways of dressing, home decorating, dining, and so on, he logically should also give the correct degree of polish to his language. Ideally, of course, he should in addition have something worthwhile to say. But a certain amount of status is conferred from just the *appearance* of acceptability; for this he should at least know how to speak and write in whole grammatical sentences, if only to make brief comment on the weather. Some social classes, to be sure, may require somewhat greater rhetorical sophistication.

Developing more and more sophistication is naturally the business of the schools and colleges, and it's time we considered the importance of education in this whole advancement process. Education, to be completely accurate, actually starts in the home, and at a very early age. "Class differences," says Vance Packard, "begin in the cradle."[8] He points out that the middle class, unlike the lower class, is lavish not only with protective love for the child, but also with early efforts at weaning and toilet training. Some writers see social class imprinting the child even then, and certainly not long after. "Status," says one, "plays a decisive role in the formation of personality at the various stages of development, for if young people are to learn to live adaptively as mature people in our society they must be trained by the informal controls of our society to fit into their places."[9] Others observe that lower-class parents, partly to save their children emotional hurt, sometimes instruct them in what parts of town to avoid. The children learn their place, away from "stuck-up" people, "where you're not wanted."

Social class, as we shall see, permeates all aspects of our lives, whether or not we're even aware of it. Sometimes it's a subtle influence, sometimes not. Middle-class parents have been known to be rather blunt: "Mary, I wish you wouldn't play any more with Sarah. The Greens—well, just aren't our kind of people."

When the child starts school, he may again find the pressure is far from subtle. Education has never been more important to the upwardly mobile person than it is today—yet the American educational system is woefully inefficient in fulfilling its obligations to the three lowest classes. There are plenty of intelligent children of the lower classes, but they are not performing so well as their higher-class cousins; they leave school prematurely; they do not go on to college in adequate numbers.[10]

It doesn't take much on our part to discover that the chief problem is the social situation in the schoolhouse. But let's hear it from a sociologist: "If the world of the child is pleasant, rewarding, and increases his self-esteem, he is likely to want to stay and do well. If it is punishing and decreases his self-respect, he is likely to do poorly and want to quit."[11]

Part of the problem is his teacher. Thoroughly middle-class herself, she is imbued with the values of the bourgeoisie, and she applies those values in every minute-by-minute judgment she makes. Studies show, not very surprisingly, that teachers "rate the school work of children from the higher classes in accordance with their family's social position"[12]—not necessarily for any sycophantic purpose but merely because, to them, such children possess all the desirable traits. This is an example of the so-called "halo" effect in grading, an extraordinarily potent factor. One consequence, early on, is the branding of gauche lower-class children as academic failures. This, in turn, becomes a self-fulfilling prophecy. Lower-class children start thinking of themselves as "losers," and soon start acting like losers. Very little is expected of a failure by his teachers, his parents—and himself.

The child's fellow pupils can also be a torment to him. Bernice L. Neugarten, writing in the *American Journal of Sociology*, reported on a study she'd made of ratings of other children by fifth and sixth graders in a Midwestern town. She found that youngsters in the upper-middle class, and above, were ranked high by all other children for qualities like "good looks, liking for school, leadership, friendship, and many other favorable personal traits"; lower-class children got low ranks or, more often than not, were given a negative rating as "bad looking," dirty, and "people you would not want for friends."[13] Many other studies confirm that social standing is recognized early in life.

Generally speaking, elementary school isn't a very happy place for the lower-class child. But high school is usually worse. Some of the most poignant passages in sociological writing are in the classic *Elmtown's Youth: The Impact of Social Classes on Adolescents,* by Yale's August B. Hollingshead. For example, in Chapter 8 he describes the freshman's agony in just selecting his school subjects. The impecunious child has to choose a set of them that is appropriate in the context of his reasonable career expectations. "The high school curriculum is organized around three courses: college preparatory, general, and commercial. Enrollment in each course is related very significantly to class position; that is, each course acts either to attract or repel students in the different prestige classes."[14] The top classes strongly favored the college-prep studies, of course; one didn't "rate" unless he was in it. Whatever course was finally chosen, it was (and is) considered a reliable indicator of one's status.

Again, in a chapter on Elmtown's high school cliques, we see the students busily evaluating and excluding each other: "The chances are 4 to 1 that a class II will be rated among the elite. The odds are 6 to 1 against a class V being rated anything but a grubby...."[15] The result of such evaluations will largely determine the degree of success one has in dealing with the opposite sex, a matter of great significance in the mid-teens. But of course we need not journey to Elmtown in the Midwest corn belt. Cities and towns close by us bear witness to their adolescent class systems. Many communities, even in our supposedly enlightened generation, unexplainedly still sanction the existence of high school fraternities and sororities. No one can calculate the pain felt by the outsider.

It can be argued that "the level at which one terminates one's formal schooling is the most precise single indicator of social level."[16] There is little wonder that, in the past, there has been a high attrition rate among the less-privileged classes. Yet real efforts have recently been made to keep all students

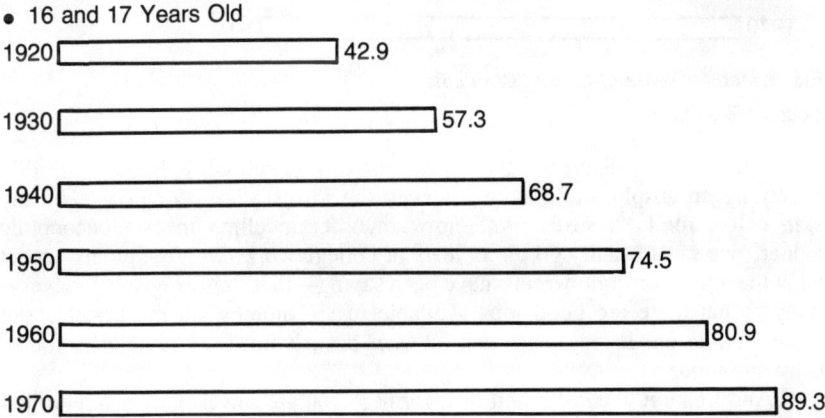

Fig. 6. *Per Cent Enrolled in School*

Source: *Graphic Summary of the 1970 Population Census,* U.S. Department of Commerce, Social and Economic Statistics Administration, Bureau of the Census (Aug. 1973).

in school, no matter their pain. And—largely, I think, because of economic realities in the "outside" world—the efforts are paying off. More and more youngsters are determinedly sticking it out till Graduation Day. Consider some remarkable statistics in Figure 6.

Those figures, please note, include students of all races. It used to be that the dropout rate among nonwhites was a national disgrace. It is still much too high, but the educational gap between whites and nonwhites appears to be slowly closing. Witness:

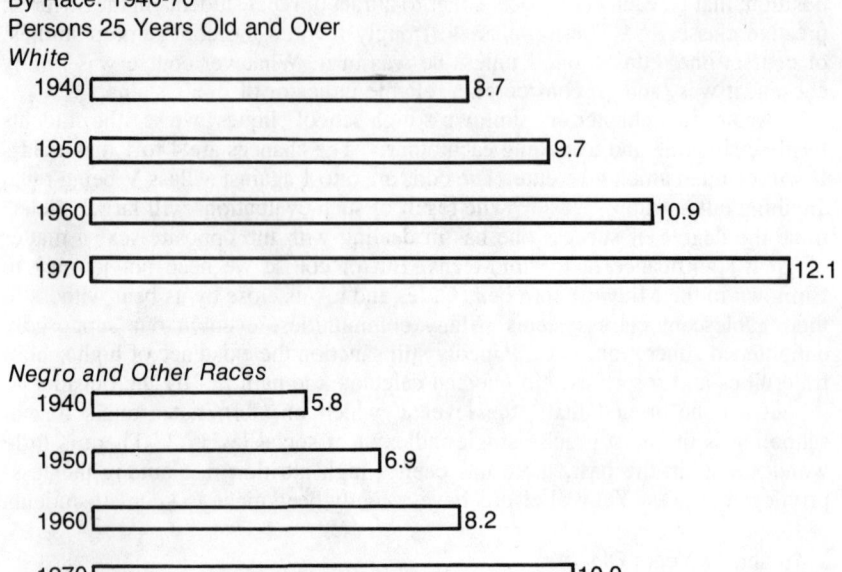

Fig. 7. Median Years of School Completed
Source: See Fig. 6.

The point of all these data is obvious: a high school diploma is steadily becoming an absolute minimum for even the lowest class, for people of any skin color, for both sexes. And now, in order to climb the socioeconomic ladder, one must usually go on to years of college work. Don't supinely accept what the television commercials have been saying—that "college isn't for everybody," that there are good jobs available in six months via the trade-school route, and so on. It may very well be true, but it's not for you. Not if you're truly ambitious.

And I take it you *are* ambitious, for here you are, investigating or enrolled in or thinking about a college English class. I take it you've recognized that college education is now the No. 1 route to success. Fifty years ago any man in business or industry could hope to rise through the ranks to high places. But times have changed. "More and more, the sons of executives are replacing their fathers in such positions," says one report. More importantly, the top jobs are increasingly being filled by men (and now women) coming *laterally* from engineering colleges, law schools, and other lofty regions of higher education. "The prudent mobile man today," says a sociologist, "must prepare himself by education if he wishes to fill an important job and provide his family with the money and prestige necessary to get 'the better things of life.' "[17]

This is not to say, however, that the thing that will appeal to you will necessarily be engineering or law. Perhaps you're ambitious, but not *that* ambitious. Maybe you have picked for yourself a nice little niche in data-processing, say, or police work. Fine; maybe a two-year college course will raise you a rung on the class ladder, and you'll be content. But whatever your plan—one year at a junior college or longer at an Ivy League graduate school—you will find this book made just for you.

How can this book fit so many individual programs? Simple: unlike most English handbooks, it lets you get off wherever you like. The chapters to come are filled with the information one needs to survive linguistically at each of the six social class levels. It is a question, you'll recall, of social acceptance, which is chiefly a matter of conducting your affairs with good taste. Good taste, that is, at *that* level. Material has been collected on grammar, mechanics, usage, and composition, and you will find it arranged in order of increasing difficulty. When you reach what you regard as your optimum or target social level, the rest of the book need not detain you.

Chapter 3, "Lower-Lower Language," is included here not because I'm suggesting you're necessarily at that level, but chiefly to give us some firm ground from which to ascend. There may also be some readers who have forgotten their grammar-school grammar, and will want to brush up a bit. Please do not be embarrassed by such temporary regressions. It happens in the best of families.

Some final remarks, though, before you begin your ascent through the mountainous wilderness of the class structure:

It is crucial that the aspirant begin his or her journey with absolutely no illusions. I hope that the first two drawings in Chapter 1 serve as startling illustration of the distances involved in your climb. In addition, be warned that the natives will not always be friendly and can at times be openly hostile. Wealth and entrenched position and power are still significant factors in the recruitment practices of the upper tribes.

Moreover, it must be admitted that education is by no means a guarantee of social success. Christopher Jencks, head of a Harvard research team, stirred a bit of a tempest with a 1972 study that plays down the influence of one's education on his degree of success out in capitalistic society. This erudite book, *Inequality*, says that some of the variation in our personal incomes can be explained by quality of school, knowledge and study skills, genetic differences, home background, or the IQ element. But by far the greatest factors are one's personality or special competence—and just plain luck. Most of one's success, according to the study, can be attributed to the fact that he's admired for some particular kind of skill he has, and has been in the right places at the right times.[18]

Perhaps that leaves you a bit nervous about your decision to invest heavily in education. You shouldn't be; there are grounds for self-confidence and optimism. Provided you do not inflate your expectations unrealistically, I see no harm in your assuming a *cheerful* attitude as you begin. If I may borrow a brewing-industry metaphor, there seems to be a certain amount of ferment in the masses these days, and perhaps you can bubble your way up by sharing in that energy. As you know, many societal elements have deliberately or by custom been deprived of rights—rights taken for granted, and yet carefully protected, by the higher-level white male. The less-privileged have long resented unfair barriers to a full participation in American prosperity and political life. And now, at last, some seem willing to struggle for their rights: the blacks and other ethnic groups, women, and various minorities whose case has never been completely heard—homosexuals, minors and the elderly, the poor on welfare, people in prisons and mental hospitals, those in the armed services, conscientious objectors to wars, and even those with long hair. All, at one time or another, have transformed resentment into agitation and turbulence. Much of this commotion has had at its core a demand for fairness in employment.

And, lo, positions are opening in nearly all of Suzanne Keller's "elites"— even at some of the top echelons. "In view of the tenacity of privilege," she says, "these proportions are still very small, but they do reflect expanding rather than contracting opportunities for lower-class aspirants . . ."[19] What it will take, in most circumstances, is conscientious dedication to one's studies, for this is a way of increasing the odds that one's luck will be good rather than bad.

Dr. Keller sees a movement away from the traditional patterns "to one more attuned to modern times, where value is placed on skill, talent, and motivation."[20] When I try peering into the future I think I see an ever-increasing stress on specialized skills, more opportunities for minority groups and women, and a continuing admiration of ambitiousness.[21] You must of course have the ambition, the motivation; but, more than this, you must somehow contrive to communicate that fact to superiors. I know of no better device than communicating verbally, skillfully, at just the right linguistic level. That's *prima facie* evidence that you've been planning and striving. The rewards, I would think, ought to follow shortly thereafter.[22] And thus do we sometimes make our own good fortune.

Perhaps your English, written and spoken, is already rather near that of your target class level. Excellent. By all means (in consultation with your instructor) just skim through whatever material you have already mastered. At the beginning, at least, no one is trying to hinder a deserving person. Onward and upward.

These capitalists generally act harmoniously, and in concert, to fleece the people.
—Abraham Lincoln

CHAPTER 3
LOWER-LOWER LANGUAGE

This chapter is included, as I said, largely because we need some base from which to begin our ascents to higher linguistic levels. It may serve some foreigners as a rather sketchy introduction to the English language. For others it might be an appropriate place to begin an intensive review of fundamentals. Still others may want merely to collect a few "don'ts" so that they may avoid at least the most horrendous of language faults—and, hence, of social perils.

And some others, struggling gamely with these highfalutin sentences, actually represent the Lower-Lower Class itself—and presumably would like to pull themselves up and out of it. Now, let us recall Figure 5 and its reminder that no class is a homogeneous unit, lacking internal variety. A careful observer of the Lower-Lower Class will witness a complex range of personalities, abilities, circumstances, and life-styles. Each class, including this one, has its swarm of little social hierarchies.

At the very bottom, whom do we find? There is a sort of grisly fascination with this question. With a shudder we pass the shadowed alley in which lies a drunken forty-year-old who looks sixty, bespattered with his vomit, half-conscious. We don't know what hell of desperation brought him to this alley; we can surmise that he will be "dried out" in a jail's drunk tank and then, maybe, at a treatment center. But we don't stop. *Am I my brother's keeper?* Before we can escape the nearly deserted neighborhood, we are accosted twice by down-at-the-heels prostitutes, one female and Spanish-looking, the other a black male. Both have serious drug problems. *There, but for the grace of God . . .* We turn a rubbish-strewn corner and with relief find this street busier, lined with defeated people, some spitting on the sidewalk, some patronizing dirty taverns and bail-bond shops and peep shows and sleazy little restaurants. This street, where there is at least some warmth, is also the L-L world. And other scenes, a bit less squalid: the Salvation Army doorway, the whiskery old men sharing a bus-stop bench and memories in the October sunshine, the nursing homes where the state provides aged widows and widowers at least some medical services.

But we must hurry to the top. Among the aristocrats of the L-L world is the hoodlum. Crime is a very big business in the United States, and of course much of it is carried on by young Lower-Lower car thieves, muggers, burglars, and armed robbers. Handguns are easily acquired in this country; possession of one brings its owner a reputation for masculine daring, so of course we find them even among ghetto teen-agers. The most daring win the most status. A

21

second top-level L-L is the virile, raffish hobo—a wanderer who, unlike his degenerate cousin, the bum, will work now and then to keep from having to scavenge in garbage cans. (He is, however, not above a little half-dignified panhandling.) Another category sometimes fairly high on the L-L social scale is the migrant laborer lucky enough to be still healthy. Besides his health, he has a wife and five children, and is sometimes able to fuel up another valued possession, a battered 1960 Ford station wagon. Welfare checks and charity will keep the family alive, during the winter, in a cheap hotel with vile odors. The migrant seems content; his brother and sister-in-law, back home, are sweating for next to nothing on a tenant farm; for years now, a sister and her kids have had no income at all but Aid to Dependent Children.[1]

> *Cusins:* Do you call poverty a crime?
> *Undershaft:* The worst of crimes. All other crimes are virtues beside it... Poverty blights whole cities; spreads horrible pestilences; strikes dead the very souls of all who come within sight, sound, or smell of it.
> —George Bernard Shaw
> *Major Barbara*

Some statistics: in 1971 about 19 per cent of America's unattached whites earned less than $1,500. Another one-fourth earned less than $3,000. Among lone nonwhites the percentages in those brackets were 31.8 and 26.9. Poverty also ravaged many families: 6.9 per cent of the white homes had less than $3,000 income; one-fifth of all nonwhite households were in that depressed and depressing category.[2]

The 1970 share of all these families in the U.S. personal-income flow was about one per cent.[3] In 1971, therefore, few L-L's had luxuries; only 13.5 per cent owned air-conditioning units (whereas 69.3 per cent of the $25,000-plus families did), and less than two per cent owned dishwashers (compared with three-fourths in that more affluent group).[4] In all aspects of poverty, as is well known, the heaviest burdens are borne by the nonwhites, and by families headed by women.

The economist John Kenneth Galbraith, one of many who have attempted to describe the causes and types of poverty, stresses some of its physical problems: "those afflicted have such limited and insufficient food, such poor clothing, such crowded, cold and dirty shelter that life is painful as well as comparatively brief."[6] Those lines come near the mark. It is well known, for instance, that poor nutrition is a factor in the general L-L dis-ease. Nutrients most often missing from their diets are ascorbic acid, Vitamin A, calcium, and iron. In late 1973, researchers from Harvard and MIT also reported that seven million Americans lived in substandard ("physically unsound") housing, another five million paid excessive rents in proportion to their incomes, and an additional one million endured overcrowding—a total of thirteen ill-housed millions.[5]

Most L-L Americans, of course, are either unemployed or seriously underemployed. (Estimates of the number of adult "functional illiterates" run as high as 21 million—21 million people who cannot really comprehend a "help wanted" ad!) But perhaps it would be instructive to examine the roles they play at least temporarily in the drama of occupations. The Census Bureau's 1973 *Statistical Abstract,* which here includes some teen-agers, gives the 1971 median income of all work categories. At the bottom of the income totem pole are farm laborers (men $2,274, women $940) and housemaids ($849).[7] They share this distinction, however, with whole armies in the lower reaches of other occupations.

In his charming *Instant Status,* Charles Merrill Smith theorizes that most of us long for a more exalted station. In particular he assumes

> that you have no interest in being part of the lower class. We would in no way cast aspersions on the virtue, patriotism, or contributions to society of the lower class. To do so would be snobbery. But it is not only an undesirable goal, it is not even a goal. Good people that they are who inhabit the lower class, it is a world of rotten jobs, hard work, low pay, graceless culture, minimum rewards, and no status. Who wants that?[8]

Who, indeed?

But let us suppose a nearby college decides to set up a store-front night school amid all this squalor. What do we tell the dark-skinned youth,[9] the ancient Jewish lady, and others, who are attracted to a remedial English class? Well, if it's a young black, say, we can tell her or him that there has been a great deal of federally financed research into the language problems of ghetto Negroes, but that so far there are few textbooks or related materials specifically designed to help him. Worse yet, we have to admit that the locutions we want him to learn will actually cause him hurt, at least in the short run.

For sociolinguists have come to know a few things about the slum. One is that school values and speech are not "reinforced" and learned in such an area; that the adolescent's peers approve different patterns—and *only* the different patterns. So the middle-class teacher marks him low; the youngster may then withdraw, or become hostile, but more often he is simply indifferent; he is soon once again in his element, on the street. Often only the child *rejected* by his slum peers does well in school. It's "the healthy, vigorous, popular child with normal intelligence who cannot read and fails all along the line."[10] The subculture has rejected the dominant culture. The subculture frequently also rejects the striving person.

Among boys, street speech habits have something to do with developing *maleness:*

> almost all males who grew up in working-class communities can probably remember their adolescent need to speak with masculinity, particularly if there was any question whatsoever about their physical prowess, their ability as athletes, or if they were tortured by...a relatively late development of facial hair and a deeper voice. Masculinity, they discovered, could be expressed by a choice of vocabulary, grammar, and pronunciation even after their bodies had unceremoniously failed them.[11]

The very last thing wanted is to be thought less than male, and over-correctness in one's speech is considered suspicious.

The same pressures, unfortunately, operate later in life, at various social levels.[12] Beyond this, there is the additional problem that few lower-class youngsters of either sex can see any immediate usefulness in middle-class speech. Most think of it as "a remote and special dialect" with "no utility for everyday life."[13] Many nonwhites doubt that they will ever know a life much different from the one they now lead.

For these reasons, and others, people from minority groups often have difficulty developing enough motivation to make the radical linguistic changes necessary for social mobility. And, make no mistake, changes *will* be necessary. There is relatively little demand in a capitalistic society for adults who read and write at the fourth-grade level, or for Americans who speak only Spanish or black-proletarian English.

For the L-L person to pull himself all the way up to the middle class, a Herculean effort may be required. It's best we get at it.

L-L SPEECH PATTERNS

Linguists sometimes point out that there are no "primitive" languages, that slum talk is as good as any other for expressing complex ideas. Although this is quite true, it is a truth they should probably keep to themselves. For no matter how efficient ghetto talk is, the fact remains that it is not approved by any of the five superior classes. The slum speaker is thus stigmatized, and especially if he uses one of the black-proletarian dialects.

I am aware that American black cultural patterns are currently rather fashionable, particularly on college campuses, and that governmental agencies, contractors, and others, are under pressure to hire a "quota" of nonwhites. But I am not convinced that all this will affect very soon the deep prejudices of many white employers—a bigotry based on class distinctions, I argue, even more than on racial differences.

No—and what I'm saying applies also to Latins and other bilinguals—if he's really in earnest about moving up, the black will consciously, deliberately, systematically, stamp out every trace of his ghetto speech. Or, if he can manage it, at least he will reserve slum talk for only a few special occasions. Outside the South, at least, he will tentatively insert the *r* in *ca'*, *fo'*, *inte'view*, and so on, and reestablish the *l* in *he'p*, *too's*, *bu'*, etc. He will slowly reverse his present tendency to simplify consonant groups at the ends of words—*passed*, *past* (*pas'*), *bend* (*ben'*), *left* (*lef'*), *told* (*tol'* or *to'*)—and to weaken final single consonants. He will carefully distinguish between words he now orally equates: *pin* and *pen*, *since* and *cents*, *poor* and *pour*, *bear* and *beer*.

If he can handle these and some other phonological variables, his progress will have been remarkable. Doubly so if, at the same time, he can remember to suppress all the black-proletarian jargon: *cat*, *honkey*, *cool*, and their more recent variants,[14] and the obscenities that now bellow so in L-L speech generally.

But mainstream U.S.A. does not regard phonological and lexical deviation, class-typed though it may be, as much of a crime. Frequently we even find it tolerated by the condescending, romanticizing higher classes. There is a subject that does evoke intolerance, however—the *grammar* of the language—and we turn to it next.

L-L GRAMMAR

The linguist Roger W. Shuy says that in dealing with grammar

it is obvious that those features which show sharp breaks between social classes are more crucial than those which show only slight differences across social-status groups. Wolfram's research clearly shows that verb third-person singular -*s* absence (*My sister go to school every day*) stratifies sharply, whereas pronominal apposition (*My brother he came home late*) has only gradient (gradual) stratification across social class.[15]

We can't organize our thoughts on grammar very well along those lines, however; we shall have to begin with its fundamentals, and hope to get to "pronominal apposition," and so on, some other time. But there's no help for it—we'll still have to use some technical terms. If we employed no useful shorthand at all, this book would be long indeed.

Now, the word *grammar* is itself a technical term, one with a number of senses, and I want to try being as clear as I can about it. First, it may be regarded as a field of scholarly study, of interest to graduate-school linguists. The term comes from the ancient Greek word *grammatikos* (pertaining to letters), which suggests the number of centuries it's been a concern to scholars, and to school teachers and their unhappy students. And many linguists feel that it's an important study; our very perceptions and thoughts may be partly formed by the grammatical structures in our heads, most put there when we are tiny children.

The Greeks and later societies recognized that a language is a set of symbols—words, chiefly—organized with enough order and regularity to warrant study of that organization. They were of course aware that a language changes continuously, but they felt that even many of these changes were predictable, or that changes came in predictable ways. Terms of Greek origin suggest an early interest in the structure of words (morphology) and of sentences (syntax). Now, occasionally the word "grammar" is stretched to include some related studies: of words' pronunciation (phonology), of their meanings (semantics), and even of their history (etymology). But not in this book.

In this book the tendency is to *shrink* the territory of grammar slightly. We will note that the domain gets fuzzy around its edges, its boundaries, and that there is a good deal of overlap of a neighboring empire, *usage*. To oversimplify considerably, we can say that grammar is an area of social conventions and neatness in the language, usage an area of more freedom of choice—and, hence, constant change and far less orderliness. In this book some things commonly thought of as grammatical formations (or problems) will be treated under the other heading. Most "usage," as we shall see, is class-conscious—some of it exceedingly so.

To repeat, one sense of *grammar* is "a field of study." The term also refers, second, to the *kind* of study. There is no unanimity among teachers and research people about the most efficient way to examine the language, or to teach it. Perhaps the simplest statement we can make about them is that they divide themselves into two large groups, the traditionalists and the modernists, with a third category reserved for those who seek various compromises. The modernist group may be subdivided into tranformationalists, structuralists, and a few other clans.[16] The traditionalist group, by contrast, is more nearly monolithic. To generalize about it: traditionalists are content with an analytic system similar to one developed long ago for describing the classical languages. Most Americans have been exposed to its elements—for example, its eight "parts of speech."

For that very reason—reader familiarity—this book is chiefly traditionalist in its bias. In recent years there has been an effort to establish the tranformational approach, especially, but I think that elementary-grade teachers haven't yet swung to it with much enthusiasm. Perhaps they have been reluctant to trade one complicated system just to get another. But perhaps its time will come.

Finally, *grammar* is often used among the masses in such expressions as "She uses good grammar" or "His grammar is awful." In this sense the word refers to some sort of standard, real or imagined, supposedly sanctioned by "educated speakers" of the language. As I indicated earlier, often this is really a reference to the subject of usage, and often to the desirability of avoiding such chuckholes and quicksand as the split infinitive and the *who-whom* distinction. These problems are partly grammatical, true, but they are in the overlap area on grammar's fringes.

But let us begin at grammar's core, where there is a consensus (inspired and developed by the higher classes) about what's proper and what isn't. All classes would agree that it's ungrammatical to say:
 There is more food than I eat can.
Such syntax would be perfectly acceptable in German, but it's just not English—not in any current dialect that I know of. Here's another bothersome construct:
 The toads squats under the bushes.
Here, obviously, we don't need to rearrange the parts; we need only change the shape of one word.
 The toads squat (or "toad squats") under the bushes.
Presto! We have a legitimate English sentence, one that we can call grammatical, one that "makes sense" without ambiguity. Finally, consider "Because he was in love." Don't call it a sentence; call it only a fragment, which we will soon discuss.

LL-G1 *Recognizing sentences*

If you have trouble distinguishing between word-groups that are sentences and those that aren't, you have your work cut out for you. It is imperative that you learn the difference, and soon; there are just too many potential writing problems, otherwise. If you don't have good "sentence sense" naturally, you'll just have to develop it painstakingly, by analysis of sentences and their parts.

A "simple" sentence is a special word-group that is said to be grammatically *independent*, which means that it meets certain formal requirements:

1. It begins with a capital letter.
2. It consists of one "clause," including both a *subject* (the main thing the sentence talks about) and a *predicate* (what is said about the subject).

The subject can also be defined as the element that controls the verb's "inflection" or form-changes.
3. It ends with a period, question mark, exclamation point, or, rarely, dots or white space.

There's also a fourth requirement (it asserts no "external dependency") that we'll talk about soon. And we must examine units that are somewhat more complicated than "simple" sentences. But consider now just these easy ones:

One-word subjects:
Fred | was re-elected.
She | drinks too much.
Phrase subjects:
Climbing these stairs | is hard work!
To get ahead | was his constant goal.

Note that the subject ordinarily is up front, ahead of the predication. There are a few exceptions:
1. In commands and requests the subject may be merely understood, not expressed: *(You)* | Be quiet! *(You)* | Come with me, please.
2. In questions the subject is often swallowed in a verb phrase: Will *you* go with her? (To see it clearly, recast it as a statement: *You* | will go with her.)
3. In inverted sentences come strange patterns: "How lucky *I* am."—or even "How lucky am *I*!"

Now, you're finding this about subjects all very interesting, of course. Actually, though, the place to begin a sentence analysis is in the predicate, and more particularly at its beating heart, the *verb*. A verb is a word or word-group that expresses something about the subject.

Sometimes we can have a one-word predicate (a verb alone):
His plan | *failed.* Honesty | *pays.*
Sometimes it will be a verb phrase:
I | *was working.* She | *should have been promoted.*
Sometimes either the verb or the subject will require a word to complete its meaning, a complete-ment or *complement*: He | *kissed* HER. The boys | *were throwing* a FOOTBALL. The building | *was* HUGE. In these sentences the verbs are in italic type, the complements in small capitals. Here they are in diagrams:

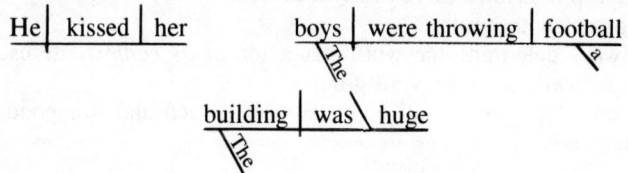

Often either the subject or the predicate, or both, will contain a number of "modifiers" or qualifying terms (shown in italics): He | kissed her *on the cheek.* All | *quickly* ran *inside. The old* woman | was *very* weary *by then.*

● We are now ready to state a rule. *In analyzing a simple sentence, always follow this sequence:* (1) *verb,* (2) *subject,* (3) *complement,* (4) *modifiers.* When

27

you think you've found a verb, look around for a suitable subject for it. If you can't find one, your "verb" just might be something else. By definition every verb must have a subject.

		Stare at this box until you have it memorized.
V	1	Verb
S	2	Subject
C	3	Complement
M	4	Modifier(s)

LL-G2 *The eight "parts of speech"*

If you are fairly clear now about subjects and predicates, it's time to consider them in some greater detail. To do this, analysts of modern English recognize eight categories of words—eight "parts of speech"—and it will be useful to know about them.[17]

How are the categories derived? By classifying every word in the language according to two or three different systems: (1) its grammatical function, as, for instance, a modifier of a verb; (2) its form, like the final *'s* of a possessive noun; (3) its kind of assertion or meaning, such as a verb's statement of an action, or a noun's naming of a place (Arizona, Boston).

Let's use an example; consider the short sentence "Chaplin's smile faded." *Chaplin's* is classified as an adjective. Why? Because of its function (modifier of the noun *smile*), its form (a noun turned into a modifier by the possesive ending *'s*), and its type of assertion (it's a descriptive and limiting word). Second, the word *smile* is a noun, partly because of its function as the verb's subject, partly because of its type of meaning (naming a thing). Finally, we recognize *faded* as a verb because of its function (it asserts something about the subject *smile*), because of its form (*-ed* ending showing past tense), and because of its kind of assertion (statement of an action).

But words are tricky. They often have more than one meaning (*e.g.*, a *leaf* may grow on a bush, or be part of a book or table-top. But, trickier still, a word also may have more than one function in a sentence. For instance, the word *long* can be a noun, verb, adjective, or adverb.

The ship tooted too *longs* and one short. (Noun)
I *long* to hear her voice. (Verb)
It was a *long* sermon. (Adjective)
Keep it as *long* as you like. (Adverb)

So here comes another rule:

• Always determine the word's function *in its context*, its use in some *particular sentence* or other word-group.

And now let's look at all eight parts of speech and, for good measure, the related "verbals."

1. *Nouns*

A noun is sometimes defined as the name of a person, place, thing, quality, concept, and so on. A much better idea, though, is to talk about the way it *functions*. What are its *uses*? Here is a list of noun functions that you may want to refer to later—when you're feeling up to it:

a. Subject of verb: The *rowboat* was waterlogged.
b. Complement (five kinds):
   (1) Direct object: Sue bought a *present*.
   (2) Indirect object: She bought her *mother* a present.
   (3) Predicate noun (a type of "subjective complement"):
       She is a sweet *girl*.
       She became the new *vice-president*.
   (4) Objective complement: We elected Bill *chairman*.
   (5) Retained object: I was asked my *opinion*.
c. Object of a preposition:... to the *store*; ... after the *game*; ... of the *king*, etc.
d. Appositive: Greta Garbo, the *actress*, was beautiful.
e. Direct address: *Bill*, please call your office.
f. Adverbial noun: He arrives *Friday* and leaves next *month*.
g. Nominative absolute: The *snow* having fallen, we got out our skis.
h. Subject of an infinitive: We knew *Dorothy* to be competent.
i. Subject of some gerunds: She disliked the *leadership* of the group being all white.

By *function*—that's one way of classifying nouns. If we happen to have other purposes, though, we can set up different classifications:

a. "Common" or "proper"
   A "proper" noun specifies a particular person, place, or thing: *Aaron Burr, New York City*, the *Mona Lisa*. A "common" noun does not so specify (*man, city, painting*) and is usually not capitalized.
b. Concrete or abstract
   A concrete noun refers to something that we perceive with our senses: *bird, table*.
   An abstract noun names a concept in our heads: *justice, love, democracy*.
c. Collectives
   A collective noun names a group as a unit: *army, band, committee, jury*, etc.
d. Singular or plural
   Most nouns have "number"—that is, they change shape to make a plural form: *window, windows; woman, women; fly, flies*. A few don't: *species, species; moose, moose*.
e. Possessive nouns
   Nouns take still another form whenever they're possessives. They usually add *'s* (*the girl's hair*) or, if it's a plural noun, *s'* (*several girls' hair*). The term "possessive" gets us into the topic of Case, which will be discussed in the next chapter. Please be patient.
f. Masculine or feminine or neuter
   Some nouns have not only number and case but also gender: *waiter, waitress; hero, heroine*. Women's Liberation people, however, resent the fact that many status-giving positions (*chair-*

man, spokesman, statesman, etc.) seem to have been appropriated by males. There is a drive on now to create neuter substitutes: *chairperson, mail carrier,* etc.

2. *Pronouns*

A pronoun is simply a word (or pair) substituting for a noun: *you, it, himself, each other.* There are a flock of them. They will get some attention in the next chapter, but here's at least a quick classification for future reference, with a few examples.

    a. Personal pronouns: *I, we, our, you, her*
    b. Relative pronouns: *who, which, that*
    c. Interrogative pronouns: *who, which, what*
    d. Indefinite pronouns: *any, some, no one*
    e. Demonstrative pronouns: *this, that, these, those*
    f. Reciprocal pronouns: *each other, one another*
    g. Reflexive pronouns: *myself, yourself, herself* (as in "I cut *myself.*")
    h. Intensive pronouns: *myself, yourself, herself* (as in "I *myself* wrote that letter!")

A Lower-Lower person cannot ordinarily be expected to make much sense out of this list. Only a few extraordinary L-L people will even give a damn.

3. *Adjectives*

An adjective's function is to modify a noun or pronoun. Ordinarily the adjective snuggles up very close to its noun: *sugarless* gum; *old* man; *one* second; *hollow* log; *the* woman, *tall* and *slender*. But a common type called a predicate adjective is used back farther to complete the meaning of a slightly foggy subject: They were by now frankly *afraid*. She seems quite *contented*.

Confusingly enough, several kinds of pronouns are classified as both pronouns and adjectives: *that* house, *our* future, *some* day, *which* way? Another irksome matter, "comparison" of adjectives and adverbs, will be discussed later. All in good time.

4. *Verbs and Verbals*

Verbs are another subject dumped into the next chapter. But we should say a few more things about them here. A verb's function is to make an assertion about its subject in terms of an action or state of being. English verbs are sometimes difficult for foreigners (and Puerto Ricans) to learn, because some important verbs take irregular shapes. Native speakers have an advantage, and therefore usually climb the social ladder with more ease.

One thing for you to do here is learn *three types of verbs*. We need some shorthand terms.

    a. An *intransitive* verb doesn't have any complement. It makes sufficient sense without one: I *am waiting*. She *types*. There it *is* [exists].

    I | am waiting

    b. A *transitive* verb, however, needs a "direct object" as its complement: The dog *chased* its *tail*. She *cashed* my *check*. ("The dog chased" and "She cashed" are meaningless fragments alone.) The verbs focus their action on their objects.

    She | cashed | check

c. A *linking* verb is entirely different. It expresses little or no action; it merely joins together the subject and an important term in the predicate—a "subjective complement," which can be either a predicate noun or a predicate adjective. (She *is* a legal secretary. The roast *smells* delicious.) These words are (1) forms of the verb *be*, (2) related verbs like *appear, seem, become,* and (3) verbs of our senses (*see, feel, smell, sound, taste*). Linking verbs set up a relationship between two terms: "The roast smells delicious" means "The roast is in the whole class of things which are delicious-smelling."

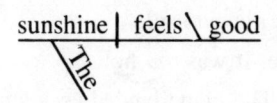

sunshine | feels \ good
            \ The

Now, a curious thing about verbs is that each has given birth to a trio of related creatures called *verbals*. These three—gerunds, participles, and infinitives—all look and act very much like verbs. For instance, they can take complements and be modified by adverbs.

• Be not deceived! Study the difference between a verb and a verbal!

A verb asserts something about a subject; a verbal has other business. A verbal looks like a verb, but actually it functions always as *another* part of speech, *never* as a verb.

GERUND (a verbal noun, always with an *-ing* ending)
   Sailing is fun. She enjoyed *swimming.*
   Sailing | is \ fun

PARTICIPLE (a verbal *adjective,* sometimes with an *-ing* ending)
   The *fleeing* convict stumbled and fell. (Present participle)
   The dog, *alarmed,* cowered under the bed. (Past participle)

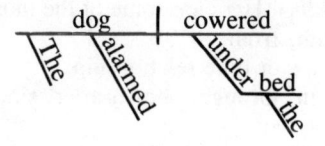

dog | cowered
 \The \alarmed \under \bed
                        \the

Participles are also used to create verb phrases: *am waiting, had been fleeing, was alarmed.*

INFINITIVE (a flexible creature that can be a noun, adjective, or adverb; ordinarily introduced with "to," the "sign of the infinitive")
   To meet her is *to fall* in love with her. (Both nouns)
   Spring is the season *to plant*. (Adjective—it's the "to plant"-season)
   I am happy *to go*. (Adverb modifying the adjective "happy"; I am "to go"-happy—that kind of happy.)

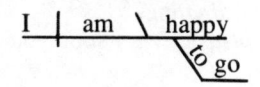

I | am \ happy
          \to go

We often omit the "to" when it follows certain verbs:
She helped (to) plan the party.
I don't dare (to) say anything.
Need I (to) go on?
Let him (to) go!

5. *Adverbs*

The function of an adverb is to modify a verb, an adjective, another adverb, or a whole clause or sentence.

    a. With a verb: She played *well*.

    b. With an adjective: It was *too* hot.

    c. With an adverb: The plane landed *very* smoothly.

    d. With a sentence: *Yes,* you may go. The ring was soon found, *luckily*.

Adverbs are popular little devices, useful in all sorts of situations. They indicate:
Time: *soon, now, tomorrow.*
Place: *here, there, everywhere.*
Manner: *softly, quickly.*
Direction: *south, left, right, up.*
Degree: *very, too, quite.*
Frequency: *often, rarely.*
Affirmation or negation, or condition: *yes, not, possibly, perhaps.*

(In "L-M Grammar" will be a unit on the handling of adjectives and adverbs. No doubt you can hardly wait.)

6. *Prepositions*

The function of a preposition is to relate a noun (or pronoun) to some other part of the sentence. That noun is called the *object* of the preposition (see Nouns). If it's actually a pronoun, it should be in the objective case (between Jerry and *me*; give it to *him*). Here are some of the most common prepositions:
    of, for, by, with, from, to

Often they express a space or time relationship:
    at, on, under, in, through, above, after, since

Occasionally they will be word-groups:
    in spite of, together with, in front of

Don't confuse the preposition *to* (followed by a noun or pronoun) with *to,* the sign of the infinitive. The infinitive usually shows action: to chop, to swim, to have voted.

Don't be afraid to end a sentence with a preposition; bans on such constructions are old-fashioned. Avoid awkwardness, though. That's one thing the reader won't put up with.

7. *Conjunctions*

A conjunction is a joining word; it hooks together words, phrases, and clauses, and even can link logically a sentence to others nearby. There are two types, *coordinating* and *subordinating.*

• *Pay close attention, please.* Very soon you'll be examining "clauses," and you'll need these terms.

a. *Coordinating* conjunctions (*and, or, but, nor,* etc.) join units of similar grammatical type or rank.
Linking words: He likes you *and* me.
Linking phrases: Put them in the kitchen *or* on the porch.
Linking clauses: He was going to leave, *but* I still wanted to dance.

b. *Subordinating* conjunctions (*if, after, although, when, where, unless,* etc.) make richer sentences by linking subordinate or "dependent" clauses to main clauses.
Because he was sick, he couldn't go.
He will stay *if* you will buy another beer.

There are very few coordinating conjunctions, but lots of these subordinating conjunctions. As we go along, try to recognize as many of the latter as you can. They will always signal that the clause following is *dependent*.

8. *Interjections*
An interjection is a word left over after all the other words were classified. It has no real grammatical reason for being in the sentence. Its only function is to express some emotion—everything from a rather bored *Well, well* through a mild *Oh* to *Ouch!* and *Ah!* (Never use more than one exclamation point, incidentally; you don't want to overdo a good thing.)

LL-G3   *Sentence types*

a. *Simple sentences*

We started out defining a "simple" sentence, you remember, with its "subject" and "predicate." By now you should have a pretty good idea of how subjects and predicates are built from parts of speech. (If not, please review.) Such a sentence, perhaps you've discovered, is not always as simple as it looks. Building a good one is a little like playing good chess. You need to know how each piece is played most effectively.

But things get still more complicated. First, let's label what it is you make when you create a simple sentence; it's called an *independent clause*. A clause is a word-group with a subject and a predicate. It's "independent" if it doesn't begin with one of those *subordinating* conjunctions we just looked at, or some other connecting word with the same function. There is no "external dependency"; it doesn't lean on any other clause; it can make perfect sense alone.
Her horse loves sugar cubes.
Larry waxes his car once a month.

Second, the simple sentence can take different syntactical shapes. Do you recall the "three types of verbs" defined a few pages back? Let's use them here to set up three basic clause patterns:

- Pattern 1, based on an intransitive verb (without any complement): $S—iV$
  He *is dancing*. She *will be talking*.
- Pattern 2, based on a transitive verb (demanding a direct object), with two variations:
  a. $S–tV–dO$
  The Israelis invaded *Egypt*.

b. *S—tV—iO—dO* (adding an indirect object)
   Sue sent *Dad* a present.
   Dan has given the *blood bank* three pints.
c. *S—tV—dO—OC* (adding an objective complement)
   She called him a *traitor*.
   We elected her *president*.

- Pattern 3, based on a linking verb and two kinds of "subjective complements":

  a. *S—lV—PN* (predicate noun)
     Senator Jones was a *dove* during the Vietnam War.
     Senator Smith is a *hawk*.
     Both seemed patriotic *men*.
  b. *S—lV—PA* (predicate adjective)
     The coat is *handsome*.
     The price seems *reasonable*.
     His offer smelled *fishy*.

In each case, we can think of the elements of the pattern as the clause's skeletal structure. Everything else is flesh.

Finally, we can deliberately introduce a little complexity into the sentence—taking care, howeer, that the flesh is not fatty:

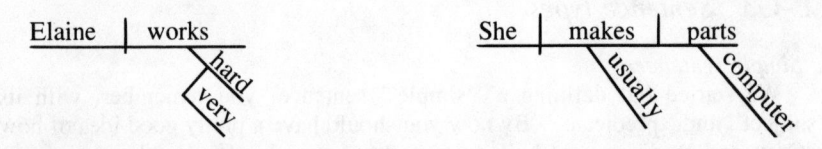

Elaine | works
         \hard
          \very

She | makes | parts
       \usually
              \computer

If we like, the front end of the sentence can be changed into a *compound* subject:

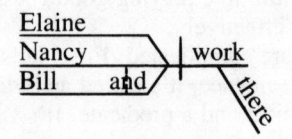

Elaine
Nancy   \ | work
Bill and /   \there

Or we can create a compound *predicate*:

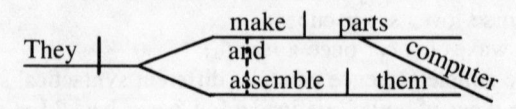

           make | parts
They | and   \computer
           assemble | them

This is still just one clause, however, so it's still called a simple sentence. So let's draw a simple diagram:

| Subject | Predicate | or | S | P |

But of course we can make sentences with more than one clause. Read on.

34

b. *Compound sentences*

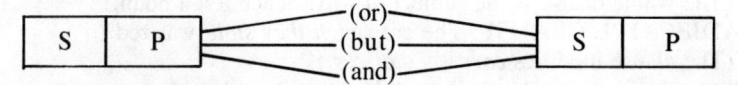

```
┌─────┬─────┐    ─(or)─      ┌─────┬─────┐
│  S  │  P  │════─(but)─════│  S  │  P  │
└─────┴─────┘    ─(and)─     └─────┴─────┘
```

Elaine works hard *and* she saves her money.

Small children sometimes use these coordinating conjunctions (*and, but, or*) to create long compound sentences. Theoretically one could hook clauses together, like boxcars, for hours and hours.

No questions? All right, let's move on to the third kind of sentence.

c. *Complex sentences*

In this case we have one main (or independent) clause, and, tacked on somewhere appropriate, at least one subordinate (or dependent) clause.

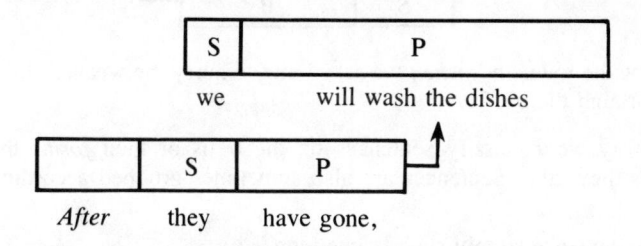

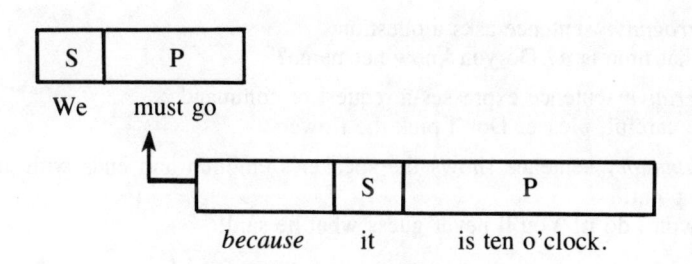

```
         ┌───┬──────────────┐
         │ S │      P       │
         └───┴──────────────┘
          we   will wash the dishes

┌──────┬───┬──────────┐
│      │ S │    P     │↑
└──────┴───┴──────────┘
 After   they  have gone,


┌───┬──────┐
│ S │  P   │
└───┴──────┘
 We   must go
      ↑
      └────┬──────┬──────────────┐
           │      │   S   │   P      │
           └──────┴──────┴──────────┘
            because   it   is ten o'clock.
```

● *A clause introduced by a subordinating conjunction automatically becomes a dependent fragment.*

"They have gone" makes sense alone. "*After* they have gone" does not. "It's ten o'clock" makes sense. "*Because* it's ten o'clock" does not.

The conjunction's meaning indicates the kind of logical relationship created as this dependent element is attached to the main clause:

It happened *before* you came. (Tells time)

If I haven't made a mistake, it should run now. (Sets up a condition) —and so on.

● *A dependent or subordinate clause functions in the sentence as a single part of speech*—a noun, adjective, or adverb.

(1) ADVERB CLAUSE: The illustrations above are all adverb clauses.

There are also noun clauses and adjective clauses.

(2) NOUN CLAUSE: *What she told us* was true.
   (The whole clause is the subject of *was*; hence it's a noun.)
(3) ADJECTIVE CLAUSE: The car *which they stole* was red.
   (The clause modifies *car*; it's *that* car.)
We'll say more, soon, about all three kinds of complex sentences.

d. *Compound-complex sentences*

This sentence type has at least one subordinate clause and at least *two* main clauses. Example:

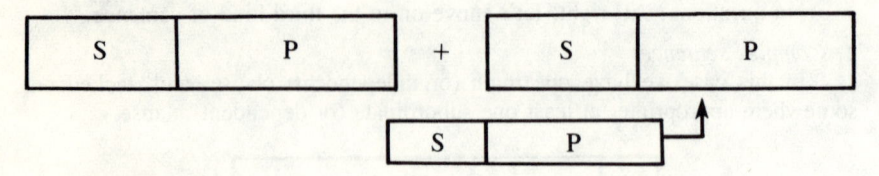

```
[  S  |  P  ]  +  [  S  |  P  ]
              [ S | P ]
```

He knew the town *and, when* we asked him to hurry, he weaved skillfully through the traffic.

That's the way we'd classify sentences on the basis of their *form*, the four basic shapes they take. Sentences are also sometimes grouped according to their *function:*

(1) A *declarative* sentence simply states something.
   That's my pen. It's raining hard.
(2) An *interrogative* sentence asks a question.
   What time is it? Do you know her name?
(3) An *imperative* sentence expresses a request or command.
   Be careful, please. Don't pick the flowers.
(4) An *exclamatory* sentence shows the speaker's emotion and ends with an exclamation point.
   I won't do it! You'll never guess what he said!

LL-G4 *Phrases*

At this point we should back up a bit, and take a closer look at some forms we hardly glanced at in our hurry. A *phrase* is a technical term meaning a word-group that does *not* have a subject and verb—but which, like the dependent clauses, functions as a noun, adjective, or adverb. (There is also a verb phrase; it will be examined later under ''Verbs.'')

You remember that we said that a verbal, like its parent verb, can beef itself up; it can take a complement and be modified by adverbs. Now we shall see it happen. Three types of phrases are merely these *extended verbals.*

a. GERUND PHRASES
   Making model ships was his hobby. (Noun—subject of verb)
   They enjoyed *pulling the taffy*. (Noun—direct object)

b. PARTICIPIAL PHRASES
   The girl *pushing the grocery cart* is his daughter.
                                    (Adjective modifying *girl*)
   The men, *obviously baffled,* grew silent.
                                    (Adjective modifying *men*)
c. INFINITIVE PHRASES
   To go there now would be dangerous. (Noun—subject)
   I want *to stop as soon as possible.* (Noun—direct object)
   Let's find a place *to have lunch.*
                        (Adjective—It's a "to have lunch"-place.)
   I'm pleased *to meet you.*
                        (Adverb—I'm "to meet you"-pleased.)
The other kinds of phrases, however, are different breeds entirely.

d. PREPOSITIONAL PHRASES
This type consists basically of a preposition and its object. Like the infinitive phrase, it's very versatile. It may be a noun, adjective, or adverb.

   After supper is the best time of the day. (Noun—subject)
   He was holding a book *of plays.* (Adjective modifying *book*)
   Dad went *to the store.* (Adverb modifying *went*)

e. NOUN PHRASES
This vague term is used here to refer to constructions in which a nonverbal noun (*mouse, ink, tree*) is modified by one or more adjectives: *the tall tree, the Bentleys' dilapidated old toolshed.*

f. ABSOLUTE PHRASES
One kind of "absolute" (syntactically independent) expression is the nominative-absolute phrase. This type is composed of a noun (or pronoun) and a participle modifying it, together with any other baggage attached to either. The whole thing is supposedly independent—but in reality it ordinarily functions as an adverb modifying the sentence to which it is loosely connected.
   The snowfall having stopped, we decided to leave the cafe.
   The old man being very tired, he tottered to the park bench.
   He sat there, *the snow piling gently on him.*
Other absolutes are a few verbal phrases which have sailed away from their sentences into autonomy. They enjoy a detached existence in some of our illogical idioms.
   Considering his age, he looks healthy.
   To sum up, the situation looks rather bleak.

LL-G5 *Clauses*

You remember, I hope, that a clause is a word-group with a subject and predicate. We have had perhaps enough examples of independent or main clauses, at least for now, but relatively few illustrations of dependent or subordinate clauses. A pity, too; they are rather interesting creatures, once you get to know them. As complex nouns, adjectives, and adverbs, they add extraordinary variety and richness to the sentence.

a. *Noun clauses*

Nouns, as you know, enjoy the distinction of holding down important positions in the sentence—subject, predicate noun, direct object, and so on. We have seen that the same eminence is attained by those verbals and phrases which exercise what I call here "the noun functions." And now we shall discover that noun clauses, too, can do anything that any other noun can do. Most noun clauses are built right into the sentence's basic skeletal structure:

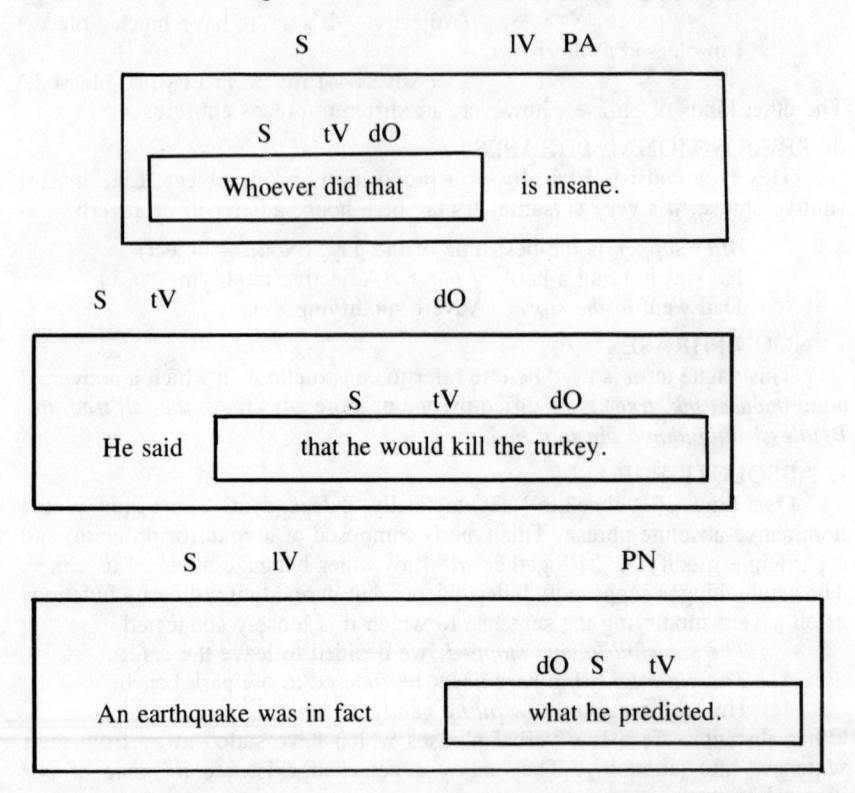

```
           S                    lV  PA
  ┌─────────────────────────────────────┐
  │      S    tV  dO                    │
  │    ┌──────────────────┐             │
  │    │ Whoever did that │  is insane. │
  │    └──────────────────┘             │
  └─────────────────────────────────────┘

   S    tV                              dO
  ┌─────────────────────────────────────────────┐
  │                   S    tV    dO             │
  │          ┌────────────────────────────────┐ │
  │ He said  │ that he would kill the turkey. │ │
  │          └────────────────────────────────┘ │
  └─────────────────────────────────────────────┘

        S   lV                          PN
  ┌──────────────────────────────────────────────┐
  │                            dO  S   tV        │
  │                         ┌───────────────────┐│
  │ An earthquake was in fact│ what he predicted.││
  │                         └───────────────────┘│
  └──────────────────────────────────────────────┘
```

b. *Adjective clauses*

Clauses that merely *modify* are ordinarily not as significant as noun clauses. Sometimes, in fact, they could be dropped right out and the sentence wouldn't really suffer. On the other hand, sometimes they are quite important indeed—even essential.

    ESSENTIAL ("restrictive")
        The cook *who was burned* has gone home.
    NON-ESSENTIAL ("nonrestrictive")
        The cook, *who was burned,* has gone home.

Do you see the difference in the two situations? (1) In the first, he is being singled out of a group of chefs; *that* one is at home. (2) In the second sentence he is the restaurant's *only* cook on this shift, and he's left. Any further information is just thrown in, between commas, as an extra dividend. (Incidentally, phrases and even single-word adjectives can be similarly "restrictive" or "nonrestrictive." See again the two participial phrases in LL-G4. Note how they are punctuated.)

It's important to distinguish between the two kinds of adjective clauses, and to remember the following rule:

● A restrictive or "essential" adjective clause is *not* set off by commas. A nonrestrictive clause is always set off—just to show that it could be lifted out, without damage to the sentence's central meaning.

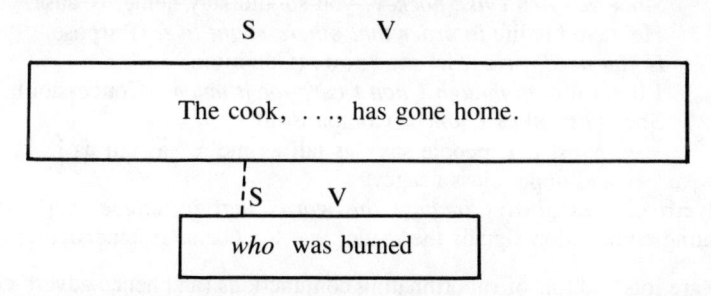

```
            S        V
┌─────────────────────────────────┐
│   The cook, ..., has gone home. │
└─────────────────────────────────┘
           │S      V
           ┌──────────────┐
           │ who was burned│
           └──────────────┘
```

The word that introduces an adjective clause is called a *relative*; it simply relates the dependent element to a noun in the main clause. Whereas a subordinating conjunction stands apart from the adverb clause's skeletal framework, the relative is usually an important structural word. (*Who*, above, is the subject of *was burned*.) Most relatives are pronouns: *who* (*whose, whom*), *whoever* (*whomever*), *what, which, that,* and so on. A few are adverbs: *when, where, why*.

I'll always remember the place *where we met*.

When speaking (and writing informally), sometimes we'll drop the "essential" relative:

The man [whom] *I called* was nice on the phone.

The time [that] *I spent with her* was wasted.

Only a few purists in the superior classes ever frown on such liberties.

c. *Adverb clauses*

Back in LL-G3c, "Complex sentences," there were several illustrations of clauses introduced by subordinating conjunctions—clauses that function adverbially. Like plain adverbs, adverb clauses are extremely useful in designing and building sentences. Just as plain adverbs often do, they can modify the main clause or its verb by telling the time, place, or manner of the action.

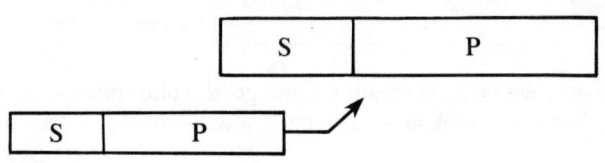

```
        ┌─────────┬─────────┐
        │   S     │    P    │
        └─────────┴─────────┘
                     ↗
   ┌─────┬─────┐
   │  S  │  P  │
   └─────┴─────┘
```

As we headed down the stairway, we spotted them coming up. (Time)
When you get there, call for a taxi. (Time)
Let's sit *where we can see well*. (Place)
I'll go *wherever you say*. (Place)
He walked *as if he were hurt*. (Manner)
Winston tastes good *as a cigarette should*. (Manner)
> ("Like a cigarette should" and "Tell it like it is" are regularly found in L-L, U-L, and L-M speech, and often in that of the Upper Middles. The upper classes don't approve of *like* as a conjunction.)

But adverb clauses do more than plain adverbs:
It rained *so* hard *that the streets were flooded*. (Result)
Since you don't like hockey, you should stay home. (Cause)
He gave his life *in order that others might live*. (Purpose)
If you need a ride, let me know. (Condition)
I'll eat it *even though I don't care for it much*. (Concession)
She is *as* tall *as I [am]*. (Comparison)
> (Most L-L people say "as tall as me"; "as tall as I" is middle and upper class usage.)

● Adverb clauses *always include the words that introduce them*. A subordinating conjunction signals the reader that the clause is dependent.

There are lots and lots of subordinating conjunctions (and hence adverb clauses) in the speech of all social classes, including L-L. So don't be intimidated by them; you're already familiar with them.

Here's a good place for you to stop and do some reviewing. In your notebook, copy the chart below (enlarging it considerably) and fill it with examples in each category. Be neat, please; your instructor may ask to see your work. Save the chart for future reference.

FUNCTION	Parts of Speech	Verbals	Phrases	Clauses
NOUN	Noun	Gerund	Ger. phrase	Noun clause
	Pronoun	Infinitive	Inf. phrase	
			Prep. phrase	
ADJECTIVE	Adjective	Participle	Part. phrase	Adjective clause
		Infinitive	Inf. phrase	
			Prep. phrase	
ADVERB	Adverb	Infinitive	Inf. phrase	Adverb clause
			Prep. phrase	

Up to now we've been creating some good, solid, middle-class models for emulation. Now let's look at some danger areas. Imitate at your own risk.

LL-G6 *The sentence fragment*

Even though we have been speaking American English for years—all our lives—we can still make mistakes with its grammar. That is, we can construct something that people in a higher class will *call* a mistake. The ambitious person, obviously, must seek to minimize the number of such incidents.

One construction often catalogued as an error is the fragmentary or incomplete sentence. Now, let's be fair; sometimes the grammarians have a point. They make sense, for instance, if they say something like this:

> It is obvious that conversational speech doesn't consist always of full sentences, with subjects and verbs neatly in place. No, frequently it's most effective to communicate in economical bursts: *Hello. Yeah. All right. When? Naah! Well— if you say so. No complaints. So long.* This sort of thing is common at all social levels. No class has difficulty handling such bits and pieces, especially since they're all given special intonations and other speech signals.
>
> But a problem arises in writing. Face it: it is deucedly difficult to *write* an effective fragment. It's hard to make it sound natural and, at the same time, both clear and graceful. As with other difficult skills, we get better at it with practice. An experienced writer also knows approximately how many readers will like his fragment and how many won't. But the college freshman often blunders and irritates too many.
>
> It all depends, of course, on the social context. If the freshman girl is merely writing colloquially to a boy friend back home, undoubtedly she will please even though she strings one fragment after another, like beads. At other times, too, she'll get away with it. For example, (1) she can answer questions that way: Which was his favorite? *The Augustan Age.* (2) She can dream up advertising copy: *Brings out the real you!* (3) She can write newspaper headlines: *Skid Road Christmas Grim.* (4) Or she might contruct a highbrow fragment beginning with *For*, sometimes called a coordinating conjunction (*For they had arrived*) or a middlebrow fragment beginning with *So*, as in *So they had a drink.* (5) She can try recording thought processes in fragments. And sometimes it will work. Sometimes. But if it is a formal writing occasion, she is urged to be careful.

Now, I'd call that a sensible comment. A good fragment *is* hard to write. In composition classes, you're well advised to avoid them entirely—at least until you're an experienced sophomore. At times the fragment is *just right* and, hence, worth a writer's gamble. But some fragments just aren't worth defending.

> She looked up quickly. *Because the prosecutor had called her name.*
> She rose from her chair.

There is an obvious ambiguity here (the *Because*-clause can point in either direction) and no evidence that the writer feels that clarity is important. How could we make the lines clearer? Well, let's begin with just the first two clauses; perhaps one of these sets will work:

1. She looked up quickly, because the prosecutor had called her name.
2. She looked up quickly; the prosecutor had called her name.
3. She looked up quickly. The prosecutor had called her name.

Here's another fragment:

> The situation now being under control.

Being is a verbal, not a verb. It just *looks* like a verb.
> FIXED: The situation *is* now under control.

The remedy for a clumsy fragment, then, is either (a) attachment to an independent clause or (b) transformation of the fragment into an independent clause. That's a simple, easy process. A nice thing about fragments is that they're easy to fix.

LL-G7 *The comma fault*

Here again we get into a swampy area where skillful writers can maneuver easily, and others get all bogged down. Most grammar books simply give us an iron law: *Don't* hook two *independent* clauses together with just a comma.

- A comma is often used to join together sentence elements of *unequal* grammatical rank. It's confusing, therefore, to find it linking two clauses of *equal* rank. Don't confuse the reader.

A violation of this rule is like signalling for a right turn and then suddenly swinging your car left. You've given the other drivers bad information. In writing, this error is called the comma fault or comma splice:
> He worked Christmas at the post office in town, the family needed extra money.
>
> Sandy wanted a swim, the water was much too cold.

There are several ways of bringing these into conformity with the writing standards of the higher classes. Among them:

1. Insert a coordinating conjunction after the comma.
> Sandy wanted a swim, *but* the water was much too cold.
2. Instead of a comma, use a semicolon.
> Sandy wanted a swim; the water was much too cold.
3. As a variant of the model above, try using a semicolon and a "conjunctive" or joining adverb.
> Sandy wanted a swim; *however,* the water was much too cold.

Be especially careful, though, with conjunctive and other adverbs. If you forget the semicolon, they can create serious ambiguity when put between two independent clauses.
> I wish I'd stayed away, *after all,* I came back just to please my mother.
>
> He's right, *at any rate,* he ought to know.

One purpose of punctuation is to make the meaning clear.
> It rained; *unfortunately,* we had to stay in.
>
> OR: It rained, *unfortunately;* we had to stay in.

(For more examples, see U-L Punctuation and LM-G3.)

4. Make two sentences.
> Sandy wanted a swim. The water was much too cold.
>
> OR: Sandy wanted a swim. But the water was much too cold.
5. Make one of the clauses subordinate to the other.
> *Although* Sandy wanted a swim, the water was much too cold.
>
> He worked Christmas at the post office in town, *because* the family needed extra money.

Now, suppose you'd written two very short clauses like this:
> He worked Christmas, he needed the money.

Or suppose you'd knotted the comma splice with a conjunctive adverb this way:
> I had a cold, *therefore* I didn't go to work.

Or, finally, suppose you'd yoked together a *series* of simple clauses (three or more) with commas:
> He had designed it, he had built it, and now he would see if it worked.
>
> She adored him, her eyes followed his every move, she would have died for him.

Those are not very troublesome, it seems to me; at least there's no ambiguity. But you gamble a little when you construct any comma fault. Ordinarily a requisite of a *good* one is a certain attention to grammatical parallelism (see L-U Grammar). As in all constructions, we want the sentence clear, natural, and graceful.

LL-G8 *The fused sentence*

I tried to suggest that sometimes a skilled writer can build a comma-spliced sentence and get away with it. But not even the Upper-Lower Class would accept the fused sentence. Here two independent clauses are run together with neither conjunction nor punctuation.

> Dick tried to join the police force he was too small.

Repair this monstrosity the way you would a comma splice. And don't write any more—or you won't make it to the U-L class.

LL-G9 *The mixed construction*

In this survey of grammatical mud-holes, the worst has been saved for last. No self-respecting L-L hobo would countenance it. Fused sentences are confusing, but this abomination is even more so:

> The fact that the boiler in the building was by that time quite old and rusty, we were afraid that it might burst.

What's happened is something like this: the writer started out to say one thing (a noun and an appositive clause, to be used together as a *subject*) and ended with a different, incompatible construction. He forgot; he thought the sentence had begun with a dependent clause; he imagined the words *Because the boiler*... This kind of mishmash usually occurs when one is tired, or when writing long and rather complicated statements, or both.

MIXED: Consider for a moment, if you will, the problems faced by the young unwed mother are often very difficult for even the most stable person to handle.
FIXED: Consider for a moment, if you will, the problems faced by the young unwed mother. They are often very difficult for even the most stable person to handle.

This section can be regarded as a kind of initiation manual for advancement to the next highest level, U-L Grammar. There is, however, frequently a gap between grammatical *standards* and the actual practices of a given social class—as the next section will demonstrate.

L-L USAGE

For some time I have been a little unhappy with such word-usage labels as *vulgate* or *vulgar* or *vulgarism*, *formal* and *informal*, *colloquial*, and *substandard*. To me, they lack the precision necessary for them to be really useful terms. One difficulty is that, as often as not, they blur or simply ignore the facts of class stratification. For example, a word or phrase substandard to one class may be solidly fixed usage in another. But a more important problem is that many usage "systems" simply do not employ enough terms—enough to allow the subtle discriminations we often wish to make. I have seen systems of only two standards (formal, informal); three (formal, informal, substandard); four (formal, general, informal, "nonstandard"). But I shall be content with no less than six, and I shall want them closely related to socioeconomic realities: L-L, U-L, L-M, U-M, L-U, and U-U.

Altering the classification system, of course, wouldn't change things much. Writers will continue to range up and down the usage scales in search of the most appropriate words they can find. In producing the grand organ tones of the English language, good writers (and speakers) play notes all over the keyboard. Yet there are also beginning writers with a much narrower range. And many of those attempting a broad range play the keyboard falteringly and clumsily. The result, often, is a good many discordant notes.

I hope sincerely that this book's six-class usage system helps us all to sharpen our images and to make finer, more delicate choices in our diction. A goal for all of us is maximum clarity. Other values cherished in writing (and other endeavors) are honesty, logicality, energy, grace, and, beyond grace, a certain sparkle. But clarity is perhaps what we must concentrate on first. And clarity depends largely upon one's accuracy and precision.

This book won't catalog all the characteristics of our class-structured language, certainly—but there will be enough examples to enable the reader to make intelligent inferences about most locutions he discovers out there in the "real" world. A careful reader will almost certainly learn something about the way a language works, and will come to appreciate the richness of American English.

Occasionally we will take note of some *jargon* (commercial, journalistic, legal, etc.), which is the special language of the pyramids mentioned and pictured in Chapter 1. A full analysis of lower-class speech would do justice to criminal jargon and to ghetto dialects (now commonly black-proletarian). Rarely, also, there will be a *localism*, a word or phrase found only in a particular region; a *slang* term, originally a flashy attempt at novelty; a *technical* term, or an *obsolete* word.

Let us begin with some illustrations of L-L usage, remembering always that our job is primarily reporting and description, and secondarily the making of various snide judgments. First, what *is* standard practice for the Lower-Lower Class? Second, why should the practice be stopped?

Ahold of. The accepted idiom is "(get) *hold of.*"

Ain't. A form derived from various ancient British contractions with "not" (*amn't, a'n't, ha'n't, i'n't*). Since many U-L and L-M speakers frown on this word as "bad grammar," it will have to rest here in disgrace. Common in speech, rarely written.

Any more. Localism for *now, these days,* etc.
    Avoid: Grandpa is feelin' better *any more.*

Be, without auxiliary support. Found chiefly in the black-proletarian dialect.
    Avoid: They *be* goin' soon. She *be* gettin' ready. He *be* home tomorrow.
    Say instead: They *are* (or *will be*) going soon.
              She *is* (or *will be*) getting ready.

Being as how. A rather tortured substitute for a subordinating conjunction like *since, because,* or *as.*

Could of. Careless mistake of *could have,* caused no doubt by the similarity of sounds. Casual speech has *could've.*

Didn't nobody (find it, etc.). A black-proletarian version of the double-negative sentence "Nobody didn't (find it)."

Didn't ought to. A substitute for *shouldn't.*
    She *shouldn't* have gone (not *didn't ought to* have gone).

Don't never, Don't have no, etc. Double negatives are stigmatized. Another to avoid: They *don't* let us use it *only* on Saturdays.

Drownded. The approved past participle is *drowned.*

Good. This adjective is often misused in place of the adverb *well.*
    Avoid: He sings *good.*

Gotta. Lower-class pronunciation of the L-M term *got to,* as in "I *gotta* go." The U-M says "I *have got* to go"; the upper classes say "I *must* go."

Had of. The approved form is simply *had.* I wish you *had* (not *had of*) called me.

Had ought, hadn't ought. Substitutes for *ought* and *ought not.* The cops *ought* (not *had ought*) to leave us alone.

Hisself. Say *himself.*

It ain't no (Santa Claus, etc.). *It* is sometimes a black-proletarian substitute for *There.* (Note the double negative, common in this dialect.) See also *They's.*

Learn. This verb means "to get knowledge (or a skill)." L-L speakers sometimes confuse it with *teach.*
    Avoid: I *learned* him a lesson he'll never forget!

Leave her do it, etc. *Leave* usually means "depart." *Let* means "permit." Say "*Let* her do it." (But "Leave her alone" is an accepted idiom.)

May of, Might of, Must of. Not *of* but *have*: May *have,* etc.

My sister she, Mr. Hayes he. The technical term for this construction is "pronominal apposition," here a superfluous restatement of the noun with a pronoun. Common in black-proletarian speech, it is also used by both L-L and U-L whites.

Nowheres. A substitute for *nowhere*.
>Avoid: He came *nowheres* near it.

Ought to of. More confusion of *have* and *of*.

Poorly: A localism for *in poor health, not well*.
>Avoid: Grandpa is feeling *poorly*.
>Avoid: Grandpa is *poorly* any more.

Should of. Confused with *should have*.

Somewheres. A substitute for *somewhere*.
>Avoid: Look *somewheres* else.

They's. Black-proletarian for *There's*.
>Avoid: *They's* no use tryin'.

This here, That there. Redundant forms of *this, that*.

Would of. L-L substitute for *would have*.

L-L PUNCTUATION

The various punctuation marks are used to suggest some of the gestures and pauses and voice tones we use in speaking. They help us to group concepts together, separate them, qualify them. They help us, in other words, to communicate with maximum clarity.

The simpler the sentence, the easier the punctuation job. Generally speaking, written sentences tend to be rather long and complicated at the highest social levels, somewhat shorter and simpler in lower-class writing. In this chapter we shall examine only three punctuation devices: those that end the sentence. Consult the index for the whereabouts of other items you're especially fond of.

LL-P1   *The question mark*

>End any direct question (sentence or fragment) with a question mark.
>>When will you be here? What time? When? Three o'clock?
>
>Occasionally you can crowd several questions into one sentence, like this:
>>Do you remember the Edsel? the Kaiser? the Cord?
>
>If it's only an *indirect* question, don't use a question mark; use a period instead.
>>He asked whether I knew her.

Some U-M letter-writers like to make requests in question form but without the question mark.
>Would you please be good enough to send me a copy of your latest catalog.

This outrageous practice should not be imitated by the lower classes. Perhaps it will die a natural death.

LL-P2   *The exclamation point*

>Following an outburst of strong feeling, use an exclamation point.
>>Stop the car! Ouch! You'll be late!

Over-use, however, will seriously weaken your writing! Employ this device only when absolutely necessary!

LL-P3 *The period*

Most sentences are declarative, like this one, and end with a period. Gentle commands and requests end the same way.
> Watch your step. Come back tomorrow.

Most abbreviations also require periods: Ms., Mrs., B.C., Ave., *e.g.*, etc. But many public agencies are abbreviated without periods: UNESCO, ROTC, NATO, and so on. Quite a few other terms are now written that way—DDT and TV, for instance, and state abbreviations in ZIP addresses (CA for California, NJ for New Jersey). This is, however, an area in which usage differs. Consult a recently published dictionary when in doubt.

Periods are also used with figures (see L-L Mechanics) and in ellipses—but only Upper Middles and the upper classes seem to use ellipses, so they needn't concern us now.

If you're asked to write a theme, it should have a title. *Don't* put a period after the title—although you might have some other mark:
> One Minute To Play! Why Didn't I Listen?

Most titles have no end-punctuation:
> *Julius Caesar*   *The Grapes of Wrath*

L-L SPELLING

Correct spelling of American English is such a complicated, mysterious business that there's little wonder this lowest social class has given it up as not worth the effort. Learning spelling rules is definitely a middle-class occupation, and therefore these rules will be found in "L-M Spelling." (There's no rule against peeking there now if you're the curious type.)

Improving one's spelling is indeed worth some effort, however, because society piles as much scorn on poor spelling as on "bad grammar"—if not more. Generations of schoolmarms and spelling bees have conditioned the higher classes to be quite bigoted on the subject. I have known some L-M people, too, to share this compulsive perfectionism.

The L-L person, therefore, should immediately begin the self-improvement process by drilling repeatedly on a few especially troublesome words. Society will expect the ambitious L-L writer to have mastered at least these:

1. all right (not *alright*)
2. a lot (not *alot*)
3. argument
4. believe
5. eighth
6. exercise
7. February
8. finally
9. its
10. it's (= it is)
11. really
12. science
13. similar
14. surprise

15. their
16. there
17. they're (= they are)
18. to
19. too
20. two

21. tries
22. truly
23. Wednesday
24. your
25. you're (= you are)

L-L MECHANICS

Grammarians often use the term *mechanics* to lump together a number of peripheral matters in a "miscellaneous" category. It includes such writing conventions as capitalization, abbreviation, and syllabication. In this chapter we shall consider only one such term—the use of numbers. For the others, please consult the index.

LL-M *Numbers*

Usage in dealing with numbers is curiously varied; practice cuts messily across class lines. The upper-class person has as much trouble being consistent as, perhaps, even the L-L night school student. For the prevention of chaos, therefore, let us all agree on a few conventions. Here are some often cited:

1. When it can be gracefully done, spell out a number that requires only a word or two. Two-word numbers from twenty-one to ninety-nine are hyphenated.

> Thirty-two years ago he stole eight hundred dollars and received a twenty-year prison term.

(Another practice, steadily becoming popular, is to spell out only the first ten numbers.)
Otherwise use figures:

> It cost $2.75. They were 215 years old. He has a 41-year-old car.
>
> The program's allocation is $2,415,632,700. (Commas separate billions, millions, thousands, and hundreds.)

Middle-class journalists, and others, occasionally use a sensible combination: 32 billion board feet; $17.2 million

2. Don't use a numeral to start a sentence. Spell it out or rephrase the sentence.
NOT: 130 steers were in the canyon.
BUT: One hundred thirty steers were in the canyon.
OR: In the canyon were 130 steers.

3. Be consistent in any one paragraph. This rule often requires you to use figures. (Statistics are best presented that way.)

> The box was 19 inches long, 6.2 inches wide, and 3 inches deep.

4. Use figures for the time of day when used with a.m. or A.M., p.m. or P.M., but otherwise spelling out is quite common.

> We got there at 2 p.m. (*not*, incidentally, 2:00 p.m.). The plane was due at 2:30 p.m. It was due at two-thirty. It landed at three o'clock.

5. The subject of dates is a bit confusing.

    a. Standard form is March 15, 1942, but gaining popularity is 15 March 1942.

    b. When no year is given, you may use one of four forms: (1) March 15, (2) 15 March, (3) March 15th, or (4) March fifteenth (this last one usually reserved for upper-class formal announcements).

    c. Some authorities forbid the ordinal number forms (*1st, 2nd, 3rd, 4th*) when the year is given: Jan. 1, 1963 (not Jan. 1st, 1963).

    d. The upper classes, and often the middle classes, are fond of formal weddings and other posh social affairs. When sending out invitations, they will sometimes spell out even the year.

    e. Usage is hopelessly divided on *century* forms. Some say centuries should always be written out and capitalized ("in the Nineteenth Century"); others authorize the informality of an abbreviated adjective form ("the 19th C. fashion") and a lower-case noun ("in the 19th century").

6. In writing addresses, most social classes use figures for street numbers (136 Main St.), although a number-as-name may be written out: 248-6th St. OR 248 Sixth St. Even when the street number is large, commas are omitted: 10543 Lundeen Ave. (not 10,543). (The upper classes have an affectation they seem to like: Forty-two Briarcliff Lane.)

7. Use figures with most percentages and all decimals:

        Only 5 per cent interest was allowed.

          (Sometimes tiny percentages are written out—one, two, three.)

        Annual rainfall there is 35.2 inches.

In dealing with money, omit unnecessary ciphers:

        $7 (not $7.00) OR seven dollars

Always omit the period if you can:

        95¢ a pound (not $.95 or $0.95) OR 95 cents a pound

8. Fractions are written in figures when attached to other figures (size 7¼) or when used in a set of numbers, such as a table. Otherwise they are spelled out (five-sixths, one-third), usually hyphenated.

9. The three highest classes—the people who publish books, write plays, design and pay for buildings—continue the 2,000-year-old tradition of Roman numerals in our culture. Lower-class strivers can impress superiors by consulting a dictionary (at "Roman") and memorizing the system. A bit more effort will enable them to translate almost any numbers they encounter. For example:

        p. xix   Page 19 in the introduction of a book. (Note that an introduction's numerals are not capitalized.)

        IV. iii. 42   Act 4, Scene 3, line 42 of a play.

        MCMLVI   [This building was erected in] 1956.

Social-class analysis may someday discover that relative familiarity with Roman numerals is an excellent indicator of class level.

    Permit me, please, to repeat myself: "A goal for all of us is maximum clarity. Other values cherished in writing... are honesty, logicality, energy, grace, and, beyond grace, a certain sparkle. But clarity is perhaps what we must concentrate on first.''

I note that we have six qualities in that list and, in the Table of Contents, six socioeconomic classes to consider. I hope no one will take it amiss if I parcel out one quality to each class. We have begun properly, I think; the clarity of the sentence's structure and diction is fundamental to our efforts at communication, and to the effectiveness of those efforts.

When the L-L person comes to understand just how important clarity is in his writing, he is probably already graduated into the Upper-Lower Class.

> *... while there is a lower class I am in it, while there is a criminal element I am of it, and while there is a soul in prison I am not free.*
> —Eugene Debs, 1918

CHAPTER 4
UPPER-LOWER LANGUAGE

Let us step a tiny notch higher on the income ladder. Measuring their meager increments of money is at least one way to measure and talk about the lower classes. In dealing with the Lower-Lowers, we looked chiefly at shabby households with less than $3,000 income in 1970. Now, in focusing on the Upper-Lower Class, let's try visualizing very modest homes where annual incomes range between $3,000 and $5,000—although, once again, there are many variables that invalidate any arbitrary income limits.

In March 1973 the two lower classes—for many purposes we can consider them together—constituted a quarter of all U.S. households. Almost half of these 17 million lower-class homes had but a single occupant, however, and that factor cuts the lower classes to just 17.1 per cent of the population. Per capita income in 1972, even with the U-L added in, was only $1,291. To be sure, in the U-L class there is more employment, mostly in service occupations and some clerical and factory work, but it is not always steady. Moreover, only 18 per cent of lower-class wives work even part-time outside the home. This lower-income group, finally, contains an extraordinarily high percentage (46.1) of household heads 66 and older.[1] The result is that many U-L individuals and families must rely, at least in part, on public assistance.

Their fortune is closely linked to their schooling. Studies in 1973 showed that only 13 per cent of the lower-class "heads of household" had had any exposure to college (nearly all of these, presumably, in the U-L class). Only 22.3 per cent more had been graduated from high school; 19.1 per cent had had "some high school"; but more than 45 per cent had only an elementary-school education "or less."[2] Nor is there much of an effort at self-education. In the lower class very little reading and almost no writing is carried on. There is instead an addiction to television.

In view of this educational record, it is not surprising that the U-L class, like the Lower-Lower, has some language habits which are unacceptable to the middle and upper classes. (We shall examine some of them soon.) Nor is it surprising that many U-L students, like the L-L's, have found American education a bitter experience. Especially (again) at high schools, which, according to Edgar Z. Friedenberg, have a "Darwinian" function. Social codes and values at these schools "endorse and support" the well-born youngsters, "while they instill in others a sense of inferiority and warn the rest of society against them as troublesome and untrustworthy. In this way the school contributes simultaneously to social mobility and to social stratification."[3] The U-L youngsters lose out on chances to develop adequate conceptions of their personal worth, or to reduce some of their anxieties, or to gain a sense of ease in dealing with life's social problems.

This incalculable loss, this cheating of millions of school children, contributes of course to the endless chain of poverty. As soon as the U-L youngster leaves school and puts himself on the job market, he or she learns all the remaining lessons about being poor. He learns, says Thomas Gladwin in his *Poverty U.S.A.*, "that most of the other people in the world are more successful and are able to do things about which the poor person can scarcely even dream, which means that the poor person sees himself as a failure, which means he has no confidence and gives up easily or perhaps does not push himself at all, and thus stays poor forever."[4] He is often condemned to a life of low status, limited competence, and powerlessness.

But suppose he does "push himself" and lands a steady job—let's say with a county road crew or some other municipal department. Because of the cultural bias of civil-service tests, he is commonly frustrated in his efforts at promotion. Failing once more, he has little to look forward to in his whole career.

He and his kind are condemned to still more "stress factors" at home, and in disproportionate numbers. The lower-class person has real reason to worry about poor health, money problems, broken marriages, neighborhood crime and violence, and so on. The result has been a high rate of psychiatric illness. A 1958 study in New Haven, Conn., indicated that the lowest of five classes had three times the rate of the three highest.[5]

This picture of the people Michael Harrington calls *The Other America* is of a class longing to be in the "mainstream" of American life, but weak and disorganized. Harrington's book records our welfare efforts on behalf of industrialists, oilmen, wealthy ranchers, and so on, and our unwillingness to attack the problems of the poor. "At precisely that moment in history where for the first time a people have the material ability to end poverty, they lack the will to do so."[6]

> The welfare state, in short, is upside-down...The protection, the guarantees, the help all tend to go to the strong and to the organized. The weakest in the society are those who are always disposed of in some congressional logrolling session.[7]

This, says Harrington, is "a monstrous example of needless suffering in the most advanced society in the world."[8] The problem is that, with less than 18 per cent of the population, the poor are a small and usually inarticulate minority group. Few, if any, politicians speak for them. Most "liberal" congressmen are willing to listen to organized labor—but labor's voice is now overwhelmingly middle class. Many unionized men and women, indeed, seem *hostile* to the lower classes. They sometimes parrot even the least sensible upper-class criticism of meager American public-assistance efforts. John Kenneth Galbraith, responding to these attacks on our welfare programs, once wryly observed that they were somewhat intemperate:

> The corrupting effect on the human spirit of a small amount of unearned income has unquestionably been exaggerated as, indeed, have the character-building values of hunger and privation.[9]

But dishonest attacks on the poor, and dishonest neglect of their problems, should not blind us to real shortcomings of the U-L class. Its members—let's face it squarely—have committed some sort of the worst imaginable grammatical offenses. They have sinned, indeed, almost as grievously as the L-L class.

U-L GRAMMAR

Centuries ago, the English language was even more vexing than it is today. It had a complex system of case forms, verb mood forms, and so on, that has dwindled now to a shadow of the former edifice. For instance, Old English had masculine, feminine, and neuter nouns, each with a different set of *four* cases.[10] Modern nouns hardly change their form at all; we rely on sentence structure to help specify the meaning—and we inquire no longer into the sexuality of, say, a table or a turnip.

Pronouns still have many inflections (*I*, *my*, *mine*, *me*) and there are several elastic verb forms (*go*, *went*, *gone*; *sing*, *sang*, *sung*). But these form-changes are only small chunks of the earlier structure. In this chapter we shall consider the surviving inflections of verbs and pronouns—and the trouble U-L people have in coping with them.

UL-G1 *Verb forms*

Verbs can be short and simple (*Go!*) or four-word phrases (*should have been going*). But they are all constructed from three "principal parts": (1) the present-tense infinitive (*to go*, but without the *to*), (2) the past-tense form (*went*), and (3) the past participle (*gone*). In assuming these principal shapes, they are either regular or irregular.

Regular verbs are no problem. They form both the past tense and the past participle simply by adding *-d* (*escaped*), *-ed* (*walked*), or *-t* (*dealt*, *burnt*). The three parts, again: *finish*, *finished*, *finished*.

Irregular verbs, on the other hand, raise hell with the morale of many immigrants. Dozens of important English verbs retain some ancient parts. Most create the past tense and past participle by a vowel change: *freeze*, *froze*, *frozen*; *swim*, *swam*, *swum*.

Your desk dictionary will be of some help, if you're in doubt. If all it gives you is the infinitive, the verb is regular. For a very irregular verb, the dictionary will list the three principal parts: *see*, *saw*, *seen*. But be careful; for other irregular verbs some dictionaries will list the infinitive (*dig*), then the past and past participle (*dug*), and then the *present* participle (*digging*). Some will even throw in, for good measure, the third-person singular, present tense (*digs*). (Among their various Protean characteristics, verbs have forms to match their subjects, whether first-person *I*, second-person *you*, or third-person *he*, *she*, or *it*—including their plurals.)

This confusing state of affairs in a dictionary entry can cause a visiting foreigner serious depression. A few have been known to catch the next transportation back to their homelands.

The native U-L person, however, has at least *heard* the correct form, on his TV set, and he should have somewhat less difficulty. He should drill incessantly, though, if he is in earnest about entering the ranks of the middle class. If this shoe fits, please cover the two right-hand columns below and recite them from memory. "Begin—began, begun." Again and again.

PRINCIPAL PARTS OF SOME
FREQUENTLY MISUSED VERBS

Infinitive	*Past tense*	*Past participle*
awake	awoke or awaked	awaked or awoke
awaken	awakened	awakened
begin	began	begun
bid (offer)	bid	bid
bid (command)	bade	bidden
bite	bit	bitten
blow	blew	blown
bring	brought	brought
burst	burst	burst
buy	bought	bought
choose	chose	chosen
dive	dived, dove	dived
do	did	done
drag	dragged	dragged
draw	drew	drawn
drink	drank	drunk
eat	ate	eaten
fall	fell	fallen
fly	flew	flown
forget	forgot	forgotten, forgot
get	got	gotten, got
give	gave	given
go	went	gone
grow	grew	grown
hang (execute)	hanged	hanged
hang (suspend)	hung	hung
know	knew	known
lead	led	led
lend	lent	lent
ride	rode	ridden
ring	rang	rung
run	ran	run
see	saw	seen
shine (give light)	shone	shone
shine (polish)	shined	shined
shrink	shrank, shrunk	shrunk, shrunken
sing	sang	sung

sink	sank, sunk	sunk, sunken
speak	spoke	spoken
steal	stole	stolen
swim	swam	swum
swing	swung	swung
take	took	taken
tear	tore	torn
throw	threw	thrown
wake	woke	waked
waken	wakened	wakened
wear	wore	worn
write	wrote	written

Many people have difficulty with *awake, awaken, wake,* and *waken*—which is not surprising.[11] For speakers in the lower classes, these pairs at times cause confusion:

raise	raised	raised
rise (get up)	rose	risen
set (put in place)	set	set
sit (be seated)	sat	sat

But the most troublesome of all, maybe, is this pair:

lay (put down)	laid	laid
lie (recline)	lay	lain

Perhaps it will help to stare at a few socially approved usages, noting that *lay* always takes an object (is "transitive") and *lie* doesn't.

Lay
Present tense: Just *lay* the letter there, please.
Present participle: *Laying* it down, he turned and left.
Past tense: He *laid* the letter on the porch swing.
Present perfect tense: He *has laid* my mail there for years.

Lie
Present tense: *Lie* down until your head stops aching.
Present participle: *Lying* down, she closed her eyes.
Past tense: She *lay* on the sofa.
Present perfect tense: She *has lain* there for an hour.

If the U-L person can master all these verb forms in both writing and speech, we can predict a promising future for him. He would bring honor to the middle class.

UL-G2 *Verb tense*

The U-L person first must leap still more language hurdles, however. We have just seen *lay* and *lie* changing their shapes to express the time or "tense" of an action. Let's examine our six tenses and memorize their uses:

1. *Present*—Be careful here; this word is a bit misleading. The present tense has several functions:
   a. Present action: The defense *rests*. Dave is *eating*.
   b. Customary action: He *eats* soul food.
   c. Historical action (the "historical present," often used in novels): As usual, Cleopatra *eats* her mid-day meal and *lets* Caesar wait.
   d. Future (!) action: Tomorrow we *eat* steak.
   e. Timeless truth: Those who *eat* green apples often get a stomach-ache.
2. *Past*—Past action that doesn't extend to the present:
   I *ate* my carrots, Pa!
3. *Future*—Future action:
   He *will eat* well there. (Upper and middle classes)
   He *is going to eat* well there. (Middle classes)
   He*'s gonna eat* well there. (U-L class)
   He *gonna eat* good there. (L-L class)
4. *Present perfect*—Past action that extends to the present:
   He *has eaten*. They *have eaten*.
   (One meaning of *perfect* is "completed.")
5. *Past perfect*—Past action completed before some particular moment in the past:
   When she came, he *had* already *eaten*.
   (Such ideas are often put in the simple past tense: I *ate* before I left.)
6. *Future perfect*—Action that will be completed in the future:
   He *will have eaten* before eight o'clock.
   (More frequently put in the simple future tense: He *will eat* before eight o'clock.)

The three highest social classes observe here a two-centuries-old ritual. In the future and future perfect tenses, where everyone else says "I will" and "we will," they at times say "I shall" and "we shall." Just in certain situations, please note. We'll discuss this curious habit at U-M Grammar.

In addition to all these tenses, there is a set of forms to show whether the verb's subject is acting (*active voice*) or is being acted upon (*passive voice*). To make matters worse, verbs also have forms designed to show the speaker's attitude toward the factuality or the likelihood of what's expressed. English verbs have an "indicative" *mood* for questions and factual statements, a "subjunctive" mood for certain doubtful or wishful statements, and an "imperative" mood for commands. We'll say a bit more about the subjunctive, the only troublesome one, a bit later on.

The whole systematic inflection of verbs, often laid out in grammar books, is called a *conjugation*. Think of it as a fast-growing hothouse plant that sends up many shoots or branches, each with several blossoms. As we watch one develop, keep your eye on those three principal parts: (1) the *infinitive* will be the stem for the present and future tenses; (2) the *past*, for just the past tense; (3) the *past participle*, for the three "perfect" tenses. Incidentally, full development of this many-flowered creature has some decidedly formal aspects (like "shall"); we are in an upper-class hothouse here.

Ready? Here we go:

CONJUGATION OF *TO GIVE* (give, gave, given)
INDICATIVE MOOD, *Active Voice*

Person	*Singular*	*Plural*
	PRESENT TENSE	
1	I give	we give
2	you give	you give
3	she (he, it) gives	they give
	PAST TENSE	
1	I gave	we gave
2	you gave	you gave
3	she gave	they gave
	FUTURE TENSE	
1	I shall give	we shall give
2	you will give	you will give
3	she will give	they will give
	PRESENT PERFECT TENSE	
1	I have given	we have given
2	you have given	you have given
3	she has given	they have given
	PAST PERFECT TENSE	
1	I had given	we had given
2	you had given	you had given
3	she had given	they had given
	FUTURE PERFECT TENSE	
1	I shall have given	we shall have given
2	you will have given	you will have given
3	she will have given	they will have given

INDICATIVE MOOD, *Passive Voice*

	PRESENT TENSE	
1	I am given	we are given
2	you are given	you are given
3	she is given	they are given
	PAST TENSE	
1	I was given	we were given
2	you were given	you were given
3	she was given	they were given
	FUTURE TENSE	
1	I shall be given	we shall be given
2	you will be given	you will be given
3	she will be given	they will be given

PRESENT PERFECT TENSE

1	I have been given	we have been given
2	you have been given	you have been given
3	she has been given	they have been given

PAST PERFECT TENSE

1	I had been given	we had been given
2	you had been given	you had been given
3	she had been given	they had been given

FUTURE PERFECT TENSE

1	I shall have been given	we shall have been given
2	you will have been given	you will have been given
3	she will have been given	they will have been given

IMPERATIVE MOOD

Active Voice   *Passive Voice*

PRESENT TENSE

give   be given

SUBJUNCTIVE MOOD
PRESENT TENSE

Singular	if I (she, etc.) give	if I (she, etc.) be given
Plural	if we (you, they) give	if we (you, they) be given

PAST TENSE

Singular	if I (she, etc.) gave	if I (she, etc.) were given
Plural	if we (you, they) gave	if we (you, they) were given

PRESENT PERFECT TENSE

Singular	if I (she, etc.) have given	if I (she, etc.) have been given
Plural	if we (you, they) have given	if we (you, they) have been given

PAST PERFECT TENSE

Singular	if I (she, etc.) had given	if I (she, etc.) had been given
Plural	if we (you, they) had given	if we (you, they) had been given

GERUNDS
PRESENT TENSE

giving   being given

PRESENT PERFECT TENSE

having given   having been given

PARTICIPLES
PRESENT TENSE

giving   being given

PAST TENSE

given   been given

PRESENT PERFECT TENSE

having given   having been given

INFINITIES
PRESENT TENSE
to give   to be given
PRESENT PERFECT TENSE
to have given   to have been given

As if all that isn't confusing enough, English verbs have a set of "progressive" forms to signal that an action is still in progress—and some "do" forms for (1) questions, (2) negations, and (3) emphatic statements.

SIMPLE FORMS: I give, she gives; I was given
PROGRESSIVE FORMS: I am giving, she is giving; I was being given
"DO" FORMS: 1. Does he give blood? Did he give any today?
        2. He does not (did not) give any here.
        3. I do give! He did give.

And then there are certain verbs that sometimes assist in creating all the tenses, voices, and moods of other verbs. These *auxiliaries* include modifications of *be, have, do, shall,* and *will,* as we have seen, but also *can, could, may, might, must,* and *ought.* Two of these, especially, present social problems.
    Can in all classes denotes an ability:
        You *can* do it easily, as you *can* see.
    It is also used by the three lowest classes to indicate or ask permission:
        Can I go to the dance?
    May, however, is the word the Establishment employs to denote permission:
        Yes, you *may* go.
(*May* is also used to suggest possibility: He *may* be the one.)

UL-G3 *Sequence of tenses*

Now, to make a sentence sound sweetly natural and logical (to refined ears), it is often necessary to make its lesser parts harmonize with its main verb. A verb in a subordinate clause, or a verbal, should fit properly with the verb of the main clause.

1. *Subordinate verbs*
    A gentleman *rises* when a lady *enters* (not *will enter*) the room.
        (The present *enters* follows the present *rises*.)
    She *has given* up hope, because no more war prisoners *have been released*.
        (Present perfect follows present perfect.)
    If he *had asked* (not just *asked*) he *could have gone*.
        (With a deadline, we need the past perfect.)
    I *wished* that I *could marry* her (not *could have married* her).
        (Back then, I was still hoping.)

2. *Verbals*

Infinitives, participles, and gerunds usually take the present tense when they show action occurring at the same time as the verb's action. This is true, at least, for the U-M Class and above.

a. *Infinitives*

I hoped *to meet* her.
NOT I hoped *to have met* her.

She had planned *to leave* by then.
NOT She had planned *to have left* by then.

They would have liked *to visit* here.
NOT They would have liked *to have visited* here.

The upper classes sometimes use the perfect infinitive to express a time earlier than that of the main verb:

I should like *to have seen* his face!

Inferior classes are not a little uncomfortable with that, however, and select something simpler:

I wish I *had seen* his face!

b. *Gerunds*

They would have liked *visiting* here.
After *visiting* his cousins, he went home. (Avoid the redundant "After *having visited* . . .")

c. *Participles*

Visiting his cousins, he lost track of time.
(Visiting and losing happened at the same time.)

The U-M and upper classes all have deep affection for the perfect participle to indicate an act preceding another:

Having spent all his money, Jack walked home disconsolately.

It's a form the U-L person might want to practice using. We have observed that it impresses L-M people, who regard it as "polite" speech.

UL-G4 *The subjunctive mood*

We come next to a set of forms the use of which exhibits marked class stratification. Centuries ago, the subjunctive seemed a firmly entrenched and lively verb mood in all of Britain's classes. The indicative mood, however, has since given it such vigorous competition that not much of the subjunctive remains in the English-speaking world. Nevertheless, all American classes use it in some traditional expressions—and, as we go up the social ladder, we find that each class employs a bit more of the subjunctive than does the one below it. It has become, it would appear, a status symbol.

We discover it chiefly in the verb *be* (*were, had been,* etc.) and, in other verbs, in their third-person singular, present tense. It is used, first, in several idioms that cross perhaps all class lines: *e.g.*, Heaven *help* us, God *forbid*, God *bless* you (after sneezes, etc.), far *be* it from me, *come* what may, if need *be*. These may all be found, at least occasionally, in L-L conversation.

In U-L speech, next, one sometimes hears a construction beginning "It's best that he/she *be told* (*stay* in bed, etc.)"; variant openers are "It's better that," "It's necessary that," and so on. Again, whereas L-L people say "if I was you," the U-L Class will sometimes use the highbrow idiom "if I *were* you." And fundamentalist church-goers, many of them U-L, are often pleased to quote Biblical subjunctive ("But if ye *be led* of the Spirit...") from a 17th-century translation.

At the L-M level, the blue-collar worker is often a union member, and this fact produces a subjunctive explosion. Unlike the typical lower-class person, who is virtually powerless, the L-M working male or female is extremely conscious of the economic strength of the union, and often vocal in making suggestions, recommendations, requests, and demands—for which the subjunctive mood is tailor-made:

We insist that he *talk* (not *talks*) to us now.

I ask that the strike vote *be scheduled* soon.

When it's business time at a union meeting, these *that* clauses can become a blizzard of formal motions and resolutions.

Will someone move *that* the minutes *be* approved?

The motion was *that* the committee *be* commended.

Resolved, *that* shop stewards *be* asked to keep better records.

I move *that* the matter *be* tabled.

If *Robert's Rules of Order* survives, it seems likely the subjunctive will also.

As we move up to the U-M Class, we find "if I *were* you" and several new idioms in common use: *suffice* it to say, *be* that as it may, as it *were*, *be* it said, and so on. In addition, U-M attorneys delight in quoting in court the ancient British common law, or perhaps last month's disputed contract, both of them laced with subjunctive verbs ("*Be* it known by these presents..."). U-M employers have also been known to utter subjunctive maledictions: "The union *be* damned!" Such oaths, however, probably are not confined to U-M chambers.

At the L-U level, many speakers and writers prefer to use the subjunctive when making wishful statements and expressing conditions contrary to fact. The practice is also quite common in the U-M class but, below that, the indicative is used.

I hoped that Agatha *were* here. (Subjunctive)

I hoped that Agatha *was* here. (Indicative)

I wish I *were* taller. (Subjunctive)

I wish I *was* taller. (Indicative)

If this *were* May, we could be sailing. (Subjunctive)

If this *was* May, we could be sailing. (Indicative)

All classes employ the indicative when the condition is not known to be contrary to fact.

If he *is* here, they will find him.

Among the Lower-Uppers, however, the subjunctive touches on conditions about which there is at least some doubt, often following *as if* or *as though:*

> She looked as if she *were* angry.
> The goldfish acted as though it *were dying.*

The middle classes use the indicative, and some authorities approve.

> She looked as if she *was* angry.

The lower classes don't like either *as if* or *angry.*

> She looked like she was mad.

When we finally reach the highest social level we find the Upper-Upper Class, ordinarily very wealthy, making much use of politely indirect imperatives in the subjunctive. Polite, but no doubt imperative:

> The terms of our Venezuelan contract require, as I am sure you are all aware, that $25 million *be* devoted to new construction.
>
> We suggest that the company *end* this Wyoming venture lest it *prove* disastrous.

In addition, the U-U person may utter some wishes, suppositions, and improbabilities that sound strange to lesser ears:

> Oh, that I *were* beautiful!
> *Were* that the case, they should have declined.
> Would (that) it *were* so!
> If he *be* here, why haven't we been told?

Some eccentric Upper-Uppers, indeed, collect rare old subjunctives as they would Italian Renaissance art, Flemish tapestries, and vintage wines.

UL-G5 *Voice*

Verbs (99 per cent of them) are either active or passive. The distinction is said to be their *voice*. When the subject acts, it's an *active* verb; when the subject is acted upon, it's a *passive* verb. Often the person or thing acting is more interesting than the receiver of the action, and usually the active voice is more direct. The U-L writer is well advised, therefore, to use the active voice most of the time. Flabby passives can drain a sentence's energy.

> WEAK PASSIVE The election *was won* by Senator Jones.
> ACTIVE VOICE Senator Jones *won* the election.
> WEAK PASSIVE A utility pole *was struck* by the swerving speeder.
> ACTIVE VOICE The swerving speeder *struck* a utility pole.

There are times, though, when the passive voice is preferable. Sometimes our interest lies chiefly with the receiver of the action:

> Lobster—a real treat—*was served* at the club dinner.

Or with the act itself:

> Trespassers *will be shot.*

Sometimes the actor is unknown or unimportant:

> The murder weapon *was found* within an hour.

Sometimes the passive is nice just for a little variety. But, again, usually the active voice produces a much more vigorous sentence.

UL-G6 Subject-verb agreement

One of the major rules of genteel grammar is this one:
- Verbs and their subjects should "agree" in *number* (singular or plural) and *person* (first, second, or third).

Probably nothing will mark a low-status person more rapidly than a violation of this subject-verb correspondence. A single "she *don't*" can bring social disaster.

Fortunately, there is a good bit of regularity in conjugations (see again *to give* in UL-G2). English verbs, for example, have rather orderly tense inflections. Unfortunately, however, there is just enough verb irregularity to serve as a middle-class barrier against the lower classes. Money is nice—but, if you want a really effective class-screening device, you will deliberately build some tricky elements into the language of "polite" society:

I give, you give, she *gives*.
I have given, you have given, she *has* given.

Verbs have a little twist like that in the third-person singular present (and present perfect). But much worse are the inflections of *to be*, which is full of twists: I *am*, you *are*, she *is*; we, you, they *are*. Look again at the complete *to give* conjugation. Note the passive voice; there you will see *to be* forms serving as auxiliaries. You might wish to scan the whole string.

Done studying that page? Very well, let us go on.

A curious thing—perhaps you've noticed—is that most nouns add *-s* or *-es* to form the plural, whereas verbs with those endings (third-person present) are *singular*.

SINGULAR   Their car *stalls*. Our tax *goes* up.
PLURAL   Their cars *stall*. Our taxes *go* up.

Maybe, as you study the next few pages, you'll discover some other oddities. Any language has lots of them.

UL-G6a

A compound subject linked with *and* ordinarily takes a plural verb.

July and August *are* usually warm here.

But if it's a singular idea give it a singular verb.

My closest friend and neighbor *lives* a mile away.
(Friend and neighbor are the same person.)

UL-G6b

Some compound subjects are linked by *or* or *nor*. In all such cases make the verb agree with the closer part of the subject.

Common "correlative" conjunctions are *either . . . or, neither . . . nor,* and *not only . . . but also.* (See also UL-G8c.)

Neither gold nor silver *was* found there. (Singular)
Either the contractor or the two painters *are* in the house. (Plural)
Either the two painters or the contractor *is* in the house. (Singular)
Either you or he *is* guilty. (Third person)
Either he or you *are* guilty. (Second person)
A clumsy-sounding formation should be rewritten:
Either you are crazy or I am.

UL-G6c   Nouns with a plural form but a singular meaning take a *singular* verb.

SINGULAR *economics, physics, mathematics, measles, mumps, news,* etc.
The news *is* good tonight.
PLURAL   *media* (plural of *medium*), *oats*, etc.
VARIABLE (1) The words *data, means, species, headquarters,* some animal names, etc., are both singular and plural.

The data on the oil supplies *is* unavailable.
(*Data* is now widely used as a collective noun.)

Their data *were* usually accurate.
(The historically correct plural of *datum*, employed by the upper classes, is considerably more highbrow.)

(2) Some nouns ending in *-ics* (*tactics, statistics*) are singular when considered a body of knowledge, but plural otherwise.
Acoustics *is* a complicated science.
The hall's acoustics *are* excellent.

(3) Words like *trousers, pants, pliers,* and *scissors* are plural, but when one is preceded by *pair of* you should use a singular verb.
These pants *need* mending.
This pair of pants *needs* mending.

UL-G6d   Collective nouns, and numbers regarded as collectives, refer to a group or quantity as a unit; they therefore take singular verbs. *However*, if the several *members* are of chief concern, use a plural verb.

SINGULAR   The band *plays* until two o'clock.
PLURAL   The band *have* all gone home.
SINGULAR   One-fourth of the crop *was* lost.
PLURAL   One-fourth of the apples *were* hail-damaged.
SINGULAR   Some of the money *is* here.
PLURAL   Some of the coins *are* here.
SINGULAR   Two thousand bushels *was* the yield.
PLURAL   Two thousand crates *were* loaded.

SINGULAR *The* number attending *was* small.
(The subject *The number* is considered a unit.)
BUT *A* number of the students *were* absent.
(*A number* means "some.")

UL-G6e   Use singular verbs with most indefinite pronouns (*another, anybody, anyone, anything, each, either, everybody, everyone, everything, neither, nobody, no one, nothing, one, somebody, someone, something*). They're all individuals.

U-L's (and others, too) are careless in speech but, in writing, they face a rather rigid rule.
   Everybody *has* blue moods now and then.
   Each man and woman *is* needed.
Among the exceptions is *none*; only a few U-U purists insist upon the invariable singular. The three highest classes use singular or plural verbs, depending on the context.
   SINGULAR   None of them *was* charged.
   PLURAL   None *are* equal to the Fighting Irish.
The three lowest classes tend to construe *none* as plural (None *are* going to jail), but it is sometimes singular, as in this U-L double negative:
   Money? There just *isn't* none.
Any, all, and *some*, and the words *more* and *most*, display similar versatility; they can be either singular or plural.

UL-G6f   The verb following the relative-pronoun subjects *that, who,* and *which* agrees with the pronoun's antecedent.

   Kay was one of the students [who *were* chosen].
   She is the only one of the students [who *was* prepared].
   She is one student [who *knows* how to study].

UL-G6g   Don't be confused by nouns or pronouns intervening between subject and verb.

Prepositional phrases are sometimes troublemakers:
   The *director*, along with various experts and assistants, *is* leaving soon.
Clauses also frequently intervene:
   The *chimpanzees* [which a psychologist studied exhaustively throughout 1974] *like* to be tickled.

65

UL-G6h Clauses beginning with the "expletives" *there* and *it* allow the writer to put the verb before the subject, for variety's sake. But their use requires some care.

It (sometimes an "anticipatory subject") always takes a singular verb.
    It *is* doubtful [that he will come].
    (The noun clause in brackets is the true subject.)
    It *was* the poor people [who felt the depression most].
    (Here *people* is the true subject, but *It* controls.)
There are (*were*) is always followed by a plural subject.
    There *are* several *ways* to do this.
There is (*was*) usually is followed by a singular subject.
    There *is* only one *way* to do it properly.
    But sometimes a compound subject is acceptable here:
    Inside there *is* a desk, a table, and two chairs.
    There *was* both courage and dignity in her manner.
    (The key nouns *desk* and *courage* are singular, please note; if they were plural the verb necessarily would match.)
There seem (*appear*) *to be* precedes a plural subject; *There seems to be* takes the singular.

UL-G6i A verb agrees with its subject, *not* with a predicate noun (or nouns).

    Sausage and eggs *are* my favorite breakfast.
    My favorite breakfast *is* sausage and eggs.

UL-G6j A title (as subject) takes a singular verb even if it has plural concepts. The same is true of a word regarded as a word.

    Emerson's Essays and Poems costs $5.25.
    Them is in the objective case.
    ("*Them*" is either underscored or quoted.)

UL-G7 *Verb-adverb combinations*

    English, especially colloquial and slang English, uses many verbs in organic combination with adverbs. This list of idioms is only a very small sample.

bang up	come out with
beg off	come up with
check out	cut out (horseplay, noise)
check up on	dig in
chip in	get across (a point)
clear away	hush up
clear out	jump at
come on!	jump on

look in on (a friend)   take in (a movie)
look out   take off
look up and down   take up with (someone)
pay off   tie down
pay up   tie up

In each case the adverb has become *part of the verb*.

UL-G8 *Pronoun agreement*

Section G6 was devoted to examining how verbs correspond with their subjects. We come now to another major pronouncement in "proper" grammar:
- A pronoun should agree with its antecedent in *gender*, *number*, and *person*.

UL-G8a   When sex is involved, always be careful. There are times when you must exercise discretion.

Our mare broke *her* leg? *its* leg?

Anyone who's rich has it all *his* own way.
(Use the masculine *his*, or at least until Women's Lib gets stronger. The clumsy *his or her* should be used very sparingly.)

UL-G8b   Compound antecedents using *and* ordinarily require a plural pronoun.

Wind and wave took *their* toll.
BUT   Mr. Baker's son and heir had *his* own office.
(Son and heir are the same person.)

UL-G8c   With other compound antecedents the pronoun agrees with the closer part. (See UL-G6b.)

Neither Jones nor Brown brought *his* lunch.
Either the Greens or Mr. Johnson honked *his* horn.
Not only Mrs. Smith but also her children had *their* cameras.

UL-G8d   Singular antecedents—including *person*, *man*, *woman*, and most of the indefinite pronouns—are followed by singular pronouns. (But see UL-G6e for a few exceptions.)

A person with a secret often shows *his* hand.
Each of the girls learned cooking from *her* mother.
Everybody jumped to *his* feet.

In such cases U-L people frequently use the plural—mistakenly:
> AVOID Each learned cooking from *their* mother.
> AVOID Everybody jumped to *their* feet.

The reason it's a mistake is that the three highest classes will often smile disparagingly at you and consider you careless. Perhaps it's not gauche in informal speech, but in formal writing, yes.

UL-G8e — Following a collective noun, use a *singular* pronoun when you're thinking of a unit, a *plural* pronoun when you're regarding the members as individuals. (See UL-G6d.)

> SINGULAR The state commission submitted *its* annual report.
> PLURAL   The jury filed out of *their* chamber and took *their* seats.

Whatever you do, be consistent. Don't say:
> The jury filed out of *its* chamber, entered the courtroom, and took *their* seats.

UL-G8f — A distinction is sometimes made between the reciprocal pronouns *each other* and *one another*.

The higher classes often prefer *each other* in references to two, *one another* when referring to more than two. In the lower classes *each other* seems preferred in all situations.

UL-G8g — "Demonstrative" pronouns, which function as adjectives, should agree in number with the nouns they point to.

In this group are *this, that, these,* and *those.* Don't say *"These kind* of tires." See LM-G1i.

UL-G8h — A pronoun should agree with the *person* of its antecedent.

This admonition usually translates, simply, "Don't shift the sentence's focus from one person to another."
> AVOID If *one* (third person) has enough will-power, *you* (second person) can lose weight.

See also LM-G6, "Shifts in point of view."

UL-G9 *Pronoun reference*

A reader is entitled to a clear noun (or pronoun) as the antecedent of the pronoun you're choosing. Make your reference exact.

UL-G9a — Avoid the ambiguity of two possible antecedents.

MUDDY	When the boss fired Pete, *he* was noisy about *it*. (Who is *he*?—The boss or Pete? What is *it*?—the act itself? Or some alleged cause? Or some supposed inequity that *Pete* is bemoaning?)
CLEAR	When the boss fired him, Pete was noisy in his protest.
OR	When he fired Pete, the boss was noisy in his complaints against him.
MUDDY	Pete told Bill that *he'd* lied.
CLEAR	Pete confessed to Bill that he'd lied.
OR	Pete accused Bill of lying.
MUDDY	He dropped the quart of beer on his toe and broke *it*.

UL-G9b Avoid remote or confused references.

TROUBLESOME	When the Peterson Company was expanding, very early in 1974, after all the big orders came in from the new sales people in Alaska, *they* asked Tom if he wanted a job.

This perhaps should start out talking about the company and end with some specific person asking Tom; "Peterson Company" is somewhat abstract. A more serious problem is that a long sentence can introduce distracting elements and, in this case, ambiguity.

UL-G9c The indefinite use of *they, it,* and *you* usually creates vague sentences and paragraphs.

LOWER CLASS	In many cities *they* (or *you*) have trouble finding parking spots.
HIGHER CLASS	In many cities motorists have trouble finding parking spots.
LOWER CLASS	*It* says in the paper that a train was derailed near here.
HIGHER CLASS	The newspaper says that a train was derailed near here.

The higher classes sanction the indefinite *it*, however, in some idioms: *it is raining, it is cloudy, it is early, it is useless to try, it seems, it is 250 kilometers to Paris.* (Incidentally, the French say *Il fait froid*, "It *makes* cold"; we say "It *is* cold." Nobody bothers to identify *it*.)

UL-G9d Be sure the antecedent and pronoun are logically related.

LOWER CLASS	Phil's father is a marine biologist, and *that's* what Phil wants to study.
HIGHER CLASS	Phil's father is a marine biologist, and *marine biology* is what Phil wants to study.
LOWER CLASS	There is a fire station downtown, and we called *them* when we saw smoke.
HIGHER CLASS	There is a fire station downtown, and we called *it* when we saw smoke.

UL-G9e   *Who, which,* and *that* are not quite
                         interchangeable.

Which refers to animals and things. *Who* is commonly used with persons, although at times it's bestowed upon favored animals. *That* usually refers to animals and things but (except in the upper classes) sometimes also to human beings.

   The man *who* is standing there is a narcotics agent.
   The cat, *which* ran up the tree, is still frightened.
   He exhibited a bear *that* could roller-skate.
   A girl *that* (or *who*) is a good dancer is always popular.

In references to animals and things, *whose* (the possessive of *who*) is sometimes used in order to avoid the awkward *of which*.

   The church *whose* steeple toppled was badly damaged.

The upper classes, however, would probably demand that the sentence be rewritten:

   The church at 16th and Broad was badly damaged when its steeple toppled.

See U-U Grammar for further upper-class thoughts on these matters.

UL-G9f   Avoid pronoun reference to a whole
                         preceding clause or sentence unless the
                         meaning is unmistakably clear.

   VAGUE When a person lights a cigarette in a restaurant, others may take offense. *This* is what I object to.

Similar vague connections are made with *that, which,* and *it.*

UL-G10 *Case*

Once again we come to a grammatical swamp—an area in which people clearly reveal their social level. It is best that you review briefly the L-L material on subjects, subjective complements, objects, etc. And, once again, recall this memory-jogger:

ANALYSIS OF A CLAUSE

V	1	Verb
S	2	Subject
C	3	Complement
M	4	Modifier(s)

Now, charting the case changes of nouns is no problem; the subjective and objective are spelled alike; the only variation is the possessive *s*-and-apostrophe, and that comes naturally enough. But the "declension" of pronouns is another matter. A half dozen common and irksome English pronouns have three different case forms: (1) subjective (*I, he, she, we, they, who*); (2) possessive (*my* or *mine, his, her* or *hers, our* or *ours, their* or *theirs, whose*); (3) objective (*me, him, her, us, them, whom*). To inflect a pronoun to its proper case, you need to know exactly what role it is playing in the clause.

UL-G10a   Subjects and (often) subjective comple-
                         ments require the *subjective* (or "nomi-
                         native") case.

LOWER CLASS   *Him* and *me* were drinking vodka.
HIGHER CLASS   *He* and *I* were drinking vodka.
(A person overimbibing, incidentally, may slip hourly in the class structure as he grows more and more intoxicated, more and more careless about his speech.)
LOWER CLASS   *Us* boys foun' some empty bottles.
HIGHER CLASS   *We* boys found some empty bottles.
But to make some finer social gradations, let's watch the people handling subjective complements:
UPPER CLASS   The first two there were *you* and *I*.
MIDDLE CLASS   The first two there were *you* and *me*. (Informal)
LOWER CLASS   The first two there were *you* and *me*. (Invariable)
U-U CLASS   It is *I* (*we, she, he, they*).
L-U and U-M   It is *I*, etc. (writing); It's *me* (most speech).
L-M and
LOWER CLASSES   It's *me* (*us, her, him, them*).

UL-G10b

Objects of all kinds require the *objective case*, sometimes called the "accusative."

They chose *her*. She gave *him* a kiss.
The chief trouble spot is the object of a preposition.
LOWER CLASS   Some of *we* boys were going.
HIGHER CLASS   Some of *us* boys were going.
The three lowest classes, aware of the quicksand here, try the supposedly "correct" subjective case in inappropriate places, as in the example above. (Try this test: drop the noun "boys"; then choose the pronoun that comes naturally—"Some of *us* were going.") Another mistake:
LOWER CLASS   They gave it to Bill and *I*.
   ("They gave it to . . . *I*?")
HIGHER CLASS   They gave it to Bill and *me*.
One of the most glaring case errors, perhaps, is the following one. *Between* is another preposition, often taking a compound object:
LOWER CLASS   They chose between *he* and *I*.
HIGHER CLASS   They chose between *him* and *me*.

UL-G10c

Some *than* or *as* clauses are elliptical (incomplete). The case of a pronoun is affected by the missing element—just as if it were there.

Diane is not as old as *I* (am).
She's a better dancer than *he* (is).
The lower classes will almost invariably use the objective (as *me*, than *him*).

UL-G10d

Appositives take the same cases as the words they refer to.

Two girls—*Shirley* and *I*—were elected.
The group elected two girls—*Shirley* and *me*.
Note: Avoid redundant appositives. See "My sister she," L-L Usage.

UL-G10e Infinitives can have subjects and complements. The subject, oddly enough, is in the *objective* case.

The judges thought *her* to have the best figure.

The infinitive *to be* creates a sticky little social-class problem. Most of us put a complement in the objective case:
How would you like to be *him*?
We expected the caller to be *her*.
But the upper classes often select the nominative case:
How would you like to be *he*?
We expected the caller to be *she*.

UL-G10f Gerunds, too, can have so-called "subjects"—which are either objective or *possessive*, never subjective.

POSSESSIVE PERSONAL PRONOUNS

	Singular	*Plural*
1	I—*my, mine*	we—*our, ours*
2	you—*your, yours*	you—*your, yours*
3	she—*her, hers* he—*his* it—*its*	they—*their, theirs*

Here again, the response to this matter is likely to be a class-formed one. The higher ranks often regard the possessive as preferable; the lower classes like the objective case most of the time. Here are some illustrations:

Gerund phrase as subject of verb
    HIGHER CLASS *The door's slamming* bothered her.
                                Its slamming bothered her.
    LOWER CLASS *The door slamming* bothered her.

Gerund phrase as direct object
    HIGHER CLASS I don't like *their smoking pot*.
    LOWER CLASS I don't like *them smoking pot*.

Gerund phrase as object of a preposition
    HIGHER CLASS My parents approve of *my working*.
    LOWER CLASS My parents approve of *me working*.

But there are exceptions to this possessive convention. The higher classes sanction the objective form, for instance, whenever a phrase intervenes between the gerund and its subject:
He warned against *anyone* in the group *lagging behind*.
Note: If you are a careful grammarian, you will distinguish between gerunds and mere participles.

Imagine *his* learning Japanese!
(Emphasis on the action in the three-word gerund phrase)
Imagine *him* learning Japanese!
(Emphasis divided between the direct object *him* and the participial phrase following)

UL-G10g   In the possessive case, nouns and indefinite pronouns have apostrophes. (Contractions also need apostrophes.) But *personal* pronouns don't.

NOUNS   John's, cows', car's
INDEFINITE   nobody's, anyone's, anyone else's, etc.
PRONOUNS
PERSONAL   yours, his, hers, its, ours, theirs
PRONOUNS
CONTRACTIONS   it's (it is), we're (we are), etc.

UL-G10h   The case of an *interrogative* or *relative* pronoun is always determined by its function in its own clause.

Interrogative pronouns (*who, whose, whom, which, what*) are used in questions. Relative pronouns hook objective clauses to main clauses (see LL-G5); they include *who, whose, whom, which, what, that*, and forms like *whoever* and the highbrow *whosoever*. (Similar pronouns are found in noun clauses, but with a reduced function.) The ones to watch most carefully are *who* and *whoever* (subjective case), *whom* and *whomever* (objective case). The old who-whom terror isn't very scary in uncomplicated sentences.

Who led the platoon?
The attack was ordered by *whom*?
Sgt. Blake, *whom* I dislike, got a promotion.

One problem, though, is that questions often scramble the natural word order:

U-U CLASS   *Whom* did you meet?
             To *whom* did you talk?
L-U CLASS   *Whom* did you talk to?

Classes other than the Uppers, perhaps you've noted, are less heedful about retaining the objective case, especially in speech.

INFORMAL   *Who* did you meet?
             Who did you talk to?

A more serious problem sometimes occurs when a second clause is jammed into the middle of the first.

Who [did you say] led the platoon?

The lesser classes become upset; "did you say'—uh—*who*?—uh—*whom*?" They think: Maybe it should be changed to "*Whom* did you say led the platoon?" But they're wrong.

• The rule here: When analyzing a sentence (V-S-C-M order!), simply ignore such parenthetical elements as *do you think, do they say, he says,* or *it is*

believed. Focus instead upon the structure of really important clauses. Otherwise you may develop migraine headaches or a nervous twitch.
Sgt. Blake, *whom* [you know] I dislike, got a promotion.
Mr. Jones, *who* [they say] had cancer, died today.

Those last two sentences contained adjective clauses introduced by relative pronouns. We've talked about relative clauses before, in LL-G5b, but a few things more need to be said.

• Rule: A relative pronoun has its case determined *not* by its antecedent but by *the structure of its own clause*.

Donna, [*who* tried skin-diving,] nearly drowned.

It's *who*, not because the antecedent Donna is a verb's subject, but because *who* is itself the subject of a verb (*tried*).

Donna, [*whom* the wave nearly drowned,] was quickly rescued.

This time the clause's subject is *wave*; *whom* is the direct object of *drowned*. *Whom* still refers to Donna but ignores Donna's case.

The diver [*whose* gear I had borrowed] went home.

Here again the first pronoun has a dual function. The possessive *whose* links the adjective clause to the main clause, and it acts as an adjective modifying *gear*.

• Be careful not to confuse adjective clauses with *noun* clauses.

Noun clause as direct object of verb

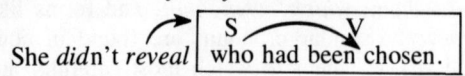

She *did*n't *reveal* | who had been chosen.

Noun clause as subject of verb

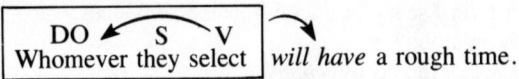

DO   S   V
Whomever they select | *will have* a rough time.

Noun clause as object of a preposition

S   V   DO
Let's give the tickets *to* | whoever wants them.

Noun clauses, as you see, can also be tricky. Faultless delivery doesn't come, usually, until one has attained at least U-M status.

U-L USAGE

Several U-L usage problems have already been discussed in this chapter—for example, the "proper" use of *can* and *may*, *who* and *whom*. But that was just a warm-up.

A, An. U-L writers sometimes forget the difference between these two. *A* is properly used before a word starting with a consonant sound (even though really a vowel, as in *union*). *An* is used before words beginning with a vowel sound. (*A* puppy, *a* ukelele; but *an* accident, *an* elephant.) A problem arises with words beginning with *h*. If it's definitely pronounced, use *a* (*a* hen, *a* habit); if it's silent, use *an* (*an* hour, *an* honorable man). If it's only lightly pronounced, usage is divided (*a, an* habitual criminal, *a, an* historian).

Accept, Except. Similar sound, different meanings. *Accept* means "to receive." *Except* is a rather uncommon verb meaning "to exclude." ("They *excepted* him from their list.") *Except* is more commonly a preposition or conjunction.

Affect, Effect. Often confused. The verb *affect* means "to influence." The rarely used verb *effect* means "to bring about"; when a noun, *effect* means "result."

    Her glance *affected* me strangely.
    We *effected* a change in the terms of the contract.
    The laxative had a good *effect*.

Allusion, Illusion. To *allude* to something is simply to make a reference to it. An *illusion* (noun) is a false conception or interpretation.

Almost, Most. Don't use *most* as a substitute for *almost*. (To reproduce colloquial speech, use *'most*.).

    AVOID   She cooks potatoes *most* every day.

Also. An adverb; not a substitute for *and*.

    She likes spinach, broccoli, *and* (not *also*) cauliflower.

Anyways. U-L for *anyway*.

Anywheres. U-L for *anywhere*.

Being that. A U-L substitute for a subordinating conjunction (*since, as, because*).

Belly, Bellyache. Somewhat inelegant when a reference to the human stomach. (*Bellyache* is also slang for "complain" or "complaint.")

Bring, brung. The principal parts of this verb are *bring, brought, brought*.

    AVOID   He *brung* along a bottle of whiskey.

Bust. The verb is *burst* (*burst, burst*), according to the higher classes. But *bust* is widely used slang for either "break" or "arrest."

    AVOID   The balloon (or bubble) is *busted*.

Buy, boughten. The principal parts here are *buy, bought, bought*.

    AVOID   It was *boughten*, not stole!
    I like the store-*boughten* kind better.

Calculate, Figure, Reckon. These verbs suggest a mathematical computation or some other kind of careful estimate. In the U-L Class, their meaning has been altered to just "guess" or "assume."

    AVOID   I *calculate* it's time to quit drinkin'.
    I *reckon* you'll be glad.

Can, May. See UL-G2.

Can't hardly, Don't hardly. Double negatives aren't acceptable in (modern) polite society.

Considerable. A class-stratifying word.

    UPPER CLASS   His efforts were *considerable* [noteworthy].
    MIDDLE CLASS   They lost *considerable* [a large amount of] ground with that maneuver.
    LOWER CLASS   They lost *considerable* [adjective turned into a noun].

Done it. Common U-L substitute for *did it*.

    AVOID   She *done* it already.

Drag, drug. The principal parts are *drag, dragged, dragged.*
    AVOID   He *drug* the body to the door.
Effect, Affect. See *Affect.*
Etc. An abbreviation of the Latin *et* ("and") and *cetera* ("other things"). U-L people often write *and etc.*, thus saying "and" twice. (The U-U Class, incidentally, regards *etc.* as a word used in business; it is not thought appropriate, therefore, in social correspondence, literature, and most college writing.)
Everyplace. U-L for *everywhere.*
Except, Accept. See *Accept.*
Feel of, Smell of, Taste of. When these are verbs, omit the *of.*
        The doctor *felt* (not *felt of*) his pulse.
But *of* is properly put after a noun.
        I like the *feel of* silk.
Figure. See *Calculate.*
Growed. The other principal parts of *grow* are not "growed" but *grew* and *grown.*
He don't, She don't, It don't. See UL-G6.
Heighth. The approved form is *height.*
Illusion, Allusion. See *Allusion.*
Is when, Is where. Putting an adverb clause after a linking verb is often frowned on as ungrammatical. Rewrite the sentence.
    AVOID   The prosecutor says the only child-support cases he handles *are when* the father is out of the county.
    TRY   The prosecutor says he handles child-support cases *only when* the father is out of the county.
Its, It's. See p. 115.
Lay, Lie. See p. 55.
Most, Almost. See *Almost.*
Noplace. U-L for *nowhere.*
Outside of. Colloquial when substituting for *besides* or *except.*
    AVOID   No one came *outside of* him and me.
Pay her no mind. The approved form of this expression is "Pay her no *attention*" or, more commonly, "Pay no attention to her."
Plenty. Another class-stratifier. Don't use for the intensives *quite* or *very.*
    HIGHER CLASS   It was a time of *plenty* (abundance).
    GENERAL USE   She brought plenty (enough).
    L-M CLASS   The truck was *plenty* big.
    LOWER CLASS   The truck was *plenty* big enough.
Piece. Unless you don't mind being considered U-L, don't use *piece* to mean "a short distance."
    AVOID   I walked a *piece* down the road.
Reckon. See *Calculate.*
Reverend. Class usage differs, but the written word is usually abbreviated.
    UPPER CLASS   The Rev. Mr. David Johnson ("Mr. Johnson")
    MIDDLE CLASS   Rev. Harold Olson ("Mr. Olson")
    LOWER CLASS   Rev. Swanson ("Hello, Reverend")

Right. A localism for *very,* as in "I'm *right* tuckered out."
Seeing as how. U-L substitute for a subordinating conjunction (*since, as, because*).
Seen. Lots of trouble here. Avoid "I *seen,*" "She *seen.*" Say instead "I *saw,*" "She *saw.*"
Set, Sit. See p. 55.
Someplace. Somewhere is preferred.
Take and. Unacceptable when used in such locutions as "Let's *take and* jump in the haypile."
Them guys. Definitely a lower-class construction. Often mistakenly used as a subject.
    AVOID   *Them guys* in Washington don't ever help the little guy.
Wait on. Acceptable in the sense of "to serve"; unacceptable as a substitute for "wait for."
    AVOID   We *waited on* his buddy for over three hours.
Way, Ways. (1) *Way* is not permitted as a substitute for *away* ("*away* down yonder"), although the informal *'way* is allowed on occasion. (2) *Ways* is often a U-L form of *way.*
    AVOID   It's just a little *ways* now.
Where at. The *at* is superfluous. Avoid "Where is it *at?*"
Who, Whom. See pp. 73-74.

U-L PUNCTUATION

> With educated people, I suppose punctuation is a matter of rule; with me it is a matter of feeling. But I must say I have great respect for the semicolon; it's a useful little chap.
> —Abraham Lincoln

In this section we shall concentrate on just

The semicolon

Despite its name, the semicolon has little if anything to do with the colon. It probably should be called a *semiperiod,* although it is also related to the comma. U-L writers seldom employ the semicolon. When they do, they are trying to avert the mysterious threat of the comma splice. Here's the convention to observe:

• Use the semicolon between major sentence parts of *equal* rank.

UL-P1   Use the semicolon to link independent clauses not joined by a coordinating conjunction (*and, or, but, nor*).

a. Stylists in the higher social classes often like to yoke two related clauses together, and, in so doing, to achieve a classical architectonic balance, with clauses of about the same length.

    For three hours the bombers droned through the dark skies; the crews, despite themselves, began to grow drowsy.

Such a balance is regarded as a distinctly formal construct.

b. Conjunctive adverbs and sentence modifiers may be placed between the clauses. See LL-G7 and LM-G3.
> She was the handsomest woman there; *moreover*, she was wealthy.
> The wedding was charming; *in my opinion*, it was the finest the town has ever seen.

UL-P2 — Use a semicolon between other coordinate clauses (1) if you wish to achieve contrast or special emphasis, (2) if your clauses have internal punctuation, or (3) if the clauses are rather long and complicated.

The bargaining committee was duly created; *but* under the circumstances it had no real power.

In 1856, with the Whigs torn by internal strife, Lincoln made up his mind; *and* so he joined a free-soil group, the new Republican Party, and vowed to attack Douglas' positions.

UL-P3 — Use a semicolon between elements in a series if any has internal punctuation.

The tour visited France for three days; Switzerland, two days; Italy, a week; and Spain, three days.

Many authorities prefer to change the final semicolon to a comma if *and* or *or* follows ("...Italy, a week, *and* Spain, three days"). This should be done, though, only when at least two semicolons remain.

> With malice toward none; with charity for all; with firmness in the right, as God gives us to see the right, let us strive on to finish the work we are in; to bind up the nation's wounds; to care for him who shall have borne the battle, and for his widow, and his orphan—to do all which may achieve and cherish a just and lasting peace among ourselves, and with all nations.
> —Abraham Lincoln, *Second Inaugural Address*

UL-P4 — Don't use the semicolon between parts of *unequal* rank.

AVOID We accidentally left the oven on for an extra hour; turning the roast a gorgeous black. (Clause and phrase)

AVOID All of us wanted to go to San Francisco; where we intended to see all the sights. (Main clause and subordinate clause)

U-L SPELLING

Some spelling rules will be found in L-M Spelling. Until then, practice on some often-misspelled words. Have someone help you drill.

1. accidentally
2. achieve
3. appearance
4. arctic
5. benefited
6. calendar
7. ceiling
8. changeable
9. changing
10. competition
11. conscience
12. conscientious

13. conscious
14. desirable
15. disappear
16. disastrous
17. environment
18. government
19. grammar
20. incidentally
21. noticeable
22. permissible
23. prevalent
24. receive
25. sophomore

U-L MECHANICS

In order to ascend the social ladder, you must not be thought too careless about society's conventions. It is wise, therefore, to learn all of its customs—including the apparently insignificant ones.

UL-M1 *Abbreviations*

UL-M1a   Classes differ somewhat in abbreviating titles with proper names.

Titles are bound up with status in any society; use them carefully lest you seriously injure someone's pride.
(1) *Ms., Mr., Mrs., Dr.*—These abbreviations may be used with either the full name or just a surname: Mr. A. K. Murdock, Ms. Becker.
(2) *Messrs., Mmes.*—On certain occasions, the three highest classes use these abbreviations (of *Messieurs* and *Mesdames*) as the plurals of *Mr.* and *Mrs.* They are occasionally to be found in a newspaper's society pages.
    Mmes. John Lee and Samuel Higginbotham
(3) *Rev., Sen., Prof., Hon.*—Except in newspapers, where practice varies, these abbreviations should be used only when a full name follows. In some upper-class circles, *Rev.* and *Hon.* are spelled out (and preceded by *the*) even with a full name.
    The Reverend Dr. Thomas Horn
    The Honorable J. J. Tewkesbury, Second District, West Virginia (a congressman)
(4) *Jr., Sr., M.D., D.D.S., D.D., LL.D.*—These are used *after* a name. Below the U-U Class, however, one may shorten academic degrees and put them almost anywhere:
    He is studying for his Ph.D.
(5) *St.* (saint, not street)—This is used with a Christian name, as in St. Mark, St. Mary's.

UL-M1b   Spell out personal names and, in most writing, days of the week.

William Jefferson was born on Wednesday, July 18.
NOT Wm. Jefferson was born on Wed., July 18.
(But initials are widely accepted: Mr. and Mrs. P. D. Jefferson ...)

UL-M1c   Some abbreviations are used only with
                   specific dates or other numerals.
   No. 1   43 Carson St.
   Aug. 13   701 Standish Blvd.
Otherwise, make it *August,* Carson *Street.*
   7:30 a.m. or A.M.   7:30 p.m. or P.M.
B.C. and A.D. may be affixed to specific historical dates or to centuries, as the Fourth Century B.C.

UL-M1d   Various other abbreviation problems:

(1) States and the District of Columbia are spelled out when used alone, but with a city they are abbreviated: Washington, D.C.; Salem, Mass. With a ZIP Code, however, the abbreviation changes: Ark., AR; Tex., TX.
(2) There are many abbreviations in technical writing (cc., L., NaCl) and in footnotes and bibliographies (see L-U Mechanics).
(3) Some Latin abbreviations are found in general writing: *e. g.* (for example), *cf.* (compare), *i.e.* (that is), *vs. (versus).* See *Etc.* in U-L Usage.
(4) In using business firm names, follow their practices: W. Jones *Co.,* but K. Smith *Company.* Occasionally a firm name will include an ampersand: J. Brown *&* Co. (Elsewhere use *and.*)
(5) In formal writing, spell out *volume, chapter, pages,* and the names of unnumbered academic subjects. Otherwise, use conventional abbreviations.
   FORMAL   In mathematics, we are to study Chapter 3, pages 78 to 99.
   INFORMAL   In math, we're to study Ch. 3, pp. 78-99.
(6) Many national organizations are familiarly known by an abbreviation (AAA, S.P.C.A.); consult your dictionary about the propriety of periods.
(7) *Mount* or *Mt., Fort* or *Ft.*—the distinctions here follow local custom.
(8) *United States* is properly spelled out when used as a noun, but often abbreviated as an adjective.
   NOUN   throughout the United States
   ADJECTIVE   U.S. prestige, the U.S. monetary situation
(9) There is great confusion in dealing with the word *century.* Is *15th C.,* used as an adjective, beyond the pale? Apparently not—but formal situations may sometimes forbid such abbreviations.

UL-M2 *Manuscript form*

Perhaps nothing will slow your rise toward the middle class more certainly than a habit of antagonizing the instructors you meet along the way. Nothing will antagonize them faster than sloppy work—reckless penmanship, not giving a damn about promptness, carelessness about content, carelessness about form. Before he (or she) certifies you've earned middle-class status, the middle-class instructor wants to know that you *care*—that you have been trying hard and will continue to do so—which is what's involved in the bourgeois "work ethic." The first thing to do in a college class, therefore, is to determine what the instructor will demand of his students, including (in an English class) his standards for the form of written work. The following suggestions are subject to his modification.

UL-M2a Follow standard practice in the preparation of the manuscript.

Originality may be desirable in a theme's content, but it is rarely a virtue in creating the purely mechanical aspects of *form*. Academic people, like many others, live according to certain conventions. What the instructor will probably expect, and want, is the following:

(1) Standard ruled theme paper (white, 8½ by 11 inches); also some unlined paper if you plan to type.
(2) Black or blue-black ink (or typewriter ribbon).
(3) Writing on only one side (except for an endorsement)—writing that is free from cute little circles dotting the *i*'s and similar distractions. (You may be asked, incidentally, to double-space; all typed themes are double-spaced.)
(4) Margins on *all four sides* of the page.
(5) A title, centered, about an inch and a half from the top. (Don't underline it or put it in quotation marks, unless it *is* a quotation.)
(6) Subsequent pages numbered, at the top, with Arabic numerals (2, 3, 4 . . .)
(7) An endorsement on the outside sheet, with your name and other necessary information. The instructor will specify its form.

UL-M2b Proofread your final draft.

(1) Check carefully all the elements—grammar, mechanics, punctuation, spelling, diction, and so on.
(2) If you must delete a word, draw a neat single line through it. Nothing else.
(3) If you must insert a last-minute word or phrase, write it *above* the line and put a caret (∧) *below* the line.
(4) If a paragraph should be split in two, indicate the splitting point with (in the margin) the symbol ¶. If two paragraphs should be only one, put "No ¶" in the margin.
(5) If this leaves things messy, recopy.

UL-M2c *Revise* the returned paper and then submit it again.

The instructor will return your paper with various little symbols on it—symbols which refer to sections in this book. Follow this procedure:

(1) Study the section indicated.
(2) If you agree that you goofed, make the correction suggested, usually by crossing out the offending item and rewriting above it.
(3) If you do *not* agree, or still don't understand, see the instructor as soon as possible. (Observe his office hours.) He won't mind explaining, or hearing your argument, but he will mind getting a paper that's only half-revised.

U-L COMPOSITION

In Chapter 3 we discussed various sentence types, noted a number of permutations, and warned the Lower-Lower writer about a few of them that are unacceptable (fused sentences, mixed constructions, and so on). The L-L person, in other words, was shown many of the basic conventions of American English sentences.

In Chapter 4 we have peeked into some more of the sentence's many chambers, and of course will continue to do so. But it is time to develop also a wider vision, to look at the sentence's "neighborhood," to consider the sentence as part of a *paragraph*. The L-L person is beginning the process of *composition—the arrangement of parts into a unified whole*—when he arranges words to make an effective sentence. Now we should examine ways of building the next larger unit of thought. To be sure, some paragraphs consist of only one sentence, but most contain more. In combining sentences, a writer should be guided by some time-tested principles of composition or "rhetoric": *unity, coherence,* and *effective development.*

UL-C1   The principle of *unity* requires that the paragraph shall have *one central thought*.

Ordinarily the central thought is expressed in a *topic sentence*. (Occasionally the main idea isn't expressed, but only implied.) This topic sentence may be the first, as in the paragraph you're reading, or it may come later, as in the two preceding paragraphs. The rest of the sentences are there to *introduce, qualify, clarify, support,* or *develop* the central idea. The paragraph is said to have unity when all its parts clearly contribute to that central statement.

In the paragraph above, for instance, Sentence No. 1 was, as I said, the topic sentence. Sentence No. 2, in parentheses, qualified No. 1 but didn't deny its validity. Sentence No. 3 sought to clarify the "central thought" by noting that its position is variable. Sentences 4 and 5 supported and also developed the topic sentence.

(*Note*: In that *last* paragraph, there wasn't any topic sentence; it was only implied. Let's try expressing it. How about this?—"*The principle of unity has been observed in each of these paragraphs.* In the paragraph above, for instance..." Yes, that will do. That was easy.)

- If a paragraph has no clear topic sentence, one should at least be implied.

UL-C2   The principle of *coherence* demands that the thought shall flow *smoothly and logically* from one sentence to the next.

Quite obviously, a paragraph is more than a strung-out series of miscellaneous ideas, many of them seemingly of equal importance. Rather, its ideas must be rigorously controlled—fitted into the paragraph's structure. There are two rules to follow to establish coherence:

- *The sentences should be arranged in some clear and reasonable order.*

- *Various devices should be employed to insure that the reader perceives that order.*

As to the first rule, the paragrapher should know that he has several possible patterns of organization to choose among. They can be classified as either natural or logical.

1. *Natural orders*
   a. *Chronological order*

Sometimes the time order can be expressed rather subtly. In one of this book's earliest paragraphs, we asked the reader to recall (1) that bonded servants were common from our "earliest colonial days" (which would be about 1619 in Virginia and the 1630's in Massachusetts Bay Colony); (2) that the French observer St. Jean de Crèvecoeur published, near the close of the Revolution, some impressions of the American class structure; (3) that, after the war, the aristocratic Founding Fathers met (in 1787) to draw up the Constitution of the United States; and (4) that James Madison of Virginia, with two others, printed in that same year a tract, *Federalist Paper No. 10,* in an effort to win public support for the Constitution—an effort finally successful in 1789.

Now, at the time, most of that was done gently, by footnotes and allusions; yet there *was* a chronological sequence coming through, covering about 170 years of our early history. A subtle treatment, we felt, was sufficient.

But in other cases the time factor should be louder and more insistent, to emphasize the relation of one phase to another. For example, in Chapter 2 came a paragraph beginning "Part of the problem is his teacher" (topic sentence). It went on to report that teachers hand out grades that often closely reflect the pupils' social positions.

> One consequence, early on, is the branding of gauche lower-class children as academic failures. This, in turn, becomes a self-fulfilling prophecy. Lower-class children start thinking of themselves as "losers," and soon start acting like losers....

If we analyze that passage, we find a sequence of four elements: (1) grades are given by the teacher and a pattern is established; (2) lower-class children are then "branded," presumably by report cards to their parents; (3) next, they start to regard themselves as failures; (4) "soon" they start to act like failures.

Finally, when the time factor is all-important, as in some narratives and physical processes, the writer must stress the order, step by step, still more. The reader likes to have the plan loom out like a fluorescent skeleton. We'll talk soon about how this may be done.

   b. *Spatial order*

A time sequence is said to be a "natural" order because it comes very easily to the mind. Also natural to human beings is a spatial arrangement, of almost anything imaginable. We have pictures in our heads, and it's not very hard to transmit those pictures to others. Russell Lynes, quoted earlier, had one in his head:

> our society has increasingly become divided vertically. Instead of broad upper, middle, and lower classes that cut across the society of the nation like the clear

but uneven slices on a geological model, we now have a series of almost free-standing pyramids...[12]

It is relatively easy, in describing a landscape or a face or a building's layout, to move clockwise, or from near to distant (or the opposite), or from north to south—or indeed in any direction that is natural and simple to follow. It is often a good idea to begin with some notable feature.

> Dominating in the room, against the bare west wall, was an ancient upright piano. Most of the easy chairs faced it in an expectant semi-circle, as if someone might suddenly favor guests with a tune for all to hum. Beyond the chairs was a small yellow-brick fireplace, its embers glowing with a gentle warmth.

And so on. After a little practice, you'll find it a simple task.

2. *Logical orders*

With material that can't effortlessly be put in a time or space matrix, the mind will have to *contrive a plan,* an order that will best clarify the subject. The emphasis is on the efficiency and effectiveness of a *logical* system of thought. The purpose is called "exposition," the business of making something clear.

Since we mean to treat this topic at some length in U-M Composition, let's be content here with a mere list of some of the techniques. The movement in the paragraph might be from something familiar (like a stove) to something unfamiliar (like an atomic reactor) or the reverse of that; from a general statement to a specific one, or vice versa; from an introductory idea to a more important one and thence to the most important; from a general statement to a set of supporting details or reasons, and so on. There are, as you can see, quite a few possibilities. The ideal one depends largely on the nature of your material.

So much for the first rule: that you should put your sentences in some clear, reasonable pattern. Now let's consider the *second* rule of coherence—that you must use various devices to *make sure* your reader sees your pattern.

Most people, perhaps, are quite familiar with these strategies. The devices, the little tricks you can play, include these: (1) using pronouns that refer to the preceding sentence; (2) inserting transitional expressions to create a logical bridge and to direct the reader onward; (3) repeating ideas and even exact words, and (4) repeating the structure of a previous sentence element (or whole sentence). Finally, we advise a negative strategy: (5) avoiding unnecessary shifts in "point of view," and especially shifts of person, tense, or number.

1. *Using pronouns*

> David very casually sat down at the piano. *He* plunked absent-mindedly at *its* keys for a moment and then...

2. *Using transitional expressions*

> In the filtration system, a slotted metal tube runs the full length of the first chamber. Its operation is simplicity itself. *First,....Second,...Next,...Finally,...*

Other time expressions include *later, soon, after a few minutes, meanwhile, in the meantime, then.* Spatial expressions might include *next to, near, to the south, above,* and so on.

But it's the logical-order paragraph that taxes your ingenuity. Fortunately, there is a wealth of transitional devices:

ADDITION	besides, and, further, furthermore, again, too, also, equally important, moreover, etc.
INTENSIFICATION	indeed, in other words
COMPARISON	in like manner, similarly
CONTRAST	however, but, yet (or *and yet*), at the same time, on the other hand, nevertheless
PURPOSE	with this in mind, for this purpose, to this end
RESULT	therefore, hence, consequently, thus
ILLUSTRATION	to illustrate, for example, for instance
SUMMARY	in brief, as I have said, as has been noted, we have seen that, to sum up

3. *Repeating ideas and words*

Sometimes an idea is rephrased for the sake of paragraph coherence. Clarity is especially enhanced by the use of examples.

> *Piped-in music* threatens to engulf us entirely. One listens to *Mantovani's violins* in the elevator. *Someone else's guitars* pursue us down the hall. In the company's rest room there is no rest...

Or a word, or a variant thereof, can be repeated:

> The American's love affair with the *automobile* shows no sign of waning. A gasoline shortage threatens; what does he do?—sell his big *car* and take the bus to work? No. He trades the big *car* in, and buys a smaller one. Meanwhile, the *auto* his wife drives...

4. *Repeating sentence structure*

An effective trick, sometimes, is the creation of "parallel" sentence structure—the repetition of structural elements, such as (here) prepositional phrase openers.

> There were plants everywhere. *Along a window seat* were African violets, purple and pink. *On a table* squatted a large Christmas cactus. *On the hearth* was a begonia, looking somewhat yellow and ill. *In a corner by the door* stood a tall philodendron, its branches threatening revolt. *Past the kitchen doorway* we could see several ferns...

The rhythm of this echo-of-form carries us along almost against our will.

Perhaps some metaphors can make all this clear. The little devices we have just been looking at serve to wire the paragraph together. They act also as bridges between sentences and as signposts indicating various logical relationships, thereby revealing the over-all structure. In short, they help to guarantee the paragraph's logicality, its continuity, and its smoothness.

UL-C3 The principle of *effective development* requires several things—that a paragraph shall be neither too short nor too long, shall be interesting, shall be continuously clear, and shall efficiently establish its points of emphasis.

a. *Avoid choppy, underdeveloped paragraphs.*

Modern newspapers customarily print very short paragraphs (thirty or forty words) but college writing, traditionally, is characterized by longer, more carefully developed paragraphs. The length depends upon the nature of the central idea, of course, and upon the stylist, but they commonly run to a hundred words and sometimes much more. The college writer should see to it that his meaning is unmistakable, and frequently that it is also persuasive. He therefore should think of *reasons,* supporting *details, examples, illustrations.* An important thing to do, occasionally, is simply to *define* one's principal terms—or any difficult or unusual concepts involved. Or, for the sake of clarity, the writer may wish to set up a *comparison* with a similar thing, or even produce an *anecdote* (or some other *narrative*) that will throw a light on the subject. He may wish to discuss its *causes,* or its *effects,* or both. Or he may decide to devote space to *description.* The number of writing problems is perhaps beyond counting—but there are also lots of solutions, and even more *combinations* of solutions. The writer's familiarity with them may help to determine, and be a good measure of, his social status.

We shall say more about these solutions in later chapters.

b. *Avoid over-long, tedious, inefficient paragraphs.*

Long-windedness—a lack of economy of language—is almost as serious an offense as stinginess in developing the paragraph. In both, there is danger of loss of clarity. In underdevelopment, we may leave out something necessary. In wordy overdevelopment, not only may we tire the reader, but we may violate the "rule of emphasis," a term some use to remind us to lay stress efficiently in reasonable places, and in reasonable degrees.

Let me explain. There are various ways to emphasize an idea. One is by using transitional devices. Another is by repeating the idea—rephrasing it because we like variety. And another is by just giving it sheer bulk. That is, all other things being equal, a writer tends to dwell long and lovingly at the points he finds both interesting and important. It's one of his signals to the reader. But suppose his point is not really very important—not greatly significant in the total composition. In such a case he has given the reader a faulty signal. Disproportionate stress may cause loss of clarity and even some confusion. (Whereupon, heeding my own advice, I conclude this paragraph.)

We will be looking at paragraph construction again in subsequent chapters, because it is, after all, a rather important subject in an English book. We'll have to take note of two special kinds of paragraphs—those in the introduction and conclusion of an essay. And we must pay attention to the techniques of building interesting *variety* into the lines, and to the ways of creating transitions from one paragraph to the next. This chapter, however, has already given the U-L writer enough practice-work to do. (Some real labor, incidentally, is only proper, for he should serve a rigorous apprenticeship before final acceptance into the great middle class.)

There is, though, one more lesson that the U-L writer should learn, which is that composition is an art—and, like all other arts, it demands of a really worthy practitioner a clear mind and an unwavering dedication to naked, cruel, beautiful honesty. To be sure, the middle class may not always be pleased to have in its midst a real, honest-to-God truth-teller and gadfly. Such a man or woman is, on the other hand, not always scorned and mocked; sometimes he makes a name for himself, wins some admiration, a certain respect. Sincerity is sometimes a rather appealing characteristic. But even if his social progress should be slowed, he would have a satisfaction. A commitment to be honest in one's expression, to be honest *with oneself,* is perhaps the highest obligation most of us will ever know. In these democratic days, when time has usurped the nobility of nobles, any person can come, if he will, into at least that inheritance.

Who are the oppressed? . . . the workers; they that make the bread that the soft-handed and idle eat. Why is it right that there is not a fairer division of the spoil all around? Because laws and constitutions have ordered otherwise. Then it follows that laws and constitutions should change around and say there shall be a more nearly equal division.
—Mark Twain, 1886

CHAPTER 5
LOWER-MIDDLE LANGUAGE

We have climbed, through diligence, to the lower reaches of the great Middle Class, foundation and bulwark of the nation, the source of much of its energy and the area where most of the work is done. The Lower-Middle group will be defined here partly in terms of 1972 household income, reported to us by the U.S. Census Bureau. Our rather arbitrary lower and upper limits will be $5,000 and $15,000.

That income span is broad enough to make this a huge social class, the largest of all, by far—as large, in fact, as all the others combined. It accounts for about half of all U.S. households and 51.5 per cent of the population. (Remember the illustrations in the first chapter? This is the big, sagging bulge in the income-and-population "tree.") Whereas a lower-class home had $1,291 per capita for an average of two people, suddenly now there are three people in an average home—and per-capita income is more than $3,000. The dollar rise is partly explained by the fact that about 39 per cent of L-M wives are now in the labor force—not as poorly paid housemaids (regarded as a lower-class role) so much as in "downtown" jobs and in school teaching.[1]

The typical L-M worker, perhaps, is a blue-collar male in the city. More than 48 per cent of all L-M occupations are in the urban blue-collar category; farm work involves fewer than four per cent at this level. We also find, as of March 1973, a substantial number of L-M people (about 39 per cent) in white-collar occupations. Again, female clerical workers account for many of that group. But more than a fifth of all L-M workers are in professional, technical, or administrative positions.[2] They're not getting rich, but they're getting by.

How have they attained these status-giving posts? The answer, clearly, is by educating themselves. We reported that in 1973 more than 45 per cent of the lower-class household heads had only an elementary school education "or less." At the L-M level that figure drops to about 22 per cent. Or we might compare the numbers of college graduates: 5 per cent among the lower-class household heads, more than 10 per cent in the L-M class. Three-fifths of the L-M heads of households have at least a high school diploma.[3]

We could, however, express the same statistics negatively. What's holding the L-M breadwinner back? Partly, at least, the fact that about 40 per cent do *not* have a high school education. Of the 33.9 million L-M household heads, fewer than eight million (about 23 per cent) have ever been in a college classroom.[4]

The Census Bureau's 1973 *Statistical Abstract*[5] tells us that a typical U-L employee is a laborer ("except farm and mine") who earned in 1971 only $4,847. Moving up a step to get a picture of the typical Lower-Middle worker, let's compare that median income with these:

Occupation	Men	Women
Craftsmen, foremen, etc.	$9,057	$4,542
Salesworkers	8,887	2,593
Clerical workers	8,426	4,726
Proprietors, except farm	9,433	3,623
Operatives, etc.	7,275	4,036
Service workers	5,529	2,635

The L-M male (if not the female) is thus in a far better income situation than his male U-L cousin. If there is even $5,000 to $7,500 coming into the home annually, the Census Bureau says, we will find in that kind of house certain amenities. In 1971 in that particular L-M stratum 22.4 per cent had a second car, 40 per cent a *color* TV set, 38.2 per cent a clothes dryer, and a quarter of them had air-conditioning[6]—all of these things bought "on time," of course, at high interest rates.

But although he has some things not enjoyed by the lower classes, the L-M worker, according to the pollsters, remains profoundly dissatisfied. Either there's monotony in his job (little chance for creativeness) or he's not earning enough (he's always in debt); these are the most frequent complaints. Our recommendations to him, or perhaps you: (1) Do something to upgrade your education; if you are earning five credits now, make it ten if you can. (2) Work especially hard on improving your speech and writing skills. If you feel you have mastered Chapters 3 and 4, begin now on the material that follows.

L-M GRAMMAR

We open this section with some rather easy material—adjectives and adverbs—but move gradually into more complex problems. Stay alert.

LM-G1 *Adjectives and adverbs*

L-M people, even the most decent among them, are forever mistaking these two functions—a confusion tolerated by the patronizing higher classes. It does no real harm; the intended meaning is clear. But it is also clear that the speaker is uneducated. Can a person call himself truly schooled if he hasn't yet learned the difference between two simple grammatical jobs?

An *adjective* modifies (describes or limits) a noun or pronoun.

An *adverb* modifies a verb, adjective, another adverb, or an entire clause or sentence.

There is no other sure distinction of the two. True, most adverbs end in *-ly* (*quickly, gracefully*), but there are too many exceptions. To make matters worse, some adjectives end with *-ly* (*womanly, friendly, saintly*) and a few *-ly* words may be either adjectives or adverbs (*only, early*). Several other common modifiers have that same dual ability: *far, fast, late, well,* and so on.

To fight your way through this thicket, you must either learn all these exceptions or use a dictionary frequently. What we described as "easy material," just now, is actually not quite so simple. If you've been careless about adjectives and adverbs in the past, it may take you some time to work flaws out of your speech patterns. Your most important job, again, is to see clearly the difference in *function*.

LM-G1a

When the thing being modified is a verb, adjective, or adverb, don't use an adjective—use an *adverb*.

With a verb
    L-M CLASS   He does it all so *easy*.
    HIGHER CLASS   He does it all so *easily*.

With an adjective
    L-M CLASS   A *real* good diver doesn't splash much.
    HIGHER CLASS   A *really* good diver doesn't splash much.

With another adverb
    L-M CLASS   She drove *awful* fast.
    U-M CLASS   She drove *awfully* fast.
    UPPER CLASS   She drove *very* fast.

LM-G1b

Following a *linking* verb, use a *predicate adjective* to modify the subject.

The linking verbs include, for example, *be* (*is, are,* etc.), *become, seem,* and the verbs of the senses (*smell, taste, look, feel, sound*). If any of these translates to *is, are,* etc., or *become(s)*, remember to use an adjective to describe the subject. ("She tasted the soup" means what it says. But "The soup *tasted salty*" means "The soup *was* salty.") There are only a few trouble spots in this area, but they can be rather treacherous.

(1) The verb *feel* (They *felt* happy, lucky, etc.) is a case in point. The predicate adjective *bad* is used after *feel* to show that a person is depressed, ill, or apologetic.
    She feels *bad* about it.
    NOT She feels *badly* about it.
The adjective *good*, on the other hand, indicates her general euphoria:
    She felt *good*.
The word *well*, which can be either an adjective or an adverb, is used as an adjective to mean that she is *not* sick.
    She felt *well*.

But *feel* is not always a linking verb; sometimes it's transitive.

    The old woman *felt* the cloth.

And sometimes it's intransitive.

    The old blind woman *felt* carefully for the doorway.

(2) The modifier is an *adverb* if it refers to the verb's action, as in the last example above. Be alert to the sentence's meaning.

| ADJECTIVE | The boy looked *glum*. |
| ADVERB | The boy looked *glumly* about him. |

LM-G1c   A few other verbs sometimes perform a linking-verb function. Use an *adjective* to modify the *subject*.

Keep awake, please. If you do use an adjective, you'll be signalling the reader to swing his attention from the verb to the subject.

| ADVERB | She grew *fast*. (Tells how quickly she grew) |
| ADJECTIVE | She grew *tall*. (Tells what she became) |

| ADVERB | The crankshaft turned *briskly*. |
| ADJECTIVE | The weather turned *brisk*. |

LM-G1d   An adverb describes a verb. But if it's really a direct object that's being modified, use an *adjective*.

| ADVERB | Keep your stamps *neatly* in an album. |
| ADJECTIVE | Keep your stamps *neat* (i.e., neat stamps). |

| ADVERB | Hold the rope *tightly*. |
| ADJECTIVE | Hold the rope *tight* (i.e., the tight rope) |

Adjectives functioning the way *neat* and *tight* do here are actually a mixed breed, with about one-quarter adverb blood. They fall in a category called "objective complement," a label for nouns or adjectives which complete the meaning of both the direct object *and* the verb. A test: If the verb were changed to passive voice, such a term would be retained as a kind of subjective complement.

    ACTIVE   Johnny colored the eggs *purple*.
    PASSIVE   The eggs were colored ["became"] *purple* by Johnny.

But not all adjectives in this position are objective complements.

    ACTIVE   Johnny colored the eggs *in the refrigerator*.
    PASSIVE   The eggs were colored *in the refrigerator* (?) by Johnny.

The phrase obviously is 100 per cent adjective and 0 per cent adverb—unless Johnny is very small and dresses warmly.

LM-G1e

Some adverbs have a common form identical to the adjective spelling, and a more highbrow form that is not.

L-M CLASS   Drive *slow*. Do it *quick*. He whistled *loud*.
HIGHER CLASS   Drive *slowly*. Do it *quickly*. He whistled *loudly*.

LM-G1f

Nouns are often used as adjectives.

POSSESSIVE FORM   A *man's* coat was stolen.
COMMON FORM   We had *grandstand* seats at the *baseball* game.

If, however, there is a well-known adjective form, the upper classes use it instead: *nasal* (not *nose*) infection; *administrative* (not *administration*) trouble.

LM-G1g

Show *degrees* of quantity or quality by forming the *positive, comparative,* or *superlative* in conventional ways.

Adjectives and adverbs, like a few other parts of speech, retain some centuries-old inflections. We "compare" (or form the comparative and superlative degrees of) most short adjectives, and some adverbs, simply by adding *-er* and *-est*. But we use *more* and *most, less* and *least*, with long adjectives, participles, and most adverbs. Your ear may tell you what's graceful and what isn't.

	Positive	*Comparative*	*Superlative*
ADJECTIVES	slow	slower	slowest
	cheap	cheaper	cheapest
	hot	hotter	hottest
But	beautiful	more beautiful	most beautiful
	frightening	more frightening	most frightening
ADVERBS	fast	faster	fastest
But	quickly	more quickly	most quickly

A few adjectives (*handsome, lonesome,* etc.) may be compared with either system. Please note, too, that some very important adjectives and adverbs are irregular in their inflection:

little	less	least
well	better	best
good	better	best
bad	worse	worst

Some adjectives and adverbs are said to be "absolute"; logically, they cannot be compared at all. It's not very logical to be, say, a *little* pregnant—or *most* perfect.

MIDDLE CLASS   Our tires are the *roundest* made.
UPPER CLASS   Our tires are the *most nearly round*.
LOWER CLASS   We have the *completest* line in town.
MIDDLE CLASS   We have the *most complete* line in town.
UPPER CLASS   We have the *most nearly complete* line in town.

Other absolutes are *dead, empty, full, wholly,* etc. Most are misused by the middle and lower classes. U-M people, however, can usually handle *unique,* which means "one of a kind."

    L-M CLASS   La Casa is the area's *most unique* restaurant.
    HIGHER CLASS   La Casa is a *unique* restaurant.

LM-G1h   The *comparative* degree refers to two things, the *superlative* to three or more.

    COMPARATIVE   That one is the *taller* of the two.
                           Both are pretty, but Ruth is (the) *prettier.*
    SUPERLATIVE   All three are pretty, but Sandra is (the) *prettiest.*

If you regularly ignore this convention, chances are that you are Lower-Middle.

LM-G1i   "Demonstrative" adjectives should *agree in number* with their nouns.

Some adjectives point to a quality in a noun (*bright* colors), whereas others merely restrict the noun to a certain size or number. Among this latter group are interrogative pronoun-adjectives (*which* boat?), possessives (*your* turn), articles (*a, an, the*), numbers (*Fifth* Amendment), and demonstrative pronoun-adjectives (*this, that, these, those*). The last-named are sometimes troublesome when used with *kind of* or *sort of.*

               These kinds of gloves won't wear out.
    OR   *This kind* of glove won't wear out.
    NOT   *These kind* of gloves won't wear out.

               That sort of weed is a pest.
    NOT   *Those sort* of weeds are a pest.

LM-G2   *Sentence modifiers* are adverbs that refer not to a particular word but to the whole clause or sentence.

a. Expressions such as *unfortunately, certainly, yes, no,* and *in my opinion* often "float" in a clause—at the beginning, at the end, or in the middle.
    Surely you jest.
    Just then, *luckily,* I saw her red hat.
b. Some related usages (*I'm afraid, I would hope, I feel, believe,* etc.) are not really adverbial but are often regarded as sentence modifiers when they appear inside a clause or at its end ("Summer, I'd say, is overdue").
c. A new middle-class sentence modifier, or a close cousin, has recently arrived on the scene. The word *hopefully,* used now to mean "I hope" or "let us hope" or "it is to be hoped," has all but lost its former adverbial sense of "in a hopeful manner." The new usage, however, is very distasteful to upper-class language conservatives. They see it as an example of Gresham's law, so to speak, operating in the language market: the bad coinage driving out the good.
d. Many more expressions commonly called sentence modifiers will be treated

under the next heading, "Conjunctive adverbs," which is a more accurate classification for them.

e. The punctuation of sentence modifiers is the same as that of conjunctive adverbs. See LM-P5, "The comma," and U-L Punctuation, "The semicolon."

LM-G3 *Conjunctive adverbs* are sentence modifiers that have the added capability of *relating one independent clause to another.*

The expressions perhaps most commonly regarded as conjunctive ("joining") adverbs are *consequently, furthermore, hence, however, indeed, likewise, moreover, nevertheless, still,* and *therefore.* But many more should be added to the list: *accordingly, after all, as a result, at any rate, besides, for example, for instance, in any event, in fact, in the first place, namely, that is, then, though, yet,* and still more. (Note that many are prepositional phrases.)

As was pointed out in UL-C2, transitions of all kinds play a major role in stitching the paragraph together. Of all the coherence-building transitions, none is more important than the conjunctive adverb. This is especially true in upper-class paragraphs.

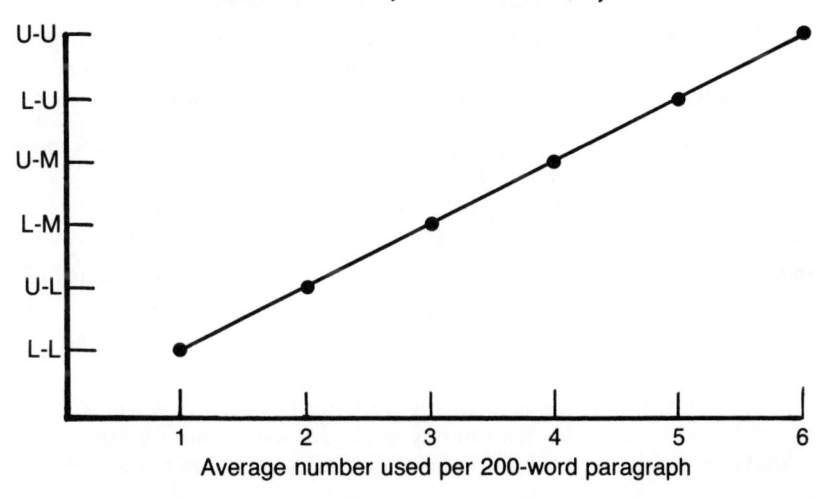

Estimated Use of Conjunctive Adverbs, by Class

As you can see in the graph, there is a remarkable correlation between rate of use of this instrument and one's class status—or so I have observed. These estimates suggest that one thing an ambitious L-M writer can do is try to double his present rate. *For instance,* if his present practice is limited to putting conjunctive adverbs at the beginnings of sentences (as in this one), he might experiment with new positions. He can tuck them, *for example,* into the middle of a clause. Or he can put them between two clauses; *indeed,* this is one of their most common positions in academic writing (U-M to U-U).

He should remember, *though,* to observe all the canons of punctuation, and especially when using the word *however.* That one is a bit tricky (see LM-P5). *Then, too,* he shouldn't overuse such expressions to the point of neglecting other connectives; he should review occasionally this book's material on co-ordinating and subordinating conjunctions and on the naked semicolon.

LM-G4 *Misplaced elements*

Old English had, as modern German has now, many case endings and other inflections to indicate the relations between the parts of a sentence. The meaning of the "bare" modern English sentence, by contrast, depends a great deal on its syntax—on the *positions* of those parts. This is especially true in writing, where we don't have the advantage of sound signals.

a. To avoid misunderstanding or just L-M awkwardness, put a modifier as close as possible to the word it modifies. In the case of some adverbs (*only, almost, even,* etc.) that means *right in front of it.*

L-M CLASS	We *only* worked six hours. (And didn't even breathe?)
HIGHER CLASS	We worked *only* six hours.
L-M CLASS	She's *just* asking for a little bit.
HIGHER CLASS	She's asking for *just* a little bit.

b. Make sure that *phrases* modify the words they're supposed to modify.

LOWER CLASS	It said that he was willing to confess *in the newspaper.*
MIDDLE CLASS	It said *in the newspaper* that he was willing to confess.
UPPER CLASS	The newspaper reported that he was willing to confess.

| AMBIGUOUS | My aunt said she'd just recovered from food poisoning *on her visit here.* |
| CLEAR | *On her visit here,* my aunt said she'd just recovered from food poisoning. |

c. Put relative clauses near the words they modify; if clumsiness results, rewrite the sentence.

L-M CLASS	She got some bread at the store *that was moldy.*
HIGHER CLASS	At the store she got some bread *that was moldy.*
LOWER CLASS	It's hard to buy shirts for boys *that won't fade.*
L-M CLASS	It's hard to buy shirts *that won't fade* for boys.
HIGHER CLASS	It's hard to buy boys' shirts *that won't fade.*

d. Don't build "squinting" expressions—modifiers that can relate to a preceding word *or,* confusingly, to one that follows.

	The man who makes a million *very quickly* makes enemies.
CLEAR	The man who makes a million makes enemies *very quickly.*
OR	The man who *very quickly* makes a million makes enemies.

e. There is danger of clumsiness and even loss of clarity whenever you divorce subject and verb, verb and complement, or the parts of a verb phrase. Often a separation is desirable—but be careful.

(1) Don't leave subject and verb *widely* separated. The reader quickly forgets what the subject was.
(2) Build no awkward constructions.

AVOID   The dog scratched, after slowly getting up, a flea.
AVOID   She *had been*, despite what she said yesterday, *talking* to him.

f. Separation (or "splitting") of *infinitives* is sometimes gracefully accomplished—but often not.

GRACEFUL   He promised *to* more than *restore* the loss.

AWKWARD   Guests are asked *to* not unnecessarily *occupy* the washer or dryer.

IMPROVED   Guests are asked not *to occupy* the washer or dryer unnecessarily.

LM-G5 *Dangling modifiers*

A "dangling" construction modifies nothing at all. It may *seem* to, but that's not the same as the real thing. Major deformities may be created through carelessness in sentence construction. They may require major surgery.

a. *Dangling participial phrases*
   Having eaten our lunch, the tour bus went on.
Tame this monster by changing the phrase to an adverb clause:
   After *we* had eaten our lunch, the tour bus went on.
Note: Less often, the dangling element may be only a verbal (not an extended phrase): *Having eaten,* the tour bus went on.

b. *Dangling infinitive phrases*
   To examine the flywheel, a cover must first come off.
Since the cover can't make the inspection, let's alter the sentence. Improve it by creating an active verb and an agent in the clause.
   To examine the flywheel, *you* first *must remove* a cover.

c. *Dangling "gerund" phrases*
   Many gerund phrases are really prepositional phrases with a gerund as the preposition's object. They too can dangle.
   After *eating* our lunch, the driver called us to the bus.
That driver is a thief and a glutton. Let's give him a smaller role:
   After eating our lunch, *we* were called to the bus by the driver.
   OR After we had eaten our lunch, the driver called us to the bus.

d. *Dangling prepositional phrases*
   At the age of twelve, my father told me to work hard in school.
It's unlikely that he sired anyone at that age. Let's revise things:
   When *I* was twelve, my father . . .

e. *Dangling elliptical clauses*
   An "elliptical" construction has a part or parts missing.
   When well oiled, you can start both motors.

97

We'd better supply the missing elements:
> When *they are* well oiled, you can start both motors.

Note: "Absolute" phrases, already discussed, are an exception to the rule that a modifier should be related logically to the clause. The following are idiomatic:
> *Judging from the reports,* his new venture is a success.
> *To make a long story short,* she agreed to marry him.

LM-G6   *Shifts in point of view*

The term *point of view,* in discussions of grammar and usage, refers to the complex set of relationships existing between agents or "actors" in the writing and whatever they're acting upon—all created by the writer. The rule here:
- Be logical and *consistent* in using subject, voice, tense, mood, person, number, etc. Avoid needless shifts, since a sensitive reader dislikes these sudden confusions.

a. *Shift of subject and voice*
> After we *finished* skiing, hot cocoa *was enjoyed.* (Shift from *we* to *cocoa*; voice shift in the verb from active to passive)

b. *Shift of tense*
> The movie *is* good, although the chief actress *was* a terrible singer. (Shift from present to past)

c. *Shift of mood*
> *Turn on* the oven, and then you can mix the ingredients. (Shift from imperative to indicative)

d. *Shift of person*
> If *you* want something badly enough, *one* can accomplish miracles. (Shift from second person to third person)

Note: One is often used idiomatically this way: "If *one* wants something badly enough, *he* can accomplish miracles." (Both are third person.)

e. *Shift of number*
> When a *golfer* is really good, *they* can drive to the green from here. (Shift from singular to plural)

f. *Shift from indirect to direct discourse*
> He asked whether it was my book and how much *did* it cost. (To fix this, simply omit the *did*.)

Besides these, there are possible shifts of the physical perspective, of the writing style, of metaphor, of the writer's attitude, and so on. There are lots of ways to confuse the reader (or at least annoy him). Still, it should be said that a slavish consistency can be a writer's hobgoblin. When he becomes skilled, he will know what liberties he may take with point of view. The important thing is to avoid the truly confusing or irritating shifts.

LM-G7 *Careless omissions*

Constructions that are incomplete sometimes put a burden on the reader. The writer should double-check his work to make it as clear and logical as possible. For example, he might ask himself:

a. In writing my final draft, have I accidentally omitted any rough-draft words or lines?
b. Do any of my sentences need qualifying phrases to make their logic unassailable?
c. Have I left out any clarifying transitions?

This can be asserted as a general rule: in written work, carelessness varies inversely with the writer's height in the social structure; the lower the position, the more frequent is the sloppiness. The basic problem, of course, is that the lower classes just don't give a damn, ordinarily; they feel that effort is useless for them.

See also the following section.

LM-G8 *Faulty comparisons*

Sometimes a careless omission occurs in the construction of a comparison. The result is some strange logic, which of course will brand the writer as Lower-Middle.

a. *Complete the comparison*
    L-M CLASS   She is as fat, if not fatter, than I am.
                    ("She is as fat ... *than* I am"?)
    HIGHER CLASS   She is as fat *as* I am, if not fatter.
    L-M CLASS   She is a very able, if not the ablest, group leader I know. ("She is a very able ... group leader I know"?)
    HIGHER CLASS   She is one of the ablest group leaders I know, if not the ablest.

b. *State both terms completely*
    L-M CLASS   I like him more than Harold. (?)
    HIGHER CLASS   I like him more than I like Harold.
    OR   I like him more than Harold does.

c. *State the basis of the comparison*

"Our newest model," says an advertisement, "costs less!" The consumer, however, has a right to be skeptical. One translation might be "costs less than a few of our competitors' models." Or "costs less than the outrageous price we had planned to charge." (Be very circumspect with *less, better, best,* and so on.)

d. *Be careful with "than any of"*
    L-M CLASS   I like "Blowin' in the Wind" better than *any of* Bob Dylan's songs.
    HIGHER CLASS   I like it better than *any other* song Bob Dylan wrote.

Again, it's a matter of logic.

e. *Don't compare incomparable things*
    L-M CLASS   The cost of new homes is higher here than any other state.
    HIGHER CLASS   The cost of new homes is higher here than *in* any other state.

L-M USAGE

About, Around. See *Around.*

Ad. "Clipped" forms of longer words are often regarded as rather informal. Other common ones are *exam, math, phone.*

Aggravate. The superior classes use this word to mean "to make worse or more severe." People in the L-M and lower classes think it means "irritate."
    L-M CLASS   The way he acted was *aggravating.*
    HIGHER CLASS   That climate *aggravates* my sinus trouble.

Aid, Aide. The higher classes like *aide* to designate a person who *aids.* They get irritated with news headlines using *aid* to refer to such a person.

All the farther, All the faster, etc. Unaccepted idioms.
    L-M CLASS   Fifty miles an hour is *all the faster* this old car goes.
    HIGHER CLASS   Fifty miles an hour is *as fast as* this old car goes.

All that. In the early Seventies it became fashionable in L-M circles to say:
    Her taste isn't *all that* good.
    The movie wasn't *all that* funny.
    I'm not sure he's *all that* smart.
The antecedent of *that* was rarely if ever given.

Anyplace. L-M for *anywhere.*

Around. This word is colloquially confused with *about* in at least two senses:
    1. Billy went *about* (not *around*) selling raffle tickets.
    2. He was done *about* (not *around*) five o'clock.
Many U-M people, too, use the colloquial *around,* but that of course doesn't make it acceptable to the genteel upper classes.

Bad, Badly. See LM-G1.

But that, But what. L-M for *that* in certain expressions.
    L-M CLASS   I don't doubt *but that* they're the same.
    HIGHER CLASS   I don't doubt *that* they're the same.

Complected. Lower-Middle for *complexioned.*

Contrary. Colloquial when used to mean *perverse* or *vexatious.*

Couple. (1) An upper-class term for a *pair*; (2) middle-class when used to mean "just a few," as in "I have a *couple* of errands"; (3) lower-class when used without the *of,* as in "a *couple* errands."

Cute. Overused term of approval (sometimes, however, used by higher classes as a disparaging term).

Day and age. Trite and redundant.
    L-M CLASS   In this *day and age* ...
    HIGHER CLASS   *Today* (or *These days,* or *In this modern age*)

Deal. L-M for *agreement, arrangement, bargain, transaction,* etc.
    We got a good *deal* on a new TV set. (Bargain)

Definitely. An L-M intensive, as in "She's *definitely* my type."
Each and every. A redundancy and a cliché.
Ecology, Environment. Sloppy L-M terms for *nature.* See a dictionary.
Enthused. Lower-Middle for *enthusiastic.*
    L-M CLASS   I'm very *enthused* about the plan.
    HIGHER CLASS I'm very *enthusiastic* about it.
Every. Used in a number of colloquial formations: *every bit as, every once in a while, every which way.*
Everyone. An accepted synonym for *everybody.* In all other uses it should be *two* words: "*Every one* of the miners was saved."
Exam. See *Ad.*
Expect. Sometimes L-M for *suppose, believe,* or *suspect.*
    L-M CLASS   I *expect* I'll be needed here.
    HIGHER CLASS I *suppose* I'll be needed here.
Extra. An L-M intensive (replacing *especially* or *unusually*), as in "He was *extra* nice to me today."
Faze. Colloquial for *bother,* as in "The explosion didn't *faze* him."
Fine. The Lower-Middles have turned this adjective into an adverb: "The clock runs *fine* now."
Fix. L-M noun substituting for *predicament*; also used to refer to various illegal activities. Most inferior classes use the verb to mean "mend" or "repair," but the lofty U-U's insist it means "make stable or firm."
Flunk. The higher classes usually prefer the verb *fail.*
Folks. L-M for *parents, family,* or *relatives.* It is often used in this sense in the U-M Class, too, but not in the upper classes. The word is also used by all classes in addressing (adult) friends ("We haven't seen you *folks* for ages!"). Middle-class salesmen are fond of the word also, presumably because it has a folksy ring.
Funny. All classes use this to mean *amusing* or *comical.* L-M people use it also for *strange.* This often necessitates a question: "Funny peculiar, or funny ha-ha?"
Get. Used in many colloquial and slang expressions, such as *get with it, get going, get away with.*
Good and. Found in certain colloquial formations: *good and warm, good and ready.*
Hopefully. See p. 94.
I could(n't) care less. If a person says "I could care less," he seems to be caring *some.* He presumably means "I *couldn't* care less."
If, Whether. Used after such verbs as *ask, know,* and *say*:
    L-M CLASS   She asked *if* he could go.
    HIGHER CLASS She asked *whether* he could go.
Imply, Infer. Don't confuse *imply* ("to hint or suggest") with *infer* ("to draw a conclusion"). Remember that the three top classes will infer unflattering things if you do.
    HIGHER CLASS The *speaker implied* that wealthy oil moguls were backing the proposal.

HIGHER CLASS   The *audience inferred* that wealthy oil moguls were backing the proposal.

In regards to. Unidiomatic version of *in regard to*, damaged in a collision with *as regards*.

Inside of. L-M for *within*, as in "A bus will be here *inside of* an hour."

Irregardless. The superior classes sanction only *regardless*.

It being. An "it being" phrase is an awkward and weak substitute for an adverb clause beginning with *since* or *because*.

Jealous. This term is used by the Lower-Middles to mean both *jealous* and *envious*. The higher classes see a distinction. Consult a dictionary, please.

Kind of, Sort of. L-M for the adverbs *rather* or *somewhat*.
    LOWER CLASS   The attorney was *kinda* flustered.
    L-M CLASS   The attorney was *kind of* flustered.
    HIGHER CLASS   The attorney was *rather* flustered.

Kind of a, Sort of a. The superior classes omit the *a* (*an*).
    L-M CLASS   Buy some *kind of a* vegetable.
    HIGHER CLASS   Buy some *kind of* vegetable.

Locate. L-M for *settle*, as in "The family finally *located* in western Pennsylvania."

Mad. L-M for *angry*. (For *insane*, the L-M Class usually employs *crazy*, although there are also several slang substitutes.)

Math. See *Ad*.

Minus. Colloquial for *lacking* or *without*. See *Plus*.

Muchly. Used jocularly by the Lower-Middles for *much*, as in "I appreciate it *muchly*."

Myself, Yourself, etc. Intensive or reflexive pronouns are not accepted as personal pronouns at the higher social levels. (See "Pronouns" under LL-G2.)
    L-M CLASS   The club chose Don and *myself*.
    HIGHER CLASS   The club chose Don and *me*.

No account, No good. L-M for *useless* or *worthless*. Often hyphenated.

Not about to. Indicates determination not to do something. A dictionary's Usage Panel voted on this locution; 40 per cent were ready to accept it, but the other 60 per cent were not about to.[7]

No way. Slang; a strong negative response to almost any question or proposal.
    L-M CLASS   "Will you do it for me?"
                              "*No way.*"

Nowhere near. L-M term for *not near* or *not nearly*.

Off of. Omit the *of* in polite society.
    L-M CLASS   Get *off of* my bed.
    HIGHER CLASS   Get *off* my bed.

Oftentimes. Archaic version of *often*. (Remember also that the *t* in *often* is silent.)

One and the same. Wordy form of the *same*.

On the average of. Wordy form of *about*.
    L-M CLASS   He visits *on the average of* once a year.
    HIGHER CLASS   He visits *about* once a year.

Over with. L-M for *done*, *ended*, or *over*.

L-M CLASS	We're glad the trial is *over with*.
U-M CLASS	We're glad the trial is *over*.
UPPER CLASS	We're glad the trial *has ended*.

Per. This Latin term (*per capita, per diem*) is Anglicized in such expressions as "miles per hour." But *a* and *an* are usually preferred.

Per cent. A Latin abbreviation meaning "by the hundred"; may be written as one word. It should almost always be preceded by a number.

Percentage. L-M substitute for *number, part, portion*.

LOWER CLASS	A large *per cent* of the group...
L-M CLASS	A large *percentage* of the group...
HIGHER CLASS	A large *part* of the group...

Philosophy. A pretentious word for *attitude* or *belief.*

Phone. See *Ad.*

Plan on. L-M variant of *plan to,* as in "I *plan on* going."

Plus. Colloquial for *and, besides* or *in addition to.* See *Minus.*

Rarely ever. L-M for *rarely, rarely if ever,* or *hardly ever.*

Real. A folksy or "cute" term for *really* or *very.*

Reason is because. The superior classes frown on the use of adverb clauses following linking verbs. Instead of *because,* use a noun or a noun clause.

L-M CLASS	The reason he's gone is *because he's sick.*
HIGHER CLASS	The reason he's gone is *his sickness* (or *that he is sick.*)

Refer back. Refer comes from the Latin *re* ("back") and *ferre* ("to carry"). Purists argue, therefore, that the addition of *back* is redundant.

Run. L-M for *manage* or *operate.*

L-M CLASS	She *runs* a bookkeeping service.
HIGHER CLASS	She *manages* a bookkeeping service.

Seldom ever. L-M for *seldom, seldom if ever,* or *hardly ever.*

Sort of. See *Kind of.*

Sure, Surely. Sure, as a sentence modifier, is used regularly by all but the upper classes, and occasionally by them ("Sure, I will"). In the L-M Class it also functions as a simple adverb ("I'm *sure* glad to see you"). The U-M Class, however, is badly divided on whether to allow that. The upper classes say no.

Sure and. Careless version of *sure to.*

L-M CLASS	Be *sure and* be on time.
HIGHER CLASS	Be *sure to* be on time.

Swell. Dated L-M slang for *good.*

Terrible, Terribly. Don't confuse the adjective *terrible* and its adverb form.

    I feel *terrible* (not *terribly*) about your news.

    His war wound aches *terribly* (not *terrible*).

Thusly. A condemned form of *thus.*

Too. Used illogically for *very* by the Lower-Middles and, often, the Upper-Middles.

MIDDLE CLASS	I'm not *too* surprised.
UPPER CLASS	I'm not *very* surprised.

Try and. Careless version of *try to*.
    L-M CLASS   *Try and* stay sober tonight.
    HIGHER CLASS   *Try to* stay sober tonight.
Type. L-M people often shorten *type of* to *type*, to the consternation of language conservatives.
    L-M CLASS   That *type* car uses too much gas.
    HIGHER CLASS   That *type of* car uses too much gas.
Verbal, Verbally. The adjective *verbal* means "in words," either spoken or written. *Oral* means "spoken" and is often a much more logical choice.
    L-M CLASS   He was given a *verbal* reprimand.
    HIGHER CLASS   He was given an *oral* reprimand.
Want to. L-M for *ought to* or *should*.
    L-M CLASS   You *want to* be nicer to her.
    HIGHER CLASS   You *should* be nicer to her.
Where. Sometimes used by Lower-Middles for *that*.
    L-M CLASS   I read *where* the Mets are looking for a new pitcher.
    HIGHER CLASS   I read *that* the Mets . . .
Where to. L-M for "Where did you go?" or "Where do you wish to go?"
    L-M CLASS   Where are you going *to*?
    L-M CLASS   "Where to?" asked the cabbie.

L-M PUNCTUATION

Again, let's focus on only one punctuation device—this time the one that's the most useful and, hence, the most common.

LM-P   *The comma*

It is assumed that, because you have arrived at this plateau, you have truly mastered all of the preceding material on sentence structure. If you haven't, you'll have difficulty with this section, since in a sense it is a *test* of your mastery. You will now examine your own ability to use a comma in the following ways: (1) to separate main clauses linked by coordinating conjunctions, (2) to separate certain introductory elements from the main clause, (3) to set off certain formations following the main clause, (4) to separate items in a series, and (5) to set off various parenthetical constructs. A middle-class person should know no less.

    LM-P1   *Main clauses* linked by a coordinating conjunction usually are separated by a comma.

The coordinating conjunctions are *and*, *or*, *but*, and *nor*. Others sometimes classed with them are the upper-class *yet* (when used to mean *but*), *for* (an upper-class variant of *because*), and the middle-class *so* (short for *and so*).

Unless two clauses thus connected happen to be quite short, put a comma before the conjunction.
    EITHER   He will stay and I shall go.
    OR   He will stay to lock up at quitting time tonight, and I shall go to the bank alone.

If one clause (or both) has internal punctuation, you may want to use a semicolon instead of a comma (see U-L Punctuation).

LM-P2

Short *introductory elements* often are not punctuated, but longer ones are.

    To him she is the loveliest creature in the world.
    When you see her you may agree.

But some expressions need a comma to prevent misreading.

    Putting it on, the old man wasn't able to find the sleeves.

The goal, you see, is always to make the sentence clear and easy to read.

    When you see her perform this evening, you may agree with him.
                                                                (Adverb clause)
    The car being loaded, the family left to pick berries. (Absolute phrase)

LM-P3

Adverbial phrases and clauses following a main clause are often set off with commas if the connection is a loose one.

    Harry ordered a big lunch, *usually about noon.*

    Harry ordered a big lunch, *because he was always very hungry by noon.*

Some adverbial elements should be more closely connected; omit the comma in such cases.

    We'll eat *whenever you say.*

LM-P4

Separate *elements in a series,* including coordinate adjectives, with commas.

    The boys gobbled cheese, ham, potato chips, and pie.
    We drove through the city, past the suburbs, and out into farmland.

Some stylists like to omit the final comma (before *and* or *or*). Others insist on leaving it in, and especially when it's needed to prevent misreading.

    She fashioned many sandwiches—cheese, peanut butter and jelly, and ham.

(See how well commas work? Proper punctuation creates maximum clarity.)

    Coordinate adjectives present a special problem. They must have equal grammatical rank; they must all modify the same noun.

    A big and soft chair
    A big, soft chair (no comma before the noun)
    A big, soft, rumpled chair

But if the adjectives aren't really coordinate, as when one is regarded as *part of the noun*, omit the final comma.

    A big, soft easy chair
    The small, square dining room

Easy chair and *dining room* are thought of as two-word nouns. One wouldn't say "a square *and* dining room." Nor are the terms reversible: "a dining square room." (Those are the two tests in such matters.) That's simple enough; the whole business gets rather messy, however, with cumulative formations of elements that aren't coordinate.

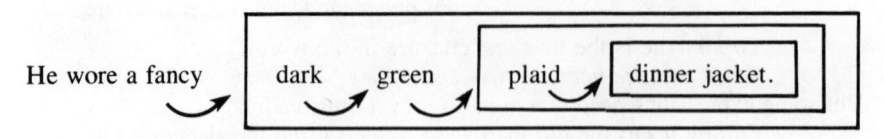

He wore a fancy dark green plaid dinner jacket.

Don't use any commas in that sentence (although you might want to hyphenate *dark-green*).

LM-P5   *Parenthetical elements, such as nonrestrictive clauses, phrases, and appositives, are set off by commas. But restrictive elements aren't.*

When an interrupting expression is placed inside the clause, you must use not one but *two* commas, or none at all. See LL-G5b ("Adjective clauses") on the difference between restrictive ("essential") and nonrestrictive ("nonessential") constructions. In the latter, the subject is *already identified*.

a. *Clauses*
    RESTRICTIVE   A course *which was difficult for him* was calculus.
    NONRESTRICTIVE   Calculus, *which was difficult for him*, was a course he didn't like.

Note: There are two tests: (1) In reading it aloud, do you need to pause? (2) Can you remove the interrupting element? Will the main clause still make sense? ("A course...was calculus" doesn't make much sense. The adjective clause is essential to the sentence's meaning.)

b. *Phrases*
    RESTRICTIVE   The dog *chained to the tree* is vicious.
    NONRESTRICTIVE   Spot, *chained to the tree*, whined in his misery.

(In the first case there were perhaps several dogs, and one had to be singled out.)

c. *Appositives*
    RESTRICTIVE   My friend *Susan* had lunch with me.
                               The poet *Walt Whitman* was a male nurse during the Civil War.
    NONRESTRICTIVE   My best friend, *Susan*, had lunch with me.
                               The "Good Gray Poet," *Walt Whitman*, was a male nurse during the Civil War.

Other parenthetical insertions usually need commas:

d. *Contrasted elements*
   Your deeds, *not your words*, are what count.
e. *Sentence modifiers*
   Your action, *unfortunately*, didn't really pacify him.
f. *Conjunctive adverbs*
   His response, *on the other hand*, was quite conciliatory.

Note: We've already discovered another common position for sentence modifiers and conjunctive adverbs—between two clauses:
   Her hair was in curlers; *therefore,* she didn't want to see him.

The comma here is optional but is often preferred by the higher classes. But you must take special care with the word *however*. When it's a conjunctive adverb, always set it off with commas:
   Sharon is intelligent; *however*, she doesn't advertise the fact.
   Sharon is intelligent; she, *however*, doesn't advertise the fact.

But if it's used as an adverb meaning "no matter how," *don't* set it off:
   However he tried, he couldn't open the box.

g. *Sentence elements out of normal order.*
   "I believe," *he said*, "that you stole the money,"
   The old man, *ill and tired*, longed for death.
   BUT The *ill and tired* old man longed for death.

h. *Addresses and other places*
   He lives at 103 Sanders St., *Lutown*, Nev.
   Nashville, *Tenn.*, is the country-music capital.

i. *Items in dates*
   Monday, *Nov. 25, 1974,* at noon

j. *Titles and degrees*
   Morton T. Friedrich, *chairman of the board*, opened the meeting.
   John Brown, *Jr.*, made the presentation. (Commas around *Jr.* and *Sr.* are occasionally omitted.)
   Eunice Peterson, *M.D.*, was the main speaker.

k. *Direct address*
   That, *old buddy*, is the real thing.
   Come here, *Art*, and help push.

Some adverbial formations can be inserted parenthetically *without* commas or pause:
   Your pay will *of course* be higher.
   He should *at least* say good-bye.
And see LM-P11, below.

LM-P6

Mild interjections and short questions are always set off.

Interjections: *Oh*, I guess you think I'm afraid to go!
Questions: You're warm enough, *aren't you*?

Often set off, also, are sentence modifiers and conjunctive adverbs: *Yes*, you're right. *In fact*, she may get a raise.

LM-P7   Use a comma to *prevent misreading*.

    NOT   After all the fuss is over.
    BUT   After all, the fuss is over.
    NOT   To begin the game is now dominated by big-name stars.
    BUT   To begin, the game is now dominated by big-name stars.

LM-P8   *Miscellaneous uses* of the comma:

a. To close the salutation in a personal letter:
    Dear John,
        I am sorry to have to say this, but...
b. To indicate an omission:
    To err is human; to forgive, divine.
c. To construct permissible comma splices:
    He worked early, he worked late. He was frantic, he was so low in funds.
d. To set up coordination of modifiers:
    The more I see you, the more I like you.
    The faster I go, the bigger my mistakes.
e. To separate figures, as in $256,338,000.

Following is a checklist of some situations in which you should *not* use a comma.

LM-P9   *Don't* use a (single) comma to separate subject and verb, the verb and its complement, or the parts of a verb phrase.

    WRONG   The life of a migrant worker in the crops(,) can be hellish.
Exception: When the subject grows long and complex, a comma is sometimes permissible before the verb. Much better ideas, though, would be (1) to reconstruct the sentence or (2) to make two sentences.

LM-P10   *Don't* (ordinarily) use a comma to separate two words or phrases joined by a coordinating conjunction.

    QUESTIONABLE   Migrants' children are cheated of an education(,) *and* a normal home life.
        (Two objects of the preposition *of*)
    QUESTIONABLE   Formal dress is not required for such an affair(,) *but* is recommended.
        (Two verbs in a compound predicate)

Exceptions: When the parts are rather long, when the stylist wants a dramatic pause, or when he wishes to suggest an afterthought, the comma becomes acceptable.

LM-P11 *Don't* set off introductory and parenthetical material unnecessarily.

As we saw earlier, many such elements fit into the sentence lightly, neatly, causing no one any confusion. Don't clutter the sentence with commas needlessly.

Perhaps you'd better go.
Flowers *in fact* can be sent by wire.

LM-P12 *Don't* use a comma (a) before the first item in a series, (b) after the last one in a series, (c) between an adjective and its noun, or (d) after a conjunction.

Omit the commas in parentheses below:
   a. The three rules at a railroad crossing are(,) stop, look, and listen. (Don't use a colon, either.)
   b. The pilot, co-pilot, engineer, navigator, and bombardier(,) all had stations in front of the wing.
   c. She is a quiet, decent(,) girl.
   d. But(,) we should act quickly. (Don't confuse *But* and *However*.)

LM-P13 *Don't* introduce a direct quotation with a comma except immediately after a "verb of saying" such as *said, whispered, shouted, asked*. Never introduce an *indirect* quotation with a comma.

The conventional practices:
   DIRECT QUOTATION   He said**,** "Don't forget to send Grandma a card."
   BUT   He reminded us to "send Grandma a card."
   INDIRECT QUOTATION He said *that* we should send Grandma a card.

Even in the first situation above, some writers would object to the comma as unnecessary clutter. They have a point. (Certainly omit it in "Say 'please'" and many similar constructions.)

As you see, occasionally you have a choice. Professional writers are often guided in such cases by their previous election of an "open" or "closed" style. Open style: A comma-less sentence like this creates a lively gait because it reduces the number of hesitations. The so-called closed style, with more commas, as in this sentence, is consonant with dignity, restraint, and a much slower pace.

L-M SPELLING

In 1852 a young Oregon Trail herd driver named Moore kept a journal of his trek westward and his painful climb into the middle class. In that diary were thirteen different spellings of the word *traveled*.[8] Few, in that individualistic age, would have complained or even thought it very unusual. Today, however, the bourgeoisie is not so tolerant; employers insist that experimentation in spelling is no longer appropriate. Middle-class schoolteachers do their best to pass along this advice to their charges.

The various spelling rules, and their numerous exceptions, create enough difficulty to serve as an excellent class-screening device. Infractions are regarded as carelessness and, almost universally, superiors subscribe to our rule: "In written work, carelessness varies inversely with the writer's height in the social structure." From this, they of course draw certain unflattering conclusions.

Pity the poor immigrant! The Filipinos, Mexicans, Cubans, and Puerto Ricans have a language (Spanish) with spelling which accurately represents its sounds. But in English, they find, the relation of spelling to pronunciation is often hard to discern. A few examples: (1) Some words sound the same but have different spelling: *right, rite, wright, write*. (2) Vowels have differing values: *ten, even, here*. (3) Various English vowels are at times pronounced "uh," which is certainly no help to the speller. And (4) somehow we have developed such sounds as *enough* and *through*, *laughter* and *slaughter*, with spellings that seem like someone's bad joke.

All of this, of course, suggests chaos. Newcomers nervously learn that English has been jerry-built, mostly from Teutonic and Latin materials, and is stuccoed with borrowings from many modern tongues. From the Spanish, we have *patio, mustang, embargo, cigar*. From the French, *ravine, naive, parole, restaurant*. From the German, *kindergarten, seminar, semester, zinc*. From the Italian, *piano, motto, volcano, umbrella*. From the Indian (Native American), *skunk, moose, hominy, succotash*. And so on. The immigrants must often grind their teeth in despair. But society is pitiless. To the superior classes, poor spelling is an immediate indicator of poor writing. (This may or may not be true, but prejudice often overcomes judgment.) So, unless they are quite extraordinary, ghetto-born and foreign-born are quickly branded incompetent.

At times, to be sure, poor spelling *is* due to mere carelessness. Society has a right to a certain amount of righteous indignation when a writer arrogantly ignores both the integrity of the language and the feelings of his readers. In such cases, superiors are justified in assuming that the writer has quit striving for higher status—has decided to settle into the *status quo*. An employer may say to himself, "Well, if he's sloppy in this, he may be sloppy in other ways, too."

If you want neither the "incompetent" label nor the *status quo*, if you sincerely want to be a better speller, you may have to endure the protracted boredom of learning certain rules and practicing them.

LM-Sp1 Start a *misspellings notebook.*

Begin immediately on a list of words you've misspelled. Make at least three columns: (1) the incorrect word; (2) the corrected spelling; (3) some "nuisance" material as a memory aid (etymology, pronunciation information, syllabication pattern, a brief definition, the word used in a sentence—or *all* of these). As you slowly write the correct spelling, say the word aloud several times. Why? Because the memory often relies on teamwork of the eye, the hand (sense of touch), and the ear. Review your notebook frequently, and keep adding to it whenever you have a new misspelling.

LM-Sp2 *Beware of mispronunciation.* Be quick to discover any such pattern in your misspellings.

a. Don't *add* any stray letters to such words as *drowned, grievous, height, mischievous.*

b. Don't omit any letters from accide*n*tally, a*r*ctic, envi*ro*nment, Feb*r*uary, gove*r*nment, quan*t*ity, recog*n*ize, use*d*.

c. Don't *change* any letters in ca*va*lry, chil*d*ren, desp*e*rate, exist*e*nce, ir*re*l*ev*ant, op*ti*mistic, p*e*rhaps, p*e*rspiration, prep*a*ration, privi*l*ege, sep*a*rate.

LM-Sp3 Be careful to *distinguish between words of similar spelling and sound.*

accept, except
advice, advise
affect, effect
all ready, already
capital, capitol
choose, chose
cite, sight, site
coarse, course
complement, compliment
conscience, conscious
council, counsel
desert, dessert
device, devise
dual, duel
dyeing, dying
formally, formerly
forth, fourth
hear, here
its, it's
know, no

later, latter
lead, led
lose, loose
moral, morale
passed, past
personal, personnel
precede, proceed
principal, principle
prophecy, prophesy
quiet, quite
respectfully, respectively
shone, shown
stationary, stationery
than, then
their, there, they're
threw, through
to, too, two
weather, whether
whose, who's
your, you're

LM-Sp4   Learn some common Greek and Latin *prefixes*, *roots*, and *suffixes*. (See U-U Usage.)

    EXAMPLE   We combine *auto-* (self), *bio-* (life), and *graphy* (writing) to form *autobiography*.

LM-Sp5   Learn the rules for *adding a prefix*.

a. Don't double its last letter if it is different from the root's first letter: *disbelief, misdeal*.

b. Don't *drop* that last letter if the root's first letter is the same: *disservice, misspelling*.

LM-Sp6   Learn the rules for *adding a suffix*, and memorize the exceptions.

a. Drop the final *e* before a suffix that begins with a vowel.

      expense   +   *ive*   = expensive
      fame   +   *ous* = famous
      shave   +   *ing*   = shaving

Some exceptions: blueing, dyeing, hoeing, shoeing, singeing, trueing.

b. Most words do *not* drop a final *e* after either *c* or *g*—if the suffix is *able* or *ous*.

      peace, peaceable   change, changeable
      courage, courageous   notice, noticeable

Some exceptions: grace, gracious; malice, malicious; space, spacious

c. Keep the final *e* before a suffix beginning with a consonant.

      rude   +   *ness*   = rudeness
      excite   +   *ment* = excitement
      love   +   *ly*   = lovely

Some exceptions: argument, awful, duly, judgment, truly

d. A monosyllable (or a longer word accented on its last syllable), *if* it ends in a single consonant preceded by a single vowel, doubles that final consonant when adding a suffix beginning with a vowel. (Got that?)

      fit, fitted   occur, occurrence
      begin, beginner   stop, stopping

But if you have a double vowel, *don't* double the consonant: *stoop, stooping; leap, leaping*. And if the word ends with *two* consonants, don't double anything: *tempt, temptation*. Finally, if the last syllable doesn't have the main accent, you should rush to a good dictionary. Some such words (*open, benefit*) never double the last letter (*opener, benefited*). Others, however, may be handled either way, depending upon your whim: *programing, programming; traveled, travelled; signaling, signalling; kidnaped, kidnapped; worshiping, worshipping*.

Exception: The middle class often allows *bus*, either as a noun or verb, to violate

112

the rule above: *buses, busing*. The upper classes frequently prefer *busses, bussing*.

e. Words ending in *l* retain it before *ly*; words ending in *n* retain it before *ness*.
   thoughtful, thoughtfully; drunken, drunkenness

f. Most words ending in *ie* change *ie* to *y* before *ing: die, dying; lie, lying; untie, untying.*

g. Except before a suffix starting with *i*, final *y* is ordinarily changed to *i*.

   rely   +   *ance*   = reliance
   mercy   +   *ful*   = merciful
   empty   +   *ness*   = emptiness
   BUT empty + *ing*   = emptying

Note: Verbs ending in *y* usually form their third-person singular, and nouns their plural, by altering *y* to *ie* and adding *s: relies, denies; ladies, cities.* But words which have a vowel before the *y* retain both: *annoy, annoys.*

h. Words ending in *c* often add *k* before *ing: picnic, picnicking; traffic, trafficking.*

LM-Sp7

Memorize the conventions dealing with *ie* and *ei*.

a. Chant this old middle-class rhyme a few times:
   Use *i* before *e*   (believe, niece)
   Except after *c*   (receive, deceit)
   Or when sounded as *a*   (freight)
   As in *neighbor* and *weigh*. (vein)

b. Memorize this outlandish sentence containing *exceptions* to the verse above: "N*ei*ther financ*ie*r s*ei*zed *ei*ther spec*ie*s of w*ei*rd l*ei*sure." (Most financiers are circumspect, or at least secretive, in their behavior; it's part of their image.) Other exceptions: *height, plebeian*.

LM-Sp8

Learn the ways of forming *plural nouns*.

a. Most nouns that don't end in *s* simply add *s*:
   cats, dogs, polliwogs, the Browns

b. Most nouns ending in *s* (or *z*) add *es*:
   mass, masses; adz, adzes; Jones, Joneses

c. Some nouns ending in *o* add *es: Negroes, heroes, potatoes.* Some add only *s: pianos, solos, sopranos.* A few, like *ghetto*, are spelled either way.

d. Some nouns ending in *f* or *fe* change the *f* to *v* and *es*:
   knife, knives; leaf, leaves; wife, wives

e. Nouns ending in *y* (to repeat) usually change *y* to *ie* and add *s: fairy, fairies; ferry, ferries.* But if a vowel precedes the *y*, we just add *s: essays, decoys*.

f. Some nouns add *en* or *ren: ox, oxen; child, children.*

g. Some plurals are formed by a change in the root vowel:
    woman, women; foot, feet; mouse, mice; goose, geese

h. With some nouns, singular and plural are the same:
    deer, deer; sheep, sheep; series, series; species, species

i. A construction with the suffix *ful* adds *s* at the *end* of the word: *cupfuls, spoonfuls*. (Don't say *cupsful, spoonsful*—or at least not at an upper-class dinner. The middle class is nervously divided on the matter. The democratic lower class sanctions *either* usage.)

j. The higher classes pluralize other compounds according to old conventions:
    passer-by, passers-by; editors-in-chief; sons-in-law

k. Plurals of letters, figures, and so on, are usually formed by adding *'s*. See L-M Mechanics, next.

Note: For many other oddities about American-English pluralizing, see U-U Spelling.

LM-Sp9

Learn the rules for spelling *possessive nouns and pronouns*.

(Please see the next section.)

L-M MECHANICS

In conjunction with the preceding lively discussion of socially approved spelling, we present here a section on socially approved use of the apostrophe. (Trumpet fanfare and applause.)

LM-M1

An apostrophe is used in forming the *possessive case* of nouns and *indefinite* pronouns.

a. With words that don't end in *s*, add *'s:*
    a woman's clothes, women's clothes, anyone's guess, the people's English, no one's business, the tree's branches

b. With singular words that end in *s*, add *'s* unless the *sound* would be awkward; in that case, add only the apostrophe:
    Jones's house, Doris's ring
  BUT Confucius' wisdom, Sophocles' play, Moses' anger
(This keeps the pronunciation *Moses,* not *Moseses.*)

c. With *plurals* ending in *s*, add just the apostrophe:
    several girls' clothes, the McCoys' lawn

d. To show joint ownership, make only the final noun possessive: *John and Winnie's house.* To show individual possession, make them all possessive: *Dan's, Mike's, and Charlie's cigars.*

e. With compounds, make only the final word possessive:
    anyone else's ticket, his son-in-law's car

LM-M2   Don't use the apostrophe with *whose* and the possessives of personal pronouns.

The relative pronoun *whose* and the personal pronouns *your, yours, his, her, hers, its, our, ours, their,* and *theirs* are already in a possessive form. They don't need (and shouldn't have) apostrophes.

LM-M3   Apostrophes are used to show that *letters or numbers have been omitted.*

    shouldn't, don't, won't, the Class of '78, the crash of '29, o'clock, it's (for *it is*), they've (for *they have*)
The apostrophe is often used to indicate colloquial speech:
    "F'r instance," he continued, "y' might get goin' faster."

LM-M4   Use an apostrophe and *s* to pluralize letters, numbers, various symbols, and words used as words.

Such usages are often underlined or in italic type:
    Dot your *i's* and cross your *t's.*
    There are six *8's,* but only two *$'s* for the signboard.
    Eliminate some *and's* from this paragraph.

L-M COMPOSITION

In U-L Composition you were exposed to some important concepts of educated writing: the principles of unity, coherence, and effective development, for example, and the so-called "natural" patterns of narration and description. All were discussed in terms of *paragraph* development, but everything said there applies also to larger constructions.

The next larger unit of organized thought might be an informal *sketch* of some kind—but is more likely to be a formal, assigned *essay* or *theme*. A theme usually contains several paragraphs and from 200 to 2,000 words (most commonly 300 to 1,500 words). Learning to write one is a traditional middle-class task, a basic freshman requirement.

LM-C1   An important part of theme-writing is the *preliminary planning.*

Here are some suggestions for the planning of any kind of home-written theme:

a. If you are asked to choose your own subject matter, select some general topic (but not *too* general) that interests you. If last year's job was in a gas station, perhaps you could write about some of your duties, or maybe about a typical day. If you like skiing, you might do well telling how to make a cross-country run or a parallel turn. If you've done baby-sitting, maybe you could discuss its pleasures or perils—but, if it's a short paper, not both.

b. Then narrow your topic still more. You'll be surprised how much your paper will benefit from being specific and concrete, rather than general and abstract.

GENERAL	SPECIFIC
The Importance of Punctuality	Don't Be Late for a Hospital Job!
Taking Good Pictures	Some Useful Filters for Your Camera
How To Increase Your Car's Gas Mileage	An Important Carburetor Adjustment—and Why It's Important
Pornographic Films	Recent Court Decisions on "Blue" Movies

Well, perhaps you get the idea from these two short lists. For more ideas, incidentally, just thumb through the yellow pages of your telephone directory. Or try a good dictionary; it has thousands of topics, every single one potentially fascinating.

c. Collect as many pieces of information as you can and then, perhaps on a single page, set down an inventory of your raw material (quotations, facts, illustrations, ideas).

d. Determine your audience; that is, know in advance what qualities your diction should have for the best effect on your reader. Now, in an English class this decision is an easy one: your audience is almost always your instructor. You should assume he (she) is a middle-class person of at least average intelligence but not necessarily with any special knowledge of your subject. Don't "talk down" to him, but don't use a lot of technical terms, either—unless they're unquestionably needed and carefully defined.

e. Decide, finally, on what you're going to say, including what attitude you will take toward your narrowed topic. Set it all down in a *thesis statement* (a sentence or two) that captures the theme in a nutshell. Your attitude might be fairly objective, as in these examples:

> Proper winterizing of a power lawnmower involves a number of steps that some people ignore.
>
> The new city park has facilities for both old and young.

Or it might be *slightly* more opinionated:

> The new city park's facilities are not really adequate for older people and even expose them to various hazards.

Once your thesis statement is phrased to suit you, you should know the direction your thoughts are going. It's time to turn to their organization.

f. Construct an outline. It needn't be your final one—it can always be revised—but it should be a pretty good guide. Our Greek ancestor Aristotle (384-322 B.C.) wrote that the end of a process is part of its beginning—which suggests a number of things. One is that a person starting to write should have a reasonably sharp mental picture of where he's headed and which route he's taking. An outline is a kind of road map of his own making. Following are two examples, one called a sentence outline, the other a "topic" outline. Both types, incidentally, will be discussed further in U-M Composition.

(1) SENTENCE OUTLINE

Thesis statement: Proper winterizing of a power lawnmower involves a number of steps that some people ignore.

  I. Draw off all gasoline.
     A. Empty the fuel tank.
     B. Exhaust gas in the carburetor.
 II. Drain dirty oil from the crankcase.
III. Put clean oil in the spark plug hole.
     A. Remove the plug.
     B. Pour one ounce of oil in the plug opening.
     C. Replace the plug but not the wire.
 IV. Prepare the mower for storage.
     A. Clean all surfaces.
     B. Wipe metal parts with an oily rag.
     C. Oil wheel bearings, etc.
     D. Find a clean, dry place for storage.

Notice first that all verbs in these short sentences are in the imperative mood. Grammatical "parallelism" is not always possible in a sentence outline, but I wanted to show that it sometimes can be arranged. Second, this is obviously a plan for a *process* narrative. That is, it outlines the steps, in suggested chronological order, that should be taken before storing the mower. (II should follow I, since the crankcase oil is best drained when the engine is warm—from exhausting the carburetor—a fact that presumably would be explained in the paper itself.

(2) TOPIC OUTLINE

Thesis statement: The new city park has facilities for both old and young. (Full sentence)

  I. Northern edge a parking lot
     A. Entrance on 26th Street
     B. Exit on Higgins Street
 II. Eastern part for adults
     A. Gardens
     B. Benches
III. Southern edge another parking lot
     A. Entrance on 26th Street
     B. Exit on Buchanan Avenue
 IV. Western part for children
     A. Wading pool
     B. Playground area
     C. Baseball field

(Note that a topic outline consists of short fragments, not sentences—except for the thesis. Parallelism, here based on a set of nouns, is important in a topic outline. It helps to clarify the relations of the parts.)

The outline above was constructed (1) to support the thesis statement, (2) to serve as a "map" of the paper's four main sections, and (3) to create a general idea of the park's terrain. Notice, please, that the spaces are arranged in clockwise fashion, going methodically around the compass from north to west. The outline's chief organizational principle is therefore *spatial,* its chief purpose apparently *description.* To be sure, there is some exposition here, and even some narration. (The writer could have us imagine ourselves getting out of a car, then walking south through the gardens, then west past the southern parking lot, until finally we reach the children's play areas.) But the writer seems primarily interested in getting us to *see clearly* the four different park sections, and the relation of those spaces to one another.

LM-C2   With the planning done, start immediately on your rough *first draft.*

Construct a short tentative title, a phrase or a short question, which is interesting but not "cute." Don't put a period at the end. (See UL-M2a.) Now comes the hard part. Your paper should fit the reader's expectations at least to this extent: he will be looking for an introduction, a "body," and a conclusion. This convention goes back at least as far as Aristotle, who wrote in the fourth century B.C. (about drama) that a composition should make "proper use" of "a beginning, a middle, and an end." We should look quickly at each.

a. *The introduction*

Your opening sentences (one or two paragraphs) are probably your most important. Great pains, therefore, should be taken with them. The introduction has a number of functions:

(1) It should begin with an *eye-catcher*—almost anything that will distract the reader's attention from coffee cup and television, and all the other competition, and draw it to your composition. Your first sentence can be serious, witty, startling, shocking, amusing, or whatever, so long as it does its job. Ideally, of course, its tone should harmonize with that of the essay—and with that of the title, a chunk of which you might want to borrow here. (But no word in the introduction should *refer* to the title.)

(2) It should usually serve as a vehicle for the *thesis statement*—brought over, perhaps verbatim, from the outline page. There are a few exceptions (some essays, for instance, have a climactic organizational plan) but these need not concern us here.

(3) It may take the time and trouble to *develop reader interest.* If the essay's topic has a great deal of *inherent* interest, as have sex, conflict, money, and some others, you needn't waste effort. But if that interest-value needs to be revealed to the reader, you might try a sentence or two of subtle salesmanship.

(4) It may even *state or hint at the essay's organizational plan.* This is commonly done in lengthy works of scholarship. (There's a rule of thumb: the longer the paper, the longer its outline and its introduction.) It may be a service to a reader, too, if he faces even a short treatise on a complex subject. You can ease him into it with "First, we shall look at ... Then ... And finally we shall..."

b. *The body*

The introduction has its counterpart in the outline's thesis statement. The introduction, in fact, is really nothing but the thesis statement somewhat amplified. And what, in the outline, corresponds to the body? The answer: all the rest of that outline, all its Roman numerals and capital letters and everything. For the fact is that those numerals and capitals are there solely to indicate the broad divisions of the territory you're creating in the body. Sometimes a III will stand for one long, important paragraph; sometimes it will stand for six or sixteen. Bulk cannot be predicted. All is relative to the writer's concerns and needs; all is determined by the Principle of Effective Development.

The real signposts of those divisions, though, are the transitional devices you will be using. The Principles of Unity and Coherence teach us to make a virtue of stubborn focus on our single main topic. Properly handled, the transitions will keep the reader focused also. Each word, ideally, will contribute to the paper's progress. Back in U-L Composition, you remember, we talked about how a paragraph is wired together by pronouns, transitional expressions, and repetitions—all of which give it both unity and coherence. Exactly the same is true on the larger scale. One paragraph can flow logically and naturally into the next, *if* the writer has planned it that way.

For example, in a *narrative* paper the reader might be guided with "First, . . . Second, . . ." just as if the Roman numerals were being translated. Another paragraph might begin with "Next" or "Meanwhile," another with "Then," still another with "Finally"—all of which emphasize the chronological pattern of development.

For another example, in a *descriptive* paper the transitions stress a spatial order: "Past the parking lot, to the south and east . . ."; "The roses end at a hedge, beyond which . . ."; "On the west . . ." The chief task in description, of course, is description. Your paper will be strewn with words charged with sense data. Try to bombard the reader with as many *kinds* as you can—aural (hearing), visual (sight), olfactory (smell), gustatory (taste), tactile (touch), kinesthetic (sense of motion), and so on. They will automatically give the descriptive paper a sense of its purpose and its direction.

Do not regard these devices as merely ornamental, like the blossoming gardens in a park. Their importance in enhancing both unity and coherence, and hence clarity, cannot be measured.

c. *The conclusion*

The story is told of a country preacher whose eloquence was remarked for miles around. Asked for the secret of his success, he answered, "Well, all I do is tell 'em what I figger to tell 'em; then I tell it to 'em; and then I tell 'em what I've told 'em."

There is a truth buried somewhere in that anecdote. We sometimes—no, *frequently*—need a summing-up of even fairly simple main points, lest many of them fly out of our memory immediately, canceled out by later points. We also like to know, for sure, that we have arrived at the end. We like to be *sure*; it's a matter of esthetics. It's nice to *see* that all is whole, complete, buttoned up. We like, also, the feeling that we've been guided by a skilled writer. "He told us at the beginning just what he was going to cover, and now, by golly, I see that he's covered it all. We've arrived just where he said we would." In such a mood, we feel we haven't wasted our time. In such a mood, we are perhaps receptive to whatever message the writer may be peddling.

Don't be afraid, therefore, to stress that message here. It's your last chance. Don't repeat your thesis statement word for word but *rephrase* it to say the same thing. Move in smoothly (avoid the hackneyed and stiff "In conclusion") and then state it boldly and confidently:

> From this little tour of the city's newest park, two conclusions can be drawn. The planners certainly haven't short-changed our youngsters. Nor have they neglected the needs of our elders . . . .

After which, you might want to end with a sentence to tie it all in a tight ribbon—a kind of punch-line:

> This is one time I'm almost pleased to part with my tax dollars.

One or two more *don'ts*: Don't end *weakly*. Don't apologize for not doing more and, above all, don't drift off into new subject areas. Remember the Principle of Unity.

LM-C3
Revise until you have a *final draft* that you're proud of.

It's a good idea to set the first draft aside for a day or two, if you can, and then have a fresh look at what you've created. Look for weaknesses of all kinds—in logic, coherence, grammar, usage, spelling, and so on. Be a tough critic.

When you have polished the paper as much as time allows, recopy neatly. Typing ability is almost mandatory for the very ambitious L-M person, and here is a fine opportunity to demonstrate your skill. If you have careful penmanship, though, you may get by with a handwritten copy.

I have tried to say a few things here about theme-writing and especially about narrative and descriptive papers. Some of these ideas, I'm confident, will be helpful. But there is one virtue the Lower-Middle writer already has, that no one, apparently, has taught him—that he just seems to come by naturally. That strength is the *energy* in his writing. Whereas the lower-class writer is much too insecure, and the higher-class writer often too preoccupied with propriety, the Lower-Middle bulldozes his way through the forests of grammar, usage, spelling, or whatever, and *says what he thinks*. Usually in short, Anglo-Saxon terms, in preference to Latin equivalents.

(If any reader is in doubt about these assertions, may I please direct his attention to this morning's or this evening's Letters to the Editor? Many Lower-Middles are regular contributors.)

One aspect of this energy is the frequent naturalness of L-M expression. There is little effort at achieving a heightened, "literary" style; instead the writing is direct, forceful, and often unashamedly propagandistic. The best of it is concise, eliminating all superfluous elaboration. Writing clearly and with compactness usually produces this kind of sinewy strength.

Now, I admire energy and directness in a sentence as much as anyone else does, and so I appeal to the L-M writer, as he moves up, not to trade away this virtue in the climb. It is too precious an asset. And he'll have no reason to part with it; some of the sprightliest, most vigorous writing I've ever seen has been what many would call formal. Let this be, then, our parting advice to the Lower-Middle as he is graduated into the Upper-Middle Class. Go ahead and take on all the highbrow, polysyllabic Latinizations you want to, but don't discard your heritage of Teutonic words. And don't be verbose. Say a thing as directly as you can, and your writing will be admirably spare and muscular.

> *Where your treasure is, there will your heart be also.*
> —Matthew 6:21
>
> *No man can serve two masters....Ye cannot serve God and mammon.*
> —Matthew 6:24

CHAPTER 6
UPPER-MIDDLE LANGUAGE

We move now into the top half of the social structure, beginning with the Upper Middles, a group of considerable size and even more social importance. Let us very arbitrarily set $15,000 and $50,000 household income as limits to frame this class. Once again, we should remind the reader that income alone will not be sufficient to purchase a situation here. Yet a candidate with a superior command of the English language (and, let us say, a good working knowledge of Brahms or Picasso or Brecht) may be accepted as Upper-Middle even without the salary qualifications. A person's appearance, occupation, cliques, church affiliation and other formal associations—and, to repeat, his writing and speech— will be taken into account by the big U-M membership committee. And of course many other things, such as one's ability to remember his anti-perspirant, or one's taste and skill in wedding a spouse.

But income, as I say, is a nice *tangible* asset. All right, just suppose the range is $15,000 to $50,000 annually. That span accounts for one-fourth of America's homes and 30.5 per cent of her people. Here *more than half* of the wives are in the labor force, and more than half of all U-M workers wear white collars. Of these, the largest sub-group is managers and administrators, a group nearly matched, though, by professional and technical people of both sexes. Most work downtown, but the typical U-M likes to live in the suburbs; about 50 per cent choose that setting, away from the central area's barely restrained hubbub and violence.[1] (Some U-M people, however, have very attractive downtown apartments, elevated several stories above the less attractive *hoi polloi*.)

According to the Census Bureau's 1973 *Statistical Abstract*, the solidly Upper-Middle (male) professional or technical specialist is self-employed, and this catapults him to the top of the occupational ladder. In 1971 the median income of doctors, lawyers, dentists, and so on, was $17,169. Salaried professionals (older teachers, assistant professors, etc.) earned a median income of only $11,571. If they were intellectual, or if their wives worked, these people perhaps had marginal U-M status.[2]

But businessmen—*i.e.*, officers in their firms or salaried managers—are the largest U-M group. Males in this category earned a 1971 median of $13,041.[3] (*Their* wives worked, too, and perhaps an older child had a part-time position in the company.) We should note, in passing, that businessmen typically have some unearned income from stocks and other investments, which begins to be significant at the higher U-M echelons.

However they made it, when these groups reached $15,000 they began to spend it on some luxuries they had been yearning for. In the $15,000-25,000 income group are about 13.2 million people. In 1971 these lower Upper-Middles were living comfortably: 62 per cent had a second car; two-thirds had a color TV set; three-quarters had clothes dryers; 43 per cent had freezers; 50.7 per cent owned a dishwasher.[4] (Only a small fraction of L-M homes had dishwashers.) Farther up, another 3.8 million people were in the $25,000-50,000 income group. Their wants were somewhat less modest. Their boats weren't rowboats or runabouts; they were cabin cruisers. Their vacation cabins were frequently as finely appointed as most American houses.

But the most common status symbol, next to one's home, is the automobile. For decades, a vast range of autos has been available to the U-M Class. Younger U-M's seem to like foreign sports cars, some quite expensive, whereas the older (and affluent) U-M settles into his Cadillac or Continental Mark IV. There are, of course, a number of perverse U-M people who see an inverted snob value in buying only inexpensive cars, such as the Volkswagen. But most observers regard the automobile as a symbol of wealth, status, and power. Those who feel deprived of those assets, it has been observed, often go in debt to buy a car to add to their self-importance.

With each rise in the social structure we have noted a higher level of educational attainment. Here in U-M country, almost half of the household heads are college graduates or, in moving up, have had "some college."[5] U-M people are also inordinately proud of their college sons and daughters, and especially if they are attending prestigious institutions or have chosen prestigious majors.

What, exactly, are the status-giving occupations these young people are aiming toward? Well, perhaps this is a good time to examine the full range, or at least some good examples at each social-class level. (I've seen several of these lists, all much alike; this one is a composite.)

THE JOB TOTEM POLE

U-U	The independently wealthy; directors of large corporations; the President, Supreme Court justices, some senators and governors.
L-U	Top-income architects, attorneys, and stock brokers; brain, heart, and some other medical specialists; widely known executives in government, business, and industry; gentlemen farmers; federal judges; top military officers; bishops.
(Borderline)	Some physicians; high-income CPA's and attorneys; local business leaders; a few editors; talented mechanical engineers; professors at prestige universities; a few army colonels and navy captains.
U-M	Younger executives in banks and other businesses (*e.g.*, department store buyers); advertising writers; accountants; small-college professors and veteran high-school teachers; some ministers.

L-M	Clerks in banks, stores, post offices, hotels; bookkeepers; small contractors; factory foremen and skilled workers; dental technicians; railroad engineers; city and county employees; truck drivers; barbers; bartenders; some grade-school teachers; army sergeants and corporals.
U-L	Taxi drivers; semi-skilled factory workers; gas-station attendants; stock clerks; gardeners; coal miners.
L-L	Under-employed domestic servants, scrubwomen, and dishwashers; laborers; migrant workers.[6]

From even a sketchy and crude list, we glimpse the structure of those occupational pyramids mentioned in Chapter 1. Some of them are extraordinarily complex, involving neat interlockings at many graded strata, precise coordination of countless moving parts. All of them have elite groups at the top. These pyramids are in every corner and level of our society. Perhaps the "most elaborate hierarchy"[7] is to be found in the United States Civil Service, with eighteen grades—16, 17, and 18 for high-level administrators, down to 3 for stenographers, 2 for mail clerks, and 1 for messengers.

(Special categories should perhaps be created for the various athletic and rock-music hierarchies. These seem to range from U-L to U-M Class; the latter is probably the ceiling no matter what income a superstar might contract for. Athletic salaries are often remarkable. In the National Basketball Association, for example, Kansas City guard Nate Archibald signed in 1973 a long-term $3,150,000 contract. The New York Knicks' thirteen players divide up $5 million a year. The Seattle Sonics have several million-plus contracts.[8] But still more remarkable are the rewards of being a top-ranked rock musician. He can apparently name any figure.)

Prestige factors in a job, says Vance Packard, include (1) its "importance," (2) the authority and responsibility connected with the job, (3) the knowledge and intelligence required, (4) the financial rewards, and (5) the "dignity" of the job. He points out that the madam of a brothel may be wealthy but may still have low prestige. And he reminds us of the strong public-relations efforts to improve group images: the undertakers who became "morticians" and then "funeral directors," the janitors who became "custodians," and so on.[9]

Nowhere does the lust for prestige burn any hotter than in the Upper-Middle Class. Carefully observed pecking orders are unspoken evidence of everyone's status in, say, a pyramidal corporate bureaucracy. The evidence, indeed, is usually made tangible: here a name and title on an office door, there some wall-to-wall carpeting and elegant furniture, over there a company car to drive. In some firms, status is conferred with the key to a private or semi-private washroom.

Status, though, is a complex thing; it involves more than just these trappings. Sociologist Ralph H. Turner has reported in *The Social Context of Ambition* that the "material ambitions" of teen-agers don't seem exorbitant demands on American society. Typically, in one survey, youngsters said they'd be content with a seven-room house and a middle-priced automobile.[10] But they have their dreams; "the boys set higher occupational goals than their fathers have achieved and ... both boys and girls have educational goals higher than their parents' attainments."[11]

The dream of many teen-agers, 35 per cent in one study, is some kind of professional status.[12] In our society, and in many others, we have rigged things so that (next to inheritance) becoming a professional person is the safest route to wealth.[13] This smoldering desire for the prestige of the attorney or the physician is fanned repeatedly by a youngster's parents. They are ambitious for him, as Michael Young has shown in *The Rise of the Meritocracy*—so much so that they will sacrifice and plan strategies and "pull strings."[14]

The all-pervasive competitiveness in American society has brought expressions of concern from psychiatrists, educators, and anthropologists.[15] Some have noted "the stress involved in pursuing high ambitions, and found ambition a contributing factor in the production of neuroses and other personality disturbances."[16] These concerns have of course been transmitted to potential spouses of ambitious people. In a survey of young women's attitudes by *Mademoiselle* magazine, it was found that few desired to marry the man who's obsessed with getting to the very top of his elite group. "They were thinking of his happiness and of his health...Throughout the answers there was a constant identification of work and achievement with ruined health, lost friends, unhappiness. It was associated with trampling on other people who are also on the ladder...."[17]

So, to forestall feelings of guilt and prevent ulcers, the person climbing his way through the Upper-Middles' steel-and-concrete mountains should ascend gradually and tactfully. There are, after all, ways to advance without savage office struggles. For many useful suggestions we are indebted to Charles Merrill Smith, who in 1972 produced *Instant Status, or How To Become a Pillar of the Upper Middle Class*. Smith's book urges, to begin with, "personality management" to achieve what he calls "the high-predictability profile." People in the U-M establishment, he says, want to be secure, comfortable, free of oddball intruders who might upset things. "Upper middle-class society values nothing so highly as predictability."[18] To facilitate your acceptance in this class, Smith has a chapter on "The Art of Creative Conformity," with advice on haircuts, dress, and conservative politics. Another chapter advises you how to select a spouse, one who will be an asset and not a liability; still another gives counsel about selection of the right car or the right club.

At one's club and at home, there are often social occasions which seem to call for the serving of alcoholic beverages. Bourbon and beer are dear to the hearts of L-M and lower-class people, but in the U-M culture, Smith says, the tastes to cultivate are those for Scotch and, more importantly, good wines. He cautions, however, against wasting time becoming an "obsessive" wine aficionado, one who "devotes his waking hours to reading about wine, and traipsing from dealer to dealer hunting down bargains in a Château Rausan-Gassies Margaux or a Haut-Médoc St. Estèphe..." No, he says, one can get by nicely being something of a fraud. "To be a synthetic wine freak is enormously less time-consuming and will serve your purposes just as well. All you need do is to memorize a few names of French wines, master the ritual of serving wine, and, of course, learn the lingo."[19]

Smith is also a good guide when shopping for a fashionable church to join. He has surveyed all surveys, he maintains, and finds this to be the descending order of denominational status:

1. Protestant Episcopal (high-class nearly everywhere in America)
2. A three-way tie of Presbyterian, Congregationalist, and Unitarian churches. (He qualifies this, though, by observing that "Unitarian prestige is largely confined to New England, where it is practically indistinguishable from Congregationalism. Outside of New England it attracts mostly intellectuals, crusaders, agnostics, World Federalists, and other unstable types."[20]
3. Methodist ("In the South and in many urban areas of the Midwest it is fully the equal of the Presbyterian church."[21])
4. Lutheran
5. Baptist
6. All others

Others also have noted the persistent dominance in our culture of the WASP, the (white) Anglo-Saxon Protestant.

Our function, though, is to remind social climbers of the importance of proper language habits. In this chapter we shall introduce material on writing *logically* and on informal documenting. But, first, some other things.

U-M GRAMMAR

Shamans and priests in primitive societies, anthropologists tell us, maintain their power by keeping secret (or at least private) the details of ancient rituals, certain mystic words and phrases, and so on. We sometimes smile at this, but in our modern English-speaking world we can find comparable techniques used to perpetuate social prestige and power.

Shall, will; Should, would

The three highest classes have entered into a pact, or so it seems, to preserve an antiquated distinction between these paired auxiliary verbs. One of the tasks of the ambitious middle class person is to learn the difference and to practice assiduously using the proper one in the proper place. (This knowledge will stand you in good stead should you later try pushing on into L-U territory).

All these auxiliaries are used with a main verb to form a verb phrase. The grammatical variations detailed here have almost disappeared from both the speech and the writing of the lower classes. In the higher classes, speech patterns are often rather informal, but the complex distinctions are regularly observed in formal writing. Ready? Here we go:

1. *Simple futurity* — With the first person, use *shall*; with the second and third, use *will*.

    I *shall* stay home tonight.
    You (She) *will* stay home tonight?

2. *Determination, promise, or command* — With the first person, use *will*; in the others, *shall*.

    I *will* stay, despite what he says.
    You (She) *shall* stay, despite what he says.

Should and *would* are technically past-tense forms but, strangely, are more often used to talk about the present and future:

3. *Duty or strong desire* — With the first person, use *would*; in the others, use *should*.

    I *would* like to stay.
    You (She) *should* stay.

4. *Weak desire* — Use *should* in the first person; in the second and third, use *would*.

    I *should* like to stay, but I don't suppose I can.
    She *would* like to stay, but she probably can't.

5. *Conditions* — Use *would* in the first person; in the second and third, use *should*.

    I *would* like to stay if the senator comes.
    You (She) *should* like to stay if he comes, you say?

6. *Habit or wish* — Use *would* with all persons.

    I *would* stay until twelve every night.
    You (She) *would* stay until twelve every night.
    I wish you *would* stay!

(The whole business is rather like learning an elaborate code. Incidentally, when asking a formal question, use the same word that you would expect in the answer: *Should* he stay? Yes, he *should*.)

Well, now, if all that gives you a headache, there is some consolation: only purists expect perfection in speech, and, even in writing, there are sometimes a few alternatives. For example, something other than simple futurity is often better expressed by *must* or *have to*; there's less chance of ambiguity ("You *must* stay." No, I *have to* go.") The informal expression "I *have got to* go") is acceptable to the middle class and even, especially in speech, to many L-U people. But be careful not to say I *gotta*, a lower-class locution.

Another informal dodge is the use of a contraction. When you're not quite sure of the proprieties, say *I'll, you'll, she'll* and no one will know that you're confused by *shall* and *will*. Instead of *should* and *would*, try *I'd, you'd* and *she'd*.

But in formal writing, you really *should* refer to your list. After a few months in the U-M Class, perhaps it will all seem natural and easy.

U-M USAGE

Some more notes on what's approved and by whom:

Action, Piece of the action. The term *action* is U-M slang for commercial or social (often sexual) transactions. (The U-M Class spawns a hedonistic sub-group called the "swinger" set.) A *piece of the action* refers to direct involvement. Both expressions have been trite for some time.

Among, Between. Among is used with several people or things, *between* with only two. Use *between*, however, to suggest a relationship in any pair of elements.

    He divided the jellybeans *among* the four boys.
    This is just *between* you and me.
    Various agreements were reached *between* the three contractors.

Amount, Number. Amount is used with a quantity or mass, *number* with a set of separate objects.

    He had a large *amount* of cash on him.
    He flashed a *number* of $100 bills.

And/or. Used by U-M attorneys in their work. Should be employed only very rarely elsewhere.

Apt, Liable, Likely. Likely is the safest to use in expressing probability. Use *apt* as a synonym only when a known tendency is involved. Use *liable* only when there is an element of risk.

    It's *likely* to rain.
    Billy is *apt* to get carsick on long trips.
    When you've been drinking, you're *liable* to be a dangerous driver.

Asset. The U-M Class employs this legal term informally in various ways:

    She has some obvious *assets*.
    The plan has a number of *assets*.
    She is a real *asset* to him.

Balance. Except when referring to money, don't use this to mean "the remainder."

U-M CLASS	I missed the *balance* of the concert.
UPPER CLASS	I missed the *rest* of the concert.

Can, May. See p. 59.

Can't help but. This double negative is used by about half of the U-M Class. The other half regards it as colloquial.

DOUBTFUL	I *can't help but* like her.
ACCEPTED	I *can't help* liking her.

Can't seem to. Regarded as slightly colloquial.

U-M CLASS	We *can't seem to* reach the governor.
L-U CLASS	We *don't seem able to* reach him.
U-U CLASS	We *seem unable to* reach him.

Center around. Illogical U-M corruption of *center on, center in,* or *revolve around*.

AVOID	The talk *centered around* his candidacy.

Claim. In formal English, this means "to assert one's right to." Less formally it's a synonym for "declared," "affirmed," and so on.
    U-M CLASS   He *claimed* he'd been there.
    UPPER CLASS   He *maintained* that he'd been there.

Contact. Commercial jargon for "talk to" or "meet with."
    U-M CLASS   I'll *contact* him in the morning.
    UPPER CLASS   I'll *see* him in the morning.
    OR   I'll *talk to* him in the morning.

Continual, Continuous. *Continuous* means uninterrupted; *continual* can mean the same but is now largely restricted to the sense of a long-term *intermittent* action.

Critical, Criticize. These terms are often used as references to fault-finding or censuring. Actually, though, upper-class purists regard them as neutral terms; the words refer simply to evaluation and judgment, which may or may not be *adverse* criticism.

Due to. Some upper-class people have strong feelings about *due to*. They like it when it introduces a prepositional phrase functioning as a predicate adjective, following a linking verb.

    The loss was chiefly *due to* bad luck.

But they don't like it doubling as an adverb. If there's a different kind of verb they want an adverbial phrase or clause.
    U-M CLASS   She stayed home *due to* illness.
    UPPER CLASS   She stayed home *because of* illness.
    OR   She stayed home *because* she was ill.

Oddly enough, the prejudice doesn't seem to apply to *owing to*, a similar form.

Educational. The upper class sees this as a somewhat sloppy U-M term for *instructive*.

Emigrate, Immigrate. The first refers to *leaving* a country, the second to *entering* one. Classes below the U-M are confused by the terms and generally avoid them. U-M's, however, have no difficulty.

Fabulous. U-M slang word of approval or admiration.

Farther, Further. The Upper-Middles emulate their superiors in using *farther* to refer to distance, *further* to degree or quantity.
    LOWER CLASSES   Let's drive a bit *further*.
    HIGHER CLASSES   Let's drive a bit *farther*.
    HIGHER CLASSES   Let's analyze this matter *further*.

Fellow. A term used informally by the higher classes to mean "person." (The lower and middle classes use it at times in a folksy way, pronouncing it *fella*.)

Fewer, Less. The higher classes insist that *fewer* refers to number, *less* to degree or quantity.
    LOWER CLASSES   *Less* than half the factories were affected.
    HIGHER CLASSES   *Fewer* than half were affected.
    HIGHER CLASSES   There is *less* chance now of a strike.

Fiancé, Fiancée. Upper-Middles, who often know a little French, observe the distinction between *fiancé* (an engaged man) and *fiancée* (an engaged woman). They also insist on the accent marks. The terms are not underscored.

First-rate. Informal U-M adjective meaning "excellent." A caution: Don't use it as an adverb.
LOWER CLASS   She sings *first-rate.*
HIGHER CLASS   She is a *first-rate* singer.

Former, Latter. The former is the first named of two, *the latter* the last named of two. The higher classes require that the terms *first* and *last* be used when there are more than two.

Gentleman, Lady. The superior classes have long been miffed about the decline of these words, and now the Women's Lib movement is also involved in the censure. Blame is put on the entertainment houses, where masters of ceremonies courteously address their audiences with the terms (which, incidentally, are also affixed to restroom doors just off the lobby). The upper classes urge that the meanings not be degraded further by using the words to mean *any* man or woman. Democratic principles notwithstanding, they say, the terms simply should *not* refer to society's lower ranks. For their part, Women's Libbers regard the use of *lady* as an often patronizing, male-chauvinist attempt to keep women enslaved as sex objects and incompetents.

I knew a *man* (not *gentleman*) who lived to be 101.

Each *saleswoman* (not *saleslady*) sold ten dresses.

Guess. The L-M employs the frequently inaccurate *I guess*; the superior classes often prefer *suppose* or *think.*

Hanged, Hung. Few people below the U-M Class recognize *hanged* as the past and past-participle verb referring to death.
LOWER CLASS   He was *hung* for murder.
HIGHER CLASS   He was *hanged* for murder.

Healthful, Healthy. The first means "producing or giving health"; the latter means having it.
It is a *healthful* climate.
He came back *healthy.*

Home. In the following context, the higher classes often like to use a formal construction.
LOWER CLASS   The McKenzies are not *home.*
HIGHER CLASS   The McKenzies are not *at home.*

In back of. Regarded as colloquial for *behind* or *back of.*

–ize. The Upper-Middle Class is immoderately fond of transforming nouns into verbs in order to save a few words per sentence. Sometimes this efficiency is colorful and otherwise laudable, as in "He *homed in* on the airbase's radio beacon," or "They *televised* the fight." But the upper class is correct, we think, in observing that this tendency can be carried to extremes and to some monstrous inventions. This is particularly true of neologisms ending in *-ize.* An advertiser wants milady to *moisturize* her skin. A social-page editor tells her readers that a certain interior decorator *accessorizes* rooms (to *personalize* them). A local garbageman asks us to *containerize* our waste. A bureaucrat tells subordinates to *prioritize* various programs. A businessman says he wants to *finalize* a deal quickly. And so on. Some of these set upper-class teeth on edge, as does a fingernail scraping a blackboard.

Lady. See *Gentleman.* The matter is complicated by the situation. Social equals have speech conventions that differ from those of, say, employer-employee relations.

Lend. See *Loan.*

Like, As, As if, As though. Unlike the others here, *like* usually is not accepted by the higher classes as a conjunction.

    LOWER CLASS   It smells good *like* a cigar should.
    HIGHER CLASS   It smells good *as* a cigar should
    HIGHER CLASS   It smells *like* [preposition] a good cigar.

Literally. The U-M Class sometimes uses this carelessly, forgetting that it means "actually"—and ignoring the possibility of using "figuratively" or "almost."

    AVOID   I was *literally* dead on my feet.

Loan, Lend. The lower classes, and some U-M people, use *loan* as both noun and verb. The upper classes want the verb to be *lend.*

Lose out on, Miss out on. Colloquial for *lose* and *miss.*

Marvelous. Sloppy U-M term of approbation.

Materialize. Illogical as a synonym for "appear".

    AVOID   The plumber finally *materialized* at noon.

Nice. Overused and vague.

O.K. Colloquial expression of assent, correctness, or well-being.

Out loud. Colloquial for *aloud.*

Over. U-M substitute for "more than." Frowned on by the upper classes.

    UPPER CLASS   *More than* 55,000 people saw the game.

Parameters. U-M jargon, as in "Can we set up some viable time-frame *parameters?*

Phenomenon, Phenomena. The U-M Class recognizes both singular and plural forms.

    SINGULAR   It is an interesting *phenomenon.*
    PLURAL   They are interesting *phenomena.*

Practically. Colloquial when used for *almost.*

    LOWER CLASS   She's *practically* broke.
    HIGHER CLASS   She's *almost* penniless.

Prior to. Stiff and awkward substitute for *before;* often used by U-M attorneys.

Put across, Put over. U-M colloquialisms for "explain persuasively," "accomplish," "meet a goal," and so on.

Put stock in. Colloquial for "rely on" or "trust."

Quote, Quote marks. Acceptance as nouns questionable. The upper classes still insist on *quotation* and *quotation marks,* although there are some signs of weakening.

Religion. Not a synonym for *denomination, faith, sect,* etc.

    LOWER CLASS   She's a member of the Baptist *religion.*
    HIGHER CLASS   She's a member of the Baptist *church.*
                               She subscribes to the Baptist *faith.*

Religious. Often grotesquely misused.

    U-M CLASS   He's very *religious* about taking his pills.

    UPPER CLASS   He's very *conscientious* (or, if there is no moral tinge, simply "very regular")...

Right along. Colloquial for "continuously" or "continually."

Right away. Colloquial for "immediately."

Shape. Informal for "condition" or "figure."
    MIDDLE CLASS   Those workouts have put me in fine *shape*.
    OR   Dieting has done wonders for her *shape*.
    UPPER CLASS   Those workouts have put me in fine *condition*.
    OR   Dieting has done wonders for her *figure*.

Show up. Means "appear" or "expose." Colloquial.

Size up. Colloquial for "estimate," evaluate," or "judge."
    U-M CLASS   He *sized up* his chances quickly.
    UPPER CLASS   He *estimated* his chances quickly.

Some. Informally substituted for various adverbs. Slang as an intensive.
    LOWER CLASS   He works *some* these days.
    HIGHER CLASS   He works *sometimes* (or *a little*) these days.
    LOWER CLASS   He's feeling *some* better.
    HIGHER CLASS   He's feeling *somewhat* better.
    SLANG   He's *some* guy!

Something else. Slang, usually showing either admiration or ironic treatment of an unusual characteristic.
    That W. C. Fields—he's *something else!*

Take in. Colloquial for either "attend" or, in the passive, "deceive."
    Let's *go to* (not *take in*) the movies.
    She's easily *deceived* (not *taken in*) by a handsome man with a good line.

Time-frame. U-M jargon, as in "Can we set up some viable *time-frame* parameters?"

Viable. U-M jargon, often. See *Time-frame*.

Want in, off, out. Informal for "want to come in," "want to get off," "want to get (or go) out."

Weird. Middle-class slang for "odd."

–wise. This suffix has a long and honorable history of turning nouns gracefully, usefully, into adverbs (*clockwise, crosswise, edgewise, lengthwise, slantwise*). It has been very helpful; it has saved much space that *otherwise* would have been devoted to cumbersome prepositional phrases; it has *likewise* saved us time and energy. But there has recently been a *-wise* explosion, causing upper-class people no little concern. The Upper-Middle Class, in its obsession with streamlining and efficiency, has once again taken this preoccupation to extremes. (See the earlier entry for *-ize*.) Especially among U-M businessmen, politicians, school administrators, and mediocre journalists, we can now hear such barbarisms as *budget-wise, economy-wise, interest-wise, legislation-wise, policy-wise, profit-wise, salary-wise, sales-wise, status-wise, tax-wise, weather-wise*—the list seems almost endless. We shall have to agree with the upper classes: U-M people should be respectfully requested to curb this unwise tendency.

Wonderful. Imprecise U-M term of approval.
Worst way. Colloquial for "very much."
    L-M CLASS   She wants to have a baby *the worst way.*
    UPPER CLASS   She wants to have a baby *very much.*

U-M PUNCTUATION

The Upper-Middles often fancy themselves language stylists and, indeed, some of them are notably accomplished in this role. Most of the nation's most distinguished poets, novelists, historians, and other writers are solidly U-M. (It could be argued, in fact, that a talented person who devotes his time to creating original writing or art, an often thankless task, has earned U-M standing no matter how little he may be recompensed.) In this section we shall examine a few more tools of the writing trade: the colon, the dash, parentheses, and square brackets, all used to set an element off from the rest of the sentence, and, finally, quotation marks.

UM-P1 *The colon*

The colon is a forceful and rather formal mark of introduction. Use it sparingly.

UM-P1a   A colon is often used to introduce a *series, quotation,* or other *statement.*

The Jones Company announces a sale on fine winter coats: lamb shearlings, suedes, leathers.
Then it was Marie's turn: "Mr. Chairman, a point of order!"
Proceed as follows: (1) Take the 30th street exit to Sheppard Avenue, (2) turn right and . . .

UM-P1b   A colon is often used before formal *appositives.*

Use of the colon creates tension before the restatement and hence adds a little drama to the sentence.
There was one thing that was clear: that we should make up our minds soon.
I have just one piece of advice: study harder.

UM-P1c   A colon is often used between two main clauses when the second amplifies the first.

We have a good chance to succeed: there are loans available at the bank and a federal guaranty plan.

UM-P1d   Some special uses for the colon:
1. After the salutation of a business letter (Dear Sirs:).
2. Between Biblical chapter and verse (Luke 3:2), although a period is also acceptable (Luke 3.2).
3. Between hours and minutes o'clock (11:59 p.m.).
4. Between city and publisher in bibliographic entries (Denver: Acme Publishing Co., 1924).

UM-P1e   *Don't* use a colon after a preposition or a linking verb.

AVOID   He pleaded guilty to: assault, battery, and resisting arrest.
AVOID   His chief interests are: wine, women, and song.

UM-P2 *The dash*

The dash is a much less formal device than the colon; it should nevertheless be used carefully. (It's important, incidentally, to distinguish it from the hyphen. We like to make the dash three times as long as the hyphen—a shorter length causes visual confusion—with no space before or after. But other fashions exist.)

UM-P2a   Use a dash to set off a *summary* or *list*.

Glue, nails, screws—we tried everything to make it hold.
We tried everything to make it hold—glue, nails, screws.

UM-P2b   A dash can mark a *sudden interruption*.

But do you think that I—
We hiked and hiked—right back to where we'd started!
I guess I'll—no, I won't either.

UM-P2c   A dash can signal an abrupt *parenthetical statement* or one with internal punctuation.

We come finally—this would be short, I promised you—to my recommendations.

UM-P2d   A dash can be used to create *special emphasis*.

I have just one piece of advice—study harder.

A final word: don't overuse the dash. Even in informal writing, it has the effect of cluttering up the page. Save it for special effects.

UM-P3   *Parentheses*

Commas, dashes, and parentheses are all used to enclose material being set off from the rest of the sentence. Gentlest, perhaps, are the commas; they keep the isolated part still tightly connected to the rest. Dashes set off parts rather abruptly—and, hence, tend to stress those parts. Parentheses, by contrast, set off parts joined only loosely to the sentence (parts playing only a minor role); the effect is to minimize the significance of the enclosed material.

The comma is the most commonly used of these three devices, by far. Please use dashes or parentheses only when you have to.

UM-P3a — Use parentheses to set off material that comments, explains, or illustrates.

It was very unusual (as I recall the matter, forty years later) to find tadpoles there.
One of the featured composers was Giacomo Meyerbeer (1791-1864).
One of the night bombers (a black B-24, usually) would go in first to drop flares.

UM-P3b — Use parentheses to enclose letters or figures in a series.

The steps are simple: (1) fill out an application form, (2) submit references from previous employers, (3) submit to an interview, and then (4) starve for six months while you wait.

UM-P3c — (Parentheses can set off an entire sentence or paragraph, such as this one. Notice that the final period falls *inside* the parentheses.)

Note: When a parenthetical addition comes at the end of a sentence, the period is *outside* the parentheses (as in this case). When parentheses are at mid-sentence and tangle with a comma (as in this example), the comma comes *after*, not before, the parentheses. These conventions are handed down by upper-class language conservatives, who like things tidy.

UM-P4   *Square brackets*

Brackets are a rare but occasionally necessary variant of parentheses. They have two principal uses in standard writing.

UM-P4a — Use brackets to indicate a *parenthesis-within-a-parenthesis*.

You may never need to construct such an oddity (but you should [at least] know what one looks like).

UM-P4b Use brackets to enclose *your own insertions or changes* inside quoted material.

> "Congress shall make no law [says the First Amendment] respecting an establishment of religion...."

Often you can *condense* a quotation this way, with or without an ellipsis (see UM-M3):

> "Congress shall make no law [establishing a]... religion...."

But the first ellipsis here isn't really needed:

> "Congress shall make no law [establishing a] religion...."

Occasionally you will quote something that is misspelled or ungrammatical. To disclaim responsibility for the error, and to show that the passage is reproduced precisely, use an underscored Latin word in brackets:

> "He was good in atheletics [sic]."

UM-P5 *Quotation marks*

The Lower-Middle Class, for some reason, cannot seem to get the hang of graceful quotation, conventionally punctuated. True, there are some little quirks about it that make it initially puzzling—but one would think that, in time, the L-M's would finally master the art. But no; it remains a task for the anointed Upper-Middle.

The purposes of quotation marks are to indicate the exact words of a speaker or writer, to indicate words being used in a special sense, and to set off certain titles.

UM-P5a Use double quotation marks to enclose a *direct quotation*.

Employ two sets of double marks to set off most direct quotations.

> "This comes as a big surprise! When are you leaving?" she asked.
>
> He paused and then said, "Tomorrow morning."

But in an *indirect* quotation the marks are omitted.

> He said that he would leave tomorrow morning.

Combinations are possible. Here is a *partial* direct quotation:

> She said that his announcement was "a big surprise."

But be careful; beware of misquoting.

> FAULTY   She said "that his announcement was a big surprise."

(In the first example above, note that each of the speakers had his own paragraph. Separating the speeches this way is standard practice in handling dialogue.)

Often the speaker tags are put inside the passage, which requires some extra punctuation.

> SPLIT QUOTATION   "This comes as a big surprise!" she exclaimed. "When are you leaving?"
>
> "When," she asked, "are you leaving?"

UM-P5b   With quotations inside others, use *single* quotation marks.

British practice is to start with single marks and to use double marks around interior material. American practice is just the opposite:

> "I can still remember old Carson almost shouting, 'Tomorrow we start on the poetry of William Blake.'"

Infrequently another box may be inside *that* box. In such cases, alternating, we return to double quotation marks.

> "He glared at me and growled, 'Please explain what Blake meant by "the chartered Thames."'"

UM-P5c   *Long quotations* and *quoted poetry* require special handling.

Whenever a quotation runs longer than one paragraph, quotation marks begin each paragraph but close *only the final one*.

> "He took poetry very seriously. For him there was a kind of spiritual pleasure in trying to connect with the mind of the poet.
>
> "This seemed to be especially true in dealing with the poems of William Blake."

When such a passage runs past ten lines (sometimes less), it's best handled with a blocked (also called "block" or "display") quotation. In such a case, we indent and *single-space* the passage. We also drop the quotation marks—except of course for something quoted inside the passage.

> He took poetry very seriously. For him there was a kind of spiritual pleasure in trying to connect with the mind of the poet.
>
> This seemed to be especially true in dealing with the poems of William Blake. He delighted in asking students if *they* had any "mind-forged manacles." Another time he might . . .

Occasionally you may wish to quote some poetry. Two or three lines can sometimes be incorporated into your paragraph, using slashes to separate the verse lines: "Bring me my bow of burning gold! / Bring me my arrows of desire!" But more commonly, perhaps, poetry is centered on the page, without quotation marks:

> I will not cease from mental fight,
>   Nor shall my sword sleep in my hand,
> Till we have built Jerusalem
>   In England's green and pleasant land.

UM-P5d   Words used in some *special sense* are often quoted.

Sometimes we want to focus on a word to be explained:

> She admired "mature" writing—clear, reasonable, and graceful sentences and paragraphs.

> The word "democracy" is very difficult to define.

(Underscoring, or italic type, is often used for the same purpose.) At other times quotation marks warn us to take a word in an ironic sense:

This is one of those "cute" little dramas that turn sensitive stomachs.
Let me tell you about that county's "justice."

But *do not* use quotation marks, please, to stress or defend nicknames, slang, well-known terms and sayings, or attempts at humor.

AVOID   Downtown we met a "Jesus freak."
AVOID   Well, back to "the old drawing board"!

UM-P5e   Use quotation marks for *certain titles*: of articles, chapters, short stories and poems, short musical compositions, and most works of art.

Blake's poem "The Tiger," from his *Songs of Experience*, has an undercurrent of terror.

But don't put quotation marks around the titles of your own college themes. It just isn't done in the U-M Class.

UM-P5f   Punctuate *carefully*.

(1) Commas and periods, in modern America, are always placed *inside* quotation marks.
"It's sweet of you," she cooed, "to come on such short notice."

(2) Colons and semicolons are always placed *outside* the quotation marks.
There was a list of "enemies": political opponents, unfriendly journalists, and the like.
The sign says "Stop"; it means what it says.

(3) Question marks, exclamation points, ellipses, and dashes go *inside* when attached to the quoted material, *outside* when they apply to the whole sentence.

INSIDE   "When will he arrive?" she asked.
INSIDE   She asked, "When will he arrive?"
OUTSIDE   Did she say, "I know him"?

(4) *Don't* use a comma with another mark.
AVOID   "Stop or I'll shoot!," he shouted.

U-M SPELLING

The Upper-Middles, though ordinarily passable spellers, must not allow themselves to fall into sloth, dissipation, and other bad habits, and hence to backslide. For the sake of their position, they should strive to become *better* spellers. They should master some of the more troublesome words, such as these:

1. accommodate
2. chauffeur
3. conceive
4. equivalent
5. exaggerate
6. exceed
7. exhilaration
8. existence
9. hypocrisy
10. incredible
11. indispensable
12. irresistible
13. misspell
14. occurred
15. perseverance

16. picnicking
17. precede
18. proceed
19. pronunciation
20. rhetoric
21. sacrilegious
22. soliloquy
23. supersede
24. temperamental
25. villain

U-M MECHANICS

The line between Mechanics and Punctuation is a thin and fuzzy one. Somewhat arbitrarily, we lump the following in the Mechanics category: (1) underscoring for italics, (2) syllabication and other uses of the hyphen, (3) ellipsis, and (4) capitalization.

UM-M1 *Underscoring for italics*

Underscore words, letters, and so on, to indicate where you would use italic (slanting) type.

UM-M1a Italicize the *titles of books, newspapers, magazines, long musical compositions, plays, films, major works of art*, and the *names of ships, trains*, and *aircraft*.

Adventures of Huckleberry Finn Gounod's *Faust*
The Scarlet Letter Rodin's *The Thinker*
Newsweek The *Titanic*
Exception: The Bible and its "books" are usually not italicized.

UM-M1b Italicize *foreign words and phrases* not yet fully accepted into the English language.

You may need a desk dictionary's help here; many of them flag a term that's still considered alien, such as *Weltanschauung* or *bon voyage*. But many words have been naturalized; for example, "bourgeois," "chauffeur," and "limousine" don't need underlining. Opinion is clearly divided, however, on how to handle the Latin abbreviations that are so common in formal writing—*e.g., ibid., i.e., op. cit.*, and even *etc*. The 1970 edition of *The MLA Style Sheet* suggests that the tendency is toward removal of all such underscoring. But it would be a good idea to check with your instructor.

UM-M1c Italicize *words, letters, symbols, and numbers used as words*.

Try to eliminate some *and*'s from your writing.
Here are six *8*'s for the signboard.

UM-M1d Don't overuse italics.

This book sets a very bad example, because its pages are littered with italicized words. Shamefacedly I admit to excesses. Sometimes I tried for emphasis or for special visual effects; sometimes I wanted to be sure we heard a word's sound. The upper classes are quite right; it's easy to overdo it.

> *If you take the hyphen seriously you will surely go mad.*
> —John Benbow

UM-M2 *The hyphen and syllabication*

Use a hyphen to create compound words, to avoid ambiguity, and to show that a word is being continued on the next line.

UM-M2a
Use a hyphen when a compound noun isn't yet accepted as a single word.

Compounds start out as separate words (*base ball*), typically become hyphenated (*base-ball*) and often are finally consolidated (*baseball*). Consult a very recent dictionary when in doubt about a term.

    mother-in-law   BUT   stepmother

UM-M2b
A hyphen is used to create a *compound adjective* before a noun.

    A well-known actress was to appear.
Exception: If the first word of the compound is an adverb ending with *-ly*, omit the hyphen.

    The quick-moving robber got away.
    BUT   The quickly moving robber got away.
Note: A compound *following* a noun usually has no hyphen.

    The actress was well known.

UM-M2c
The hyphen helps in *clarifying* a sentence.

There may be a difference, for example, between *antique-lovers* and *antique lovers*. There might also be confusion about a *light blue jacket*—but not if, in writing about a pastel coat, you say *light-blue*.

UM-M2d
The hyphen is used to form *compound numbers* from twenty-one to ninety-nine, and to express *fractions*.

    one-sixth   two-thirds   three-fourths

UM-M2e
Use a hyphen to avoid a troublesome union of letters.

    NOT   preeminence   BUT   pre-eminence
    NOT   reenter   BUT   re-enter

In some words, though, the hyphen is often omitted: *cooperation, coeducational.*

In other cases, the hyphen may allow you to assert your intended meaning: *recreation* or *re-creation*, *recovered* or *re-covered*.

UM-M2f   Hyphenate such affixes as *all-*, *ex-*, *self-*, *-elect*, and a few others.

    all-Conference   self-appointed
    ex-President Nixon   Givernor-elect Smith

Usage differs in dealing with many others, such as *half-*, *multi-*, *pre-*, *-like*, and *-wise*.

    pre-Columbian   swan-like
    prehistoric   swanlike

In general, there seems to be a slow drift away from the hyphen in such combinations.

UM-M2g   At the end of a line, *divide words carefully*, using a hyphen.

(1) Divide between syllables. Consult a dictionary when in doubt about the breaking-points. Examples: *ab-rupt*, *ac-cede*, *ac-ces-sory*.

(2) Never divide words of one syllable. Newspapers used to follow this rule but in the 1970's relaxed their typographical standards, thereby creating abominations like *vie-wed*, *tw-elve*, and *thro-ugh*.

(3) In dividing a compound that's already hyphenated, split it where the hyphen is.
    NOT   well-de-signed, All-Amer-ican
    BUT   well-designed, All-American

(4) Never leave a single letter hanging.
    NOT   a-way, creep-y,   BUT   away, creepy.

UM-M3 *Ellipsis*

The term *ellipsis* (plural *ellipses*) sometimes refers to an expression that's clear even though it's grammatically incomplete.

    Whenever [it is] possible, [you] please stop and see me.

Here, however, it's a technical term in mechanics: an intentional omission of something in shortening a quotation. Its mark: three spaced periods. (Pay attention now; these are important lessons for the U-M writer to learn. You will be needing this expertise soon in dealing with documented writing.) Consider this treatment of a fragment from Lincoln's "Gettysburg Address":

    "But, in a larger sense, we cannot dedicate . . . this ground."

If you want to show that a sentence ends but the paragraph continues, use *four* dots (a period snuggled close to the final letter and then three spaced dots).

    "But in a larger sense, we cannot dedicate . . . this ground. . . ."

The more common practice, though, is to ignore the paragraph's continuation.

When the quoted portion is only a short fragment, you may (should) quote without an ellipsis. Be sure that the quotation is integrated grammatically.

But, said Lincoln, "we cannot dedicate" the battlefield.
If there is any chance of misunderstanding, however, always indicate the ellipsis.
The ellipsis dots are standard when the quotation is nearly a full thought.

"The brave men, living and dead, who struggled here have consecrated it..."

Notice that no comma is used when a speaker tag is affixed.

"The brave men, living and dead, who struggled here have consecrated it..." he added.

Other uses:

(1) To suggest a pause in conversation or action:

"Well... I guess I can."

(2) To show the continuation of a series:

The odd numbers are 1, 3, 5...

(3) To create special effects in advertisements, promotional material, etc.:

Friday night... The musical event of the season!... See you there?

UM-M4 *Capitalization*

U-M business leaders, in their correspondence and other official utterances, tend to capitalize somewhat more than is necessary. They seem to feel that it adds elegance or distinction to be "Personnel Manager" or "Treasurer" instead of merely lower-case "personnel manager" or "treasurer." There are, however, quite a number of capitalization conventions generally recognized in our society—fewer than a century ago, but still quite a few.

UM-M4a Capitalize the *first word of a sentence,* the pronoun *I,* and the old-fashioned interjection *O.*

When I see her, O how I long for her!
But don't capitalize *oh* unless it's the first word.

UM-M4b Capitalize also the first word of a quoted *sentence* incorporated in another, and, in *most verse,* the first word of every line.

He asked, "When may I see you again?"
Things are in the saddle,
And ride mankind.—Ralph Waldo Emerson

UM-M4c Capitalize (sometimes) an *independent clause following a colon.*

There is no unanimity among U-M stylists on how to handle such clauses, but there are certain tendencies: (1) If a *set* of sentences follows, as here, all are capitalized. (2) If only one follows, it is capitalized if it is long and complex, or if the writer wants it stressed. If it is short and merely an appendage of another clause *before* the colon, it is not capitalized. (3) If the element before the colon is not a full clause, the clause following is often capitalized, whether long or short.

To repeat: Those chosen for the positions were all white males.
(4) If the element *following* the colon is not a complete clause, it is usually not capitalized.
We had a choice: to stand and fight or to run and be called cowards.

UM-M4d   Capitalize *proper nouns* and their modifications.

(1) Persons and places:
W. A. Mozart; Texas, Texan, El Paso, Tex.

(2) Races, nationalities, and languages:
Caucasian, Indian, Negro; Swedes; Polish

(3) Most organizations and their official members:
Republican Party, Communist Party, a Communist, the Senate, the Girl Scouts, R. J. Reynolds Tobacco Co.

Exception: Classes in school and college are sometimes capitalized, when they're thought of as officially organized groups. But a member is in lower case: sophomore, senior.

(4) Historical events, eras, and documents:
the Civil War, the Renaissance, the Constitution

(5) Days of the week, months, and holidays:
Monday, February, Yom Kippur

(6) Sacred terms:
Brahma, Allah, Zeus, God the Father, Jesus the Son, the Lamb of God, the Virgin, the Great Spirit, Jehovah.

(7) Some personifications (common in sayings and older poetry):
Justice is blind; the Almighty Dollar

Let not Ambition mock their useful toil,
   Their homely joys, and destiny obscure;
Nor Grandeur hear with a disdainful smile
The short and simple annals of the poor.
—Thomas Gray,
"Elegy Written in a Country Churchyard"

(8) Sections of the country, and derivatives:
Far West, Westerner, the South, Southern hospitality, the Northeast

But if only a *direction* is meant, make it lower case:
The plane flew off toward the northeast.

(9) Seasons when part of formal academic terms or commercial promotions:
Fall Semester, the Summer Quarter; Fall Coat Sale

But seasons used alone are not capitalized: winter, spring.

(10) Specific academic courses:
History of the Ottoman Empire; Biology 205

But broader disciplines are capitalized only if they are languages: history, biology, Spanish.

(11) Sometimes capitals are used in an ironic sense:
He was convinced he was spokesman for the One True Religion.

UM-M4e *Capitalize titles preceding a name.*

General Eisenhower, Secretary Ickes, Judge Hall

But when a title *follows* a name, we must observe some class distinctions:

(1) Two U-U positions are regularly entitled to capitals:
Woodrow Wilson, President of the United States
Earl Warren, Chief Justice of the United States

(2) Lower-class and L-M positions are regularly lower case:
Woodrow Jones, apprentice bricklayer
Joan Warren, waitress

(3) Between these extremes, usage is guided by the distinction of the office and the formality of the occasion. In informal situations, even a U-U person may be lower-cased (Robert L. Deane, chairman of the board). In formal situations, however, even a U-M person may get a formal, capitalized title (William Hayes, Professor of History).

Family relationships are capitalized when used as titles, or used alone in place of names, but not if a possessive comes first: Dear Cousin Sue, my cousin; Mother, our mother; Grandpa.

UM-M4f *With titles of books, films, student papers, etc., capitalize conventionally.*

(1) Capitalize the first word and all other "important" words.

(2) "Unimportant" words are ordinarily put in lower case. These include the articles (*a, an, the*) and conjunctions and prepositions with fewer than five letters.

The Oxford Book of American Verse
The Man Without a Country

UM-M4g *Capitalize common nouns only when part of a proper noun.*

Newspaper usage sometimes differs here, but terms like *river, lake, park, street, building, county, college, high school*, and *club* are ordinarily capitalized when part of a proper name and in lower case when used alone.

Whitman College, the college
the Pennsylvania Railroad, the railroad

When the generic term is plural, it is often not capitalized: Main and Lewis streets; 13th and 14th centuries.

UM-M4h *Avoid unneeded capitals.*

A reminder: the gradual tendency in recent decades has been toward fewer and fewer capital letters. Seasons used to be capitalized regularly; now rarely.

A.M. and P.M. used to be standard; now they're in competition with a.m. and p.m.

In some situations capitalization has a significant prestige value, however, so we suggest tactfulness.

U-M COMPOSITION

Back in L-M Composition you were given some suggestions on the planning and writing of themes—especially narrative and descriptive themes, both based on easy, "natural" patterns of organization. In this chapter we move to more difficult papers—exposition and argument—which have no natural plan. Here you must depend upon your mind's ability to create *some kind of "logical" set of ideas*.

UM-C1 *Exposition*

Expository papers have a simply stated but sometimes complex task: to inform and explain; to make something clear. Such papers make up the great bulk of the writing a college student will do: "The Growth of Commercial Aviation in the United States," "Acoustical Problems in the Hayes Auditorium," "New Uses for Tungsten," "The Species of Rocky Mountain Amphibians."

Once again I should stress the importance of the planning stage—indeed, here more than ever, since the writer must choose among many possible treatments of a given thesis. Take this section you're now reading, for example. I have had one hell of a time trying to figure out the best way to organize it. I doubt that I finally chose the ideal arrangement, but it's too late to tinker with it now.

UM-C1a *Outlining expository papers*

In my early organizing I decided, for no particular reason, to set up a "topic" outline rather than a sentence outline. A topic outline, you recall, begins with a full-sentence thesis but supports that thesis with mere fragments. These are not just random bits, however; for one thing, their form ideally displays a great deal of grammatical parallelism. This helps to clarify and emphasize the *coordinate* nature of the elements in each section.

FAULTY   I. *Stripping* the old wax (Verbal)
             II. *Application* of the new (Noun)
           III. *How to buff* (Phrase)
                 A. By hand
                 B. With a machine (Prepositional phrases)
                     1. ...
                     2. ...

(Instead let's, for example, start out with three verbals: *Stripping*... *Applying*... *Buffing*...)

Note also the typographical features—the indenting, the Roman numerals, capitals, Arabic numerals, and so on. These are arranged with some care to rank together coordinate points and to subordinate any *subordinate* points. (The latter, again, are supposedly coordinate to one another in any one group.)

As I began, I reminded myself of a few rules.

- An outline covers its subject, no more and *no less*.
- It is organized cautiously, so that an A doesn't *overlap* the subject of a B.

FAULTY   A. Earliest settlements
               B. Below the Falls

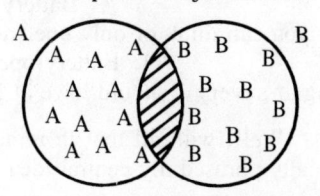

The problem here is that A is organized on a time principle and B according to a spatial principle. This is extremely bad form, as the circles suggest. Beware of all types of "cross-classification." Always divide according to a *single* principle, or at least *one at a time*. Suppose you're considering the settlements along the Ohio River. You might arrange them chiefly by time periods, with the geography subordinated.

Thesis: Town-building on the Ohio River has had a long history.

   I. Earliest settlements
      A. Above the Falls of the Ohio
      B. Below the Falls
  II. Town-starts in the 19th Century
      A. Above the Falls
      B. Below the Falls
 III. Modern townsites
      A. Above the Falls
      B. Below the Falls

For some reason, your chief interest might be in the difference between those two parts of the river, with the chronology this time slightly less important:

   I. Settlements above the Falls of the Ohio
      A. The earliest period
      B. The 19th Century
      C. The 20th Century
  II. Settlements below the Falls
      A. The earliest period
      B. The 19th Century
      C. The 20th Century

Note that an expository paper can make good use of narrative and descriptive material and structure. I have been leading up to this point: that in writing, as in nature, no elements exist pure, but always in compounds or combinations. Thus we can have "narrative description" or "descriptive narration" or, as here, one or both playing handmaiden to expositon.

Two more outlining rules:

- *Don't use vague terms* such as "Introduction," "Body," and "Conclusion."
- Don't construct any *single* subheadings.

Since the I or A promises a division into at least two parts, it's a breach of faith to deliver only one.

  FAULTY I. The types of portable radios
        A. Battery-operated

If you can think of only one, rewrite your main heading:

      I. Battery-operated portable radios

Again, every 1 should have at least a 2; every *a* should have a least a *b*.

Well, with all that in mind, I inched forward. After much deliberation I finally phrased my central idea and hammered out a tentative outline.

Thesis: The mind can devise several main "logical" patterns (and a huge number of combinations), any of which can form the structure of an expository essay.

 I. Inductive statements
  A. Classification
  B. Causal hypothesis
  C. Generalization
 II. Deductive statements
  A. The categorical syllogism
  B. The hypothetical syllogism
  C. The disjunctive syllogism
 III. Analytic statements
  A. Analysis by partition
   1. Formal
   2. Informal (the "details" paper)
  B. Analysis by division
   1. Formal
   2. Informal
    a. Illustration(s)
    b. Examples
 IV. Synthetic statements
  A. Analogy
  B. Comparison-and-contrast
  C. Scales and hierarchies
  D. The set of reasons
  E. Definition
  F. Climactic arrangements
  G. Miscellaneous combinations

With that outline completed, I was ready to begin writing. I decided to make full use of headings and subheadings (which are rarely found in a short essay), and I began to type.

  The human mind, an amazingly capable computer, works with several basic "programs" and, from these, creates an almost infinite number of thought patterns. Each may serve as the structure of an expository essay. Let's survey the possibilities very quickly, beginning with a fundamental set—our inductive ideas.

UM-C1b *Induction*

In this process our thoughts move from specific data *into* some generalized statements about those data. Induction is one of our prime efforts to push back the chaos of experience and to create as much order as we possibly can. Inductive logic forms a major part of the so-called "scientific method." For example, we can *classify* items, or seek to *explain* them or their behavior, or *make generalizations* about them.

(1) *Classification*

Attempts to classify take various shapes: "This A has characteristics X and Y." "This A is a B," "These A's are B's," or, with more sophistication, "An A is a B if A has characteristics X and Y." The word *is*, however, shouldn't be translated as "equals"; instead it means "belongs to the class of." This is most easily seen in a circle diagram. Consider: "That station wagon is an Opel—a Buick import."

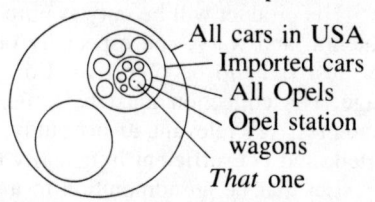

All cars in USA
Imported cars
All Opels
Opel station wagons
That one

As you can see, classification is the basis for most of our attempts to define something. There are two steps in this kind of definition; first, we put the term into a class or "genus," and then we differentiate it from all other terms or "species" in that class.

TERM	GENUS	DIFFERENTIATION
A lectern	is a stand	that supports a speaker's notes or books.
Gluten	is a mixture of proteins	found in cereal grasses.

When writing a theme, never hesitate to define carefully and completely any term with which your reader might not be familiar.

Formal classification of an item can be quite elaborate. In biology, for instance, we could begin with the organism itself, put it into a "variety," that into a larger "species," that into a "genus," that into a "family," that into an "order," that into a "class"—and thence to a huge "phylum" and even a larger "kingdom." Circles and circles, expanding past the horizon...

Perhaps the most common use of classification is the effort to assert something about a *group* of items. We can classify motorcycles according to their horsepower rating, their place of manufacture, and so on—whatever basis suits our need *at that moment*. Later, of course, we can shuffle the deck and use a different basis of classification.

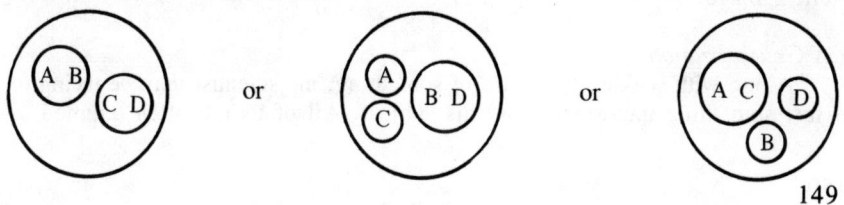

There are several rules for proper classification, but they are more rigorously applied in a related activity, formal *division*; the rules are listed there.

Incidentally, this section you're now reading can be viewed as a classification of various types of thought patterns.

(2) *The hypothesis of causation*

The model of logical thought is very often that of the scientist, busy in his laboratory with his data. Frequently he goes a step beyond mere classification to seek reasons *why* the data fall into a class, or behave as they do. Scientific procedures include (a) collection of the data, (b) formulation of a tentative causal hypothesis, (c) processing and analysis of the data, and finally (d) a series of tests of the hypothesis. If the tests verify and support the hypothesis fully, the scientist may publish his findings in some scholarly Upper-Middle Class journal as a "theory" or even a "law." "An A is a B," he might say, *"because of* X and Y."

His product will be only as pure as his processes. At every step he must be watchful and wary, and especially of his own wishful thinking. At every step he must fight to be objective. For just one example, consider the very first stage. His collection must be limited to data which are (1) clear, bona fide examples, (2) relevant to his study, (3) "unweighted" and otherwise undistorted, and (4) sufficient in quantity or numbers. Otherwise, he gets *garbage*.

Let that be an admonition to a student (of, say, the Civil War) asked to write a paper inquiring into either *causes* or the *effects* of some causative factor. And a further caution: Rarely, if ever, do we find one cause producing one effect. Rather, the picture gets quite messy, even in a simple process:

C_1, C_2, C_3 → $E_1 = C_4$ → E_2, E_3, E_4; C_5

This is a pluralistic world we're living in. Rise, if you can, above the kind of simplistic thinking one often sees in Letters to the Editor or hears in a bar.

    Habitual marijuana smoking causes damage to chromosomes.

    The rise in beef prices is the dirty work of Omaha middlemen.

There may indeed be some truth in such statements—but, unless you can show you have looked at other possible causative factors, your idea may seem—well, garbage.

(3) *Generalization*

Along with seeking the cause of something, the scientist may be trying to *assert* something important about his subject. All of us are often tempted to move from the simple classification "This A is a B" to the embrace of "*All A's are B.*" And if we think we know some of the causative factors, we feel daring; we take the step. This is called "the inductive leap." When a laboratory experiment produces time after time the same results, or when a professionally handled survey yields the same results again and again, the time is ripe for a statement. We don't know *for sure* that "All A's are B," but we are willing to assume its truth until some negative evidence overwhelms it.

| Warning: The Surgeon General Has Determined that Cigarette Smoking Is Dangerous to Your Health. | means "All cigarettes are dangerous." |

But be careful; hasty and/or sweeping generalizations may be just more rubbish. Suppose someone says:

> A radical youth always turns conservative when he grows older and more affluent.

Always? Not even *one* exception? It's often best to hedge a little, you see, using words like *often, usually, seldom,* and the like. As some wag with a taste for paradox has put it, "All generalizations are invalid, including this one."

UM-C1c *Deduction*

So much for induction. Now, *deduction* is a thought process that moves in a different direction. Induction begins with bits of data and ends with a classification, a "proved" hypothesis, or a supported generalization—in other words, with some broad statement. Deduction, by contrast, *begins* with one of these general propositions and proceeds to draw from it *some related statement.* In deductive logic we are still concerned with the search for truth, but now our attention swings to a related subject, *validity.* Producing valid statements is a matter of following all the rules of this logical game. Or rather of three games— three *syllogisms,* which is the name for the little machines used in deductive logic.

(1) *The categorical syllogism*

>All pharmacists are Upper-Middles.
>Swenson is a pharmacist.
>∴ (Therefore) Swenson is an Upper-Middle.

As you can see, there is no special magic in a syllogism. All it does is announce explicitly some simple, ordinary thoughts. It takes a statement, rubs it against a second statement, and produces a third. These are called the major premise, minor premise, and conclusion.

What we are after is a sound, reasonable conclusion—that is, one which has *both truth and validity.* It is quite possible to get one without the other. The only way to produce both is to start with true premises (does everyone agree that *all* pharmacists are U-M?) and then make no errors in operating the syllogism.

Now, a *categorical* syllogism can work only if it has exactly three different terms—found in either the subject or the predicate of the statements. Each of these three must appear exactly twice in the syllogism. One of the three, the "middle term," appears in the two premises but *not* in the conclusion. Its only function is to relate the other two terms *to each other.* Here the middle term is *A*:

All A's are B.
c is an A
c is a B.

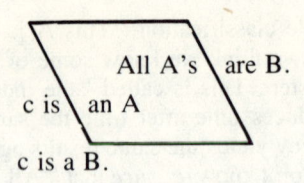

There is also a kind of double-talk, or double-think, to be learned at the outset. When we say "All pharmacists are Upper-Middles," we should think "All (things known as) pharmacists are (*in the class of* things known as) Upper-Middles." Our thoughts must form class-pictures like these:

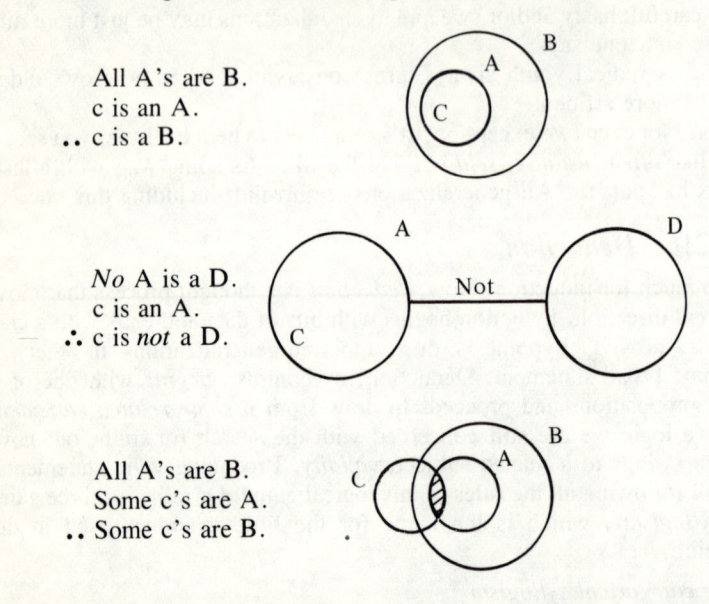

All A's are B.
c is an A.
∴ c is a B.

No A is a D.
c is an A.
∴ c is *not* a D.

All A's are B.
Some c's are A.
∴ Some c's are B.

With these little circles, one can see at a glance how valid his thinking is. The syllogism is said to have 256 possible patterns, of which only two dozen produce valid conclusions. It pays, it would seem, to *follow the rules*. Here are the six most important ones for the categorical syllogism:

(a) There must be only three terms, and they must be used in the *same sense* throughout. (Otherwise you might create a fourth term.) We want no ironic word-plays, no equivocation, when running this machine.

(b) The syllogism can't have two negative premises or two "particular" premises (using the word *some*). It's easy to see why.

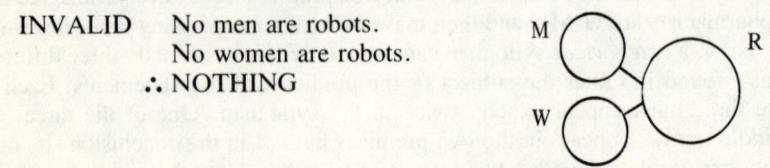

    INVALID   No men are robots.
                         No women are robots.
                        ∴ NOTHING

INVALID   Some men are Americans.
          Some Americans are women.
          Some men are women?

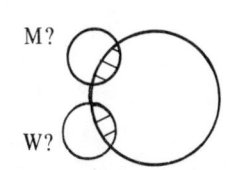

Those circles, you see, must be forced to show a definite, clear, inescapable relationship. Nothing less will do.

(c) The premises can't have the same predicate *unless* one premise has a negative term.

INVALID   All drug addicts are sick people.
          Joanne is (a) sick (person).
          ∴ NOTHING

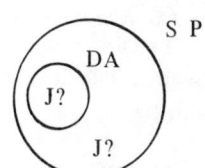

BUT   All drug addicts are sick people.
          Joanne is *not* sick.
          ∴ Joanne is not a drug addict.

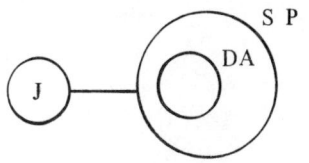

(d) Retain in the conclusion any *qualification* in the premises. If a premise is negative or particular, the conclusion is the same.

VALID   All obsessions are dangerous.
          Some hobbies are obsessions.
          ∴ *Some* hobbies are dangerous.

(e) The middle term must be "distributed" at least once. Briefly, this means that it must refer to a whole *class* of things—at least once. Otherwise it doesn't set up any relationships.

          No priests are thieves.   (Valid, because the
          Father Johanson is a priest.   negative term involves
          ∴ Father Johanson is not a thief.   the *whole* class)

BUT   (All) Preachers are eloquent people.
          Some eloquent people are lawyers.
          ∴ NOTHING

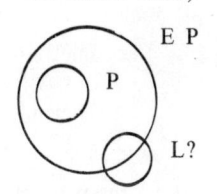

You can assume the subject "Preachers" means all preachers—but you're not allowed to make the same assumption about a *predicate* term, such as "eloquent people." Here that term has *not* been distributed.

(f) A term distributed in the conclusion must also be distributed in the premise in which it first appeared.

All U-U's are wealthy people.
All U-U's are happy people.
∴ All wealthy people are happy people?

Invalid, since "wealthy people" wasn't distributed in the major premise. See (e), above.

(2) *The hypothetical syllogism*
In using this second machine we start with the premise that *if* A (the "antecedent") happens, B (the "consequent") will also happen.

(a) It is sound practice to "affirm the antecedent."

                    A   B
VALID   If he has Disease X, he will die soon.
             He has Disease X.
             ∴ He will die soon.

(b) We can also "deny the consequent" and produce a valid conclusion.

VALID   If she is quiet, she will get some candy.
             She is not getting any candy.
             ∴ She has not been quiet.

But if we do either of these backward, the resulting construction is unsound.

INVALID   If he has cancer, he will die.
               He doesn't have cancer. (Denying the antecedent)
               ∴ He won't die? (Not ever?)

Again: To produce validity, we must either affirm the antecedent or deny the consequent. There's no other way.

(3) *The disjunctive syllogism*
The disjunctive or "alternatives" syllogism has two types, inclusive and exclusive. In both we assume that one possibility must be correct.

(a) Inclusive—Here one *or both* can be true:

    The burglary was committed by either A or B.
    But A has been proved *not* guilty.
    ∴ The burglar must be B.

But note that, even if A were found guilty, B might *also* be guilty.

(b) Exclusive—Here *only one* can be true:

    He is either 64 or 65.
    We find he is 64.
    ∴ He is *not* 65 (not quite eligible for a full Social Security payment).

I have not been taking pains, though perhaps I should have, to point out how each of the thought patterns being surveyed can be useful to you. All along

I've hoped you could visualize some paragraph or whole essay based on this classification or that syllogism. But let us pause for one quick example. Suppose you know that your town or city is faced with a true "either-or" problem, one of these disjunctions, one of life's common situations where a *decision* must be made. Suppose that the assumed causes of a water-pipeline break have finally been narrowed down to two, one of which makes a contractor guilty of gross negligence. If it's *only* the other cause, the contractor is exonerated. Let's pretend further that it's determined, some days later, that it's either A or B but not both. Now the municipal stage is set for drama. (I have seen some excellent themes based chiefly on students' collections of news clippings.)

A caution: Always make sure that what you call an "either-or" situation is that in fact. Many careless thinkers reduce all of life to a set of polarities, usually with strong moralistic convention. They see only good guys and bad guys everywhere. (See "Scales and Hierarchies," below.)

There. So much for formal logic for the time being. Now you can go about the campus continually poking holes in your friend's arguments. Unless, of course, you value their friendship.

In this sketchy examination of induction and deduction, what we have been looking at is the scientific method at work. Induction begins with particular data and projects them, as if with a magic lantern, against a huge screen: *All* A's are B.

INDUCTION

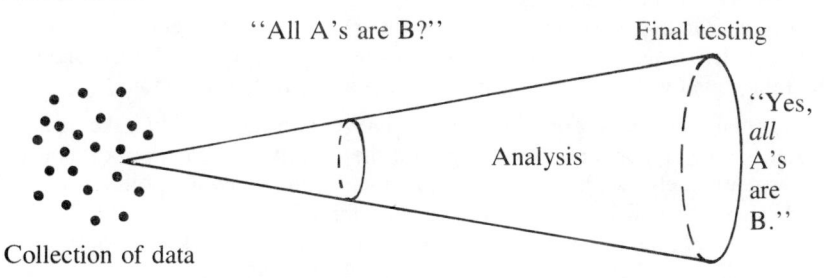

"All A's are B?"   Final testing

Analysis   "Yes, all A's are B."

Collection of data

Deduction, by contrast, begins with an all-embracing proposition and moves to a restricted statement.

DEDUCTION

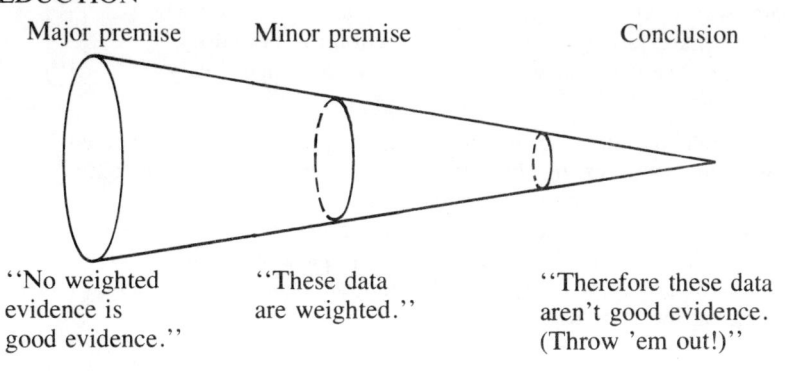

Major premise   Minor premise   Conclusion

"No weighted evidence is good evidence."   "These data are weighted."   "Therefore these data aren't good evidence. (Throw 'em out!)"

Perhaps you can see that deduction's *interaction* with induction is indispensable to the scientist. It acts as a check on induction at every step along the way toward "proof." Something like this, then, might be our best picture of the scientific method:

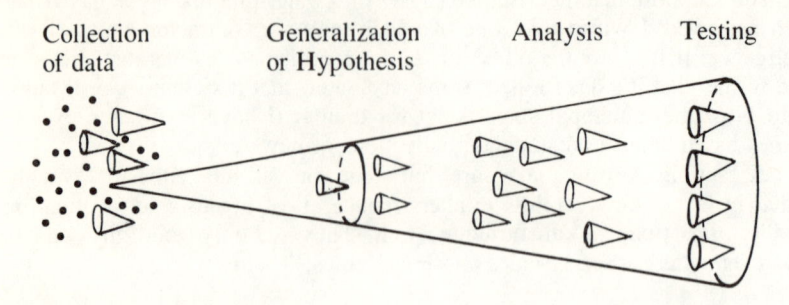

Collection of data   Generalization or Hypothesis   Analysis   Testing

UM-C1d *Analytic statements*

That rough analysis of the scientific method leads us bumpily into our next topic—analysis itself, which can be defined as a separation of a whole into its various elements, in order to examine their nature or their relationships. There are several methods.

(1) *Analysis by partition*

In *partition* we are dealing with a thing or process thought of as a single entity, rather than a collection of many examples or species. We are cracking the thing open to look at its jigsaw-puzzle *parts* and their functions.

(a) Formal partition—For example, whenever we laboriously take apart a watch, or the contents of a desk (or even the desk itself), and then catalog the pieces completely, we have made a formal partition. When the political science teacher separates the U.S. Government into three branches—executive, legislative, and judicial—he has made a formal partition that students busily jot down in their notebooks. When the chemist tells us that sulphuric acid is H_2SO_4 or that water consists of H_2O (two parts of hydrogen and one of oxygen), we can construct a little inventory. By the way, if we could take a part away—say the oxygen—would we still have water? No; we'd have just hydrogen, which you don't want to drink. If we take away the hands of a watch, we no longer really have a watch.

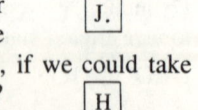

E.
L.
J.

H
H
O

(b) Informal partition—In dealing with complex entities (the United Nations organization, the Boeing 747, the latest steelworkers' union contract), it is often impractical to make an exhaustive inventory of parts. Here we settle for what's called the paragraph (or essay) of *details*—just enough of them to give us a reasonably clear picture of the thing in question. Incidentally, that's what I was attempting in writing, just a bit ago, about some of the stages and other elements of the scientific method.

(2) *Analysis by division*

> *The world is divided into two classes of people: those who divide the world into two types of people, and those who do not.*
> —Anonymous

In *division*, by contrast, we are working with something thought of as essentially *plural*—that is, a grouping of many types and specific examples of the class being examined. (Note that if we extracted an element here it *would* come out whole: a watch classed under "Timepieces" would come out a *whole* watch.)

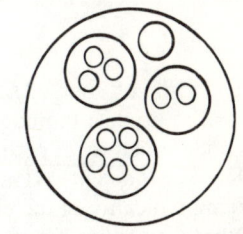

(a) Formal division: For instance, you might want to write a paper in which you distinguish between all the various species and subspecies of falcons or of land-grant colleges or of rye grasses. In such a case, provided your analysis is thorough, we can call it a formal division. A purist would insist upon one that is completely exhaustive (and often we would, too). But there are times when this isn't very practical; in such a situation, you are advised to indicate to the reader what ground you *are* covering. To illustrate:

Thesis: There were many causes of the Vietnam War.
  I. Economic factors (A., B., C....)
  II. Political factors (A., B., C....)
  III. Other factors

Now, in dealing with III you might cite two or three of these miscellaneous causes and then decide you're running out of space and time. All right; tell the reader there were these *and others,* so he's aware that you know you haven't completed the list.

The principle of exhaustiveness holds, incidentally, down to the most minor subdivision of your paper. In *each* section you are urged to be complete or, at the very least, to use "such as" or "and so on" as signals of incomplete lists.

The alert reader can see by now that division is the other side of the coin of *classification*. Classification, you recall, is a building-up process; items are categorized until all species are full, species are catalogued until larger classes are full, and so forth. In division, the process is reversed; here we want to break down a large class to see its smaller components clearly.

In both classification and division, and especially in formal efforts, we should be governed by certain rules or principles. First, by the rule of exhaustiveness or inclusiveness, already discussed. Second, by the rule of exclusiveness, which requires us to take pains to avoid "cross-classification." The meticulous writer will apply consistently a single basis of classification, or at least one at a time, thus keeping all his categories *mutually exclusive*.

AVOID   I. Cold-blooded animals   II. Vertebrates

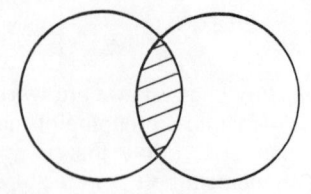

Reptiles and fish, of course, fit *both* categories. The only way to resolve this difficulty is first to deal thoroughly with blood temperature in animals and *then* with their bone structure, or perhaps vice versa. (See again the outlining of a paper on Ohio River settlements.) Third, there are various rules having to do with the relevance and typicality of the evidence by which items are to be classified. For example, there is neither justice nor logic in labeling a person a "drunkard" on the basis of a single overindulgence. Finally, the rule of clarity demands that all species be crisply delineated to eliminate problems with fuzzy or marginal cases.

(b) Informal division: Here we're often making no real attempt at exhaustive analysis. Our chief concern is with the clarity of a general idea or concept. How best to make it clear? Well, two techniques come quickly to mind.

    (1) An *illustration* or two, if well chosen, can do wonders to throw light into murky corners. (The word comes from the Latin *illustrare,* to light up, illuminate.) Allow me, please, to illustrate: Suppose you're writing about the operation of a large downtown hotel. You might mention casually a cadre of cooks and helpers, a genus of desk clerks, of waiters and waitresses, of cleaning people, and so on until you bump into "bellhops." Suddenly it occurs to you that you don't known much about bellhops, and that maybe others don't either. So you do some research (you buy coffee for a talkative bellhop) and then you devote several paragraphs to telling what he does around the place in a typical day. If you get lucky, that section not only tells us what a "hotel employee" is, but also a little of how the various species interact to operate that hotel.

    (2) A few *examples,* as few as two or three, perhaps, often can do as much as illustration to clarify a complex topic. You want to write about salt-water fishing? For salmon, and maybe some other kinds? Well, you don't need to describe all the salmon species (chinook, coho, sockeye, and so on); mention of just two or three of them may be sufficient to cover that fishing ground. Then on the tuna, farther offshore . . .

    The reason why illustrations and examples have such power to clarify is this: In trying to communicate swiftly, to cover a lot of matters fast, man often babbles away at a high level of *abstraction* (*i.e.,* removal from the specific and concrete). He talks about "black power," "Western democracy," "peace with honor," "justice," etc., and often gets away with it. But sometimes his ideas begin to lose contact with the actualities his listener or reader is familiar with. As soon as he senses this, a good speaker will pause and provide some specific (and usually concrete) link with the world his audience knows. Such a link is often vivid and memorable.

This has been called "coming down the abstraction ladder," which metaphor suggests to us that there are various *levels of abstraction,* and that "abstraction" is a relative term. "Working dogs" is less general than "dogs" but it is more general than "collies." Citing of something quite specific and concrete suddenly floods the abstraction with meaning.

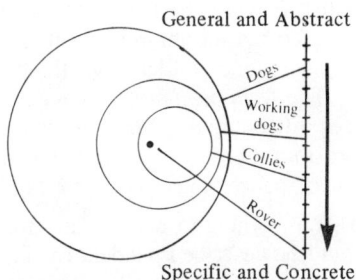

General and Abstract

Dogs
Working dogs
Collies
Rover

Specific and Concrete

Examples sometimes have another function—merely to stand as *typical* of the class. They thus serve as support of a generalization about that class. You say you have happy memories of your early teens? What you need for a paper is a set of examples of such memories. The effect will of course be to clarify, but also to prove your point; you weren't just faking it.

Both illustrations and examples seem to have a special flavor when they come from the writer's own experience. They are often not only more vivid and interesting, but also more convincing. Readers have a natural trusting relationship with a writer who's giving them memoirs. Moreover, continuation of the examples builds cumulatively a sort of intimacy in that relationship. We often grow fond of a particular narrator.

UM-C1e   *Synthetic statements*

We have been discussing analysis by partition and by division, a distinction involving a sense that some topics are singular whereas others are plural. Analysis is one very important way of clarifying something, but this "tearing down" is of course not the only way. We come next to efforts to *build* clarity.

The term *synthesis* refers to a combining of elements into a whole. Some kinds of inductions would obviously fit under the heading, but I'm thinking here of concepts ingeniously devised or *contrived*—compounds constructed from a limited set of simple concepts. Perhaps some examples and illustrations will explain my meaning.

(1) *Analogy*

When, in a song, a youth says that his love for a certain maiden is like a flower, he has created a tender little simile. He may go on to develop and extend that simile: like the flower, his love grows larger and stronger every day; like the flower, it is a beautiful thing, and so on. He has now created a full-fledged analogy—a brief comparison of two very unlike things. It's brief because analogies break down rather quickly. There are just too many *differences* involved.

(2) *Comparison (and contrast)*

But when two things are in the *same* class (two trees, two people, two philosophic positions, and so on) a comparison can be strung out almost indefinitely. You can compare Marge with Denise down to the color of their toenails, or their taste in boy friends and booze. Comparison is a common assignment in English classes; the reason is that it's an excellent means of clarifying something. To put an unfamiliar subject into sharp, clear relief, simply compare it with something similar, something well understood by the reader.

The term *compare* technically means to show both similarities and differences. In common usage, however, it is often limited to the similarities. To do a more thorough job with a subject, therefore, we set up a *comparison-and-contrast* paper. There are three types:

(a) The "whole-to-whole" method, applied for example to two politicians, might first describe President Kennedy in full and then President Johnson in full, the Johnson half showing both similarities of and differences between the two men.

(b) The "part-to-part" method might treat the background of each, then their political views, their concepts of government's proper role, their programs, their influence and success in dealing with Congress, their problems, and finally their general contribution.

(c) The "likeness-difference" method ordinarily begins with a set of similarities and then ends with a set of differences. You might, however, wish to stress similarities, in which case you might want to reverse the order.

(3) *Scales and hierarchies*

Based on our faculty to perceive likeness and difference is our capacity to *appraise* everything we experience. We human beings hate chaos, love order; we want a certain niche, a label, a value, for everything we encounter. Products and people and lots of other things are hourly—nay, more often—rated on various scales. In exposition, we commonly seek objectivity and use measurable quantities and qualities in describing the world about us. Some things are heavier than others, costlier than others, more solidly built than others. We have scales for effectiveness, efficiency, permanence, liquidity, fire-resistance—you name it. Once the scales have been established, we can easily sort competing elements into a hierarchy. (This book works informally with several scales in describing the hierarchy of the U.S. social classes.)

Exercises in scale-thinking are valuable insofar as they sharpen our perceptions. They also set up invaluable alternatives to sloppy "either-or" thinking.

(4) *The set of reasons*

The "reasons" paragraph or paper, very common in argument, can be used in exposition, too—if, for instance, you're merely explaining why *someone else* holds a given position. (That makes it, you see, a supposedly objective treatment.)

> The reasons why Morrison despised his son-in-law were manifold.
> One was that Jason's speech was invariably coarse . . .

Reasons can be synthesized out of anything known about the subject. For instance, they can be based on our scale-thinking.

> The party allowed John Martin to lead the way near the crevasse, for he was much taller, stronger, and more experienced than the others. He stood six foot three, slim but well muscled...

A list of reasons can also produce a kind of cause-and-effect paper, one showing the history and dimensions of an issue.

> The city council next month faces a serious problem with the public works budget. Street Supt. A. J. Mallory has reviewed for council members the emergency allocations of recent weeks, necessitated by the washout on Anderson Drive, the cracking of the First Street Bridge, the frost damage on several arterials, the...

(We shall return to the set-of-reasons shortly under the heading "Argument.")

(5) *Definition*

A whole "definition" paper, one given over completely to the task of defining some difficult abstraction like *love*, is potentially the longest and most complicated of all essays. Why? Because it can make use, if the writer wishes, of all the techniques we have so far discussed—narration and description, and any induction, any deduction, any analysis, any comparison, any set of reasons. Such an essay may fill a whole book.

A simple definition paragraph, by contrast, can be just two or three lines long.

These extremes are created by the nature of the subject matter, chiefly, although the situation and audience might also be important factors. In ordinary conversation, we have little trouble; we clarify with a synonym, a phrase, or perhaps a sentence. But there are times when a sentence isn't enough. Permit me, please, to illustrate with a hypothetical problem.

A child or a foreigner inquires about the game called *pool*. (a) You respond with a synonym, "pocket billiards," but that proves to be no help at all. (b) You try a classification: "It's a game played with fifteen hard balls on a felt-covered table that has cushioned edges and six pockets around the edges." A dictionary produces a bit more, but—well, he still looks rather puzzled. (c) You suddenly remember to try naming some *types* of pool. "There's rotation, and black ball, and straight..." But these examples, which sometimes help greatly, are here only increasing his confusion. (d) You have a few minutes before dinner, so you two rush downtown and peek in at a poolhall. You exhibit an example, which of course is of great value in building understanding. (e) After dinner, you have plenty of time—time for the clincher, an "operational definition." You've tried a synonym, a classification, examples, and actual exhibition of an example; but what works when all else fails is the definition put in terms of the *processes* involved:

> The person starting the game plays from any point behind a certain line, called the balk line. His opening shot, or "break," should hit...

Once again, we have "come down the abstraction ladder" to the specific and concrete, and with an operational definition we stay there until understanding is complete.

An extended definition, as we said, can combine many techniques. Suppose

161

you want to elucidate "heroin addiction." After opening with a few horrible *examples*, you might show the *process* from its inception. Your research will give you theories about *causes*; news stories may reveal street crimes and other *effects*. Perhaps you could *describe* a typical addict, and *compare* him with, say, an alcoholic. A scholarly study might be material for a *précis* or some other summary. Or you could consider several addicts and *classify* them according to the social problems they have experienced. . . .

Well, you get the idea. The writing of a good extended definition is a special art form.

(6) Climactic arrangements

We can imagine various situations in which a writer might select certain material he's analyzed and arrange it in special ways.

(a) The "order of interest" might dictate a narrative leading to a climactic moment, or a set of ideas building gradually to the one with most interest.

(b) The "order of familiarity" might require the writer to begin with details that a reader will be comfortable with, and then to move gradually into less familiar territory.

(c) The "order of complexity" takes the reader systematically, slowly, from the simple to the complex.

(7) Miscellaneous combinations

This category is a catch-all for any pattern I've neglected to mention, and for all the combinations that a writer's ingenuity may devise.

If you are overwhelmed by this lengthy list of possible expository patterns, take heart. The instructor has his limits; he can assign and criticize perhaps one set of themes a week. Typical expository assignments are comparison-and-contrast, partition or division (or both), cause-and-effect, and definition papers. Instructors are also fond of descriptive and narrative assignments; narrative exposition is the basis of "process" themes.

Before the term is over your instructor may also try to get from you at least one "argument" paper. We turn to that topic next.

UM-C2 *Argument*

The boundary between exposition and argument is so misted over that it is almost invisible. In a sense, all exposition *is* argument; it says, "Look here, what I'm telling you is true" (*i.e.*, as opposed to some other views of reality). Here, however, we want the term *argument* to mean a forceful appeal to the listener's (or reader's) intellect—an appeal to him to accept a proposition, whether that entails ultimate action or mere silent acquiescence. In L-U Composition we shall consider a related rhetorical form, persuasion, which appeals largely to the emotions and seeks quick responses. But let us confine ourselves now to somewhat less passionate disagreements.

Among the higher social classes, there are stylized debate situations which call for distinctly formal arguments, rather like those of ancient Greece. At one

Ivy League college we might hear this sequence: the proposition or basic premise ("The operation of international law requires the participation of all nations"); the "issue" ("The question is whether this premise dictates the UN's acceptance of renegade country X"); the presentation of inductive, deductive, analytic, or synthetic evidence; and finally the speaker's conclusion. In the tradition of this little drama, it has all been an "objective" search for truth. Elsewhere, say at a prestigious state university, debaters might use a different pattern, one going something like this: the presentation of a "problem" which needs a solution; the speaker's proposed solution; the evidence confirming this position, and finally the refutation of any opposing argument. (The last two parts, incidentally, may be reversed if the speaker feels he can end with a stronger point that way.) There are, of course, opportunities for opponents' rebuttal.

Another ritualized debate pattern is that found in courts of law. There, U-M and L-U attorneys enter an arena to do battle about divorces, torts, patent cases, and so on, with a judge acting as a referee. The winner is often the side with the most ingenuity in presenting evidence, and sometimes this involves us more in persuasion than in argument—especially if a jury is present. Nevertheless, many courtroom disputes are rather interesting, and you may find it cheap entertainment to attend sometime.

> *The law, in its majesty equality, forbids the rich as well as the poor to sleep under bridges, to beg in the streets, and to steal bread.*
> —Anatole France

Still another ritual is sometimes observed by engineers and other technical experts. They are often asked to justify a proposal in terms of specified factors:

a. Feasibility—Will it do the job?
b. Superiority—Will it produce better results than some alternative proposal?
c. Acceptability—Are process difficulties, undesirable side effects, and costs all within acceptable limits? Will safety and health provisions meet approved standards? And so on . . .

Among those of us who are not debaters, lawyers, or engineers, arguments are a good bit less formal. We have opportunities as adults to write Letters to the Editor, for instance, and in college we are regularly invited to express opinions. No one prescribes the exact shape, but a common pattern is the so-called "reasons" paper, just introduced as an expository technique. It is just as useful here.

The "reasons" paper, even an informal one, must be planned with at least as much care as any other type. You should first set up an outline, following the suggestions in UM-C1a. Your proposition may sometimes be a broad generalization, but it is more likely to be a judgment about a rather specific matter: Why the B-1 Bomber Is a White Elephant; The Energy Problem Is Here To Stay; Robert Frost—Our Best Poet; Why We Should Fluoridate Our Water Supply, and so on. After you have phrased both title and thesis statement, arrange your reasons in some reasonable order. Find as many as you can, for it is often true that the more you have, the stronger the argument. Then begin to write, remembering to address yourself to the mind and not the passions.

What you write will be largely expository—facts, dates, a division, a definition—because argument is merely an *extension* of exposition. It is based on exposition and, hence, will be only as detailed and as pure as the underlying expository data. How can you best support your thesis? By selecting carefully from a wealth of possibilities: Sometimes personal *experience* will be appropriate, sometimes historical *research*. For other situations, you may need to report some known *principles* of the physical or social sciences, or some recent *controlled study*. Still others may call for expert testimony on *standards*; remember that many products can be rated on a scale of usefulness, efficiency, cost, durability, or whatever. Quoting a respected expert or *authority* will also aid your cause immeasurably.

In the fields of artistic or literary criticism, standards are not always universally revered or even observed. Nonetheless, evaluations by people of sound experience usually count for something, and usually for much more than the half-baked notions of a tyro. Certainly you can get valuable help from these older writers' critiques.

But in argument we want *your* carefully considered judgment, whether you're a tyro or not. One thought-pattern not very common in exposition is "X is *better than* Y." In argument that pattern may give structure to a very interesting paper.

UM-C3 *Informal documentation*

When we come to L-U Mechanics we shall be dealing with formal documenting techniques, but *right now* we should remind the reader that when he borrows explicit ideas, or exact language, he has a responsibility to acknowledge the debt.

Occasionally this can be a very simple procedure. Suppose you are writing a 500-word theme reviewing a single book. You must figure a way of presenting the publication details. One suggestion is to state early in the text the book's title and the author, and then to stick in an asterisk(*). This signals the reader to look for another asterisk at the bottom of the page, where you'll give him the place of publication, publisher, and publication date.

That done, you can start quoting special words and phrases and perhaps a sentence (but no long passages in a short paper). At the close of each quotation, direct or indirect, simply put the page number in parentheses:

"... am willing to wait" (p. 162). Then he ...

Real *research* to support a position, however, will involve more than one source, and will involve you in formal documentation.

Research is a difficult activity, but it doesn't seem to bother the Upper-Middles; many seem to thrive on it. In fact, the U-M's appear to be somewhat happier in *whatever* they're doing than the classes below them. Whether it's their jobs they like, or the money, or something else, isn't clear; perhaps what they like is their whole life-style. Research people have shown, though, that money seems to be a strong factor. In one 1970 survey, only one-fourth of the lowest income class regarded themselves as "very happy." As the research went into successively higher income classes, the percentage of "very happy" people climbed steadily. It reached almost 50 per cent among the highest identified group (over $15,000), our Upper-Middle Class.[22]

It may be that the cause-and-effect relationship could be turned around. Perhaps happy people are the ones who, being productive, earn promotions and hence higher pay. There's a problem for our U-M logicians to work on.

> *We have no more right to consume happiness without producing it than to consume wealth without producing it.*
> —George Bernard Shaw,
>   *Candida*

A final word: Logical thinking has been stressed in this chapter, appropriately in one dealing with the U-M Class. Of all the characteristics of good writing, logicality seems to be the one typically contributed by the U-M writer. His writing sometimes lacks the vigor of Lower-Middle religious and political tracts, but he compensates with his relative detachment and cool rationality. There is much that we can all learn from him.

The country is governed for the richest, for the corporations, the bankers, the land speculators, and for the exploiters of labor.
—Helen Keller, 1911

CHAPTER 7
LOWER-UPPER LANGUAGE

The last two chapters have been a portrait of the great American middle class, which, the way we have skewed things, accounts for 82.1 per cent of the population. That figure squares with the popular mythology, too; survey after survey testifies that practically all Americans regard themselves as middle class. The L-L and U-L classes together totalled only 17.1 per cent, you remember. That leaves a tiny 0.8 per cent for the household-income category $50,000 and above—the nation's upper class.

Less than one per cent of the population—yet this upper class is so influential in guiding the life of the nation, and in setting the tone of its culture, that it deserves a great deal of attention. To begin, let's note a few random statistics: Two-thirds of the household heads are college-educated and most of them hold a degree. More than 89 per cent assert that they have white-collar jobs, many of them as "managers or administrators." Not surprisingly, the number of working wives plummets in this class to a small fraction of the total.[1] The wife's income clearly isn't needed to maintain the upper-class standard of living. Instead, she plays the role of gracious hostess; upper-class people have a lot of big parties.

At this point we should begin to distinguish the lesser rich, the Lower-Uppers, from the *really* rich, the Upper-Uppers. And since income statistics on this mountain-top are neither readily available nor very helpful, we shall have to use other measuring-sticks—wealth, position, prestige, influence, taste, and sophistication with language. These scales may upset our previous statement that fewer than one per cent of the people enjoy upper-class incomes. We may sometimes be talking about *two* per cent, perhaps—but so what? We've been saying right along that income isn't everything.

The government has difficulty making adequate studies, apparently, in the rarefied atmosphere of these heights. In the Census Bureau's 1973 *Statistical Abstract* we find not much Internal Revenue Service information about upper-class personal wealth, and what's there is out of date. But it will help some. We learn that, as the U.S. population grows, so does the upper class, but sometimes much faster. The number of American millionaires and multi-millionaires (gross estate size) was about 47,000 in 1958, when General Eisenhower was in the Presidency. Four years later, in the administration of Pres. John F. Kennedy, it had grown to 71,000. By 1969, in President Nixon's first term, the number had doubled to 147,000. Of these, about 4,000 had gross 1969 estates of more than $10 million.[2] This smaller group, each person rivalling Croesus, can perhaps be tentatively regarded as Upper-Upper.

167

As to the positions occupied by the Lower-Uppers, we can rely to some extent on common knowledge and on local standards. Let's go back to the "Job Totem Pole" of the previous chapter. We hedged considerably in defining U-M positions by creating a "borderline" category, members of which can be either U-M or L-U. These include doctors, lawyers, and businessmen with annual incomes of only about $35,000 or $40,000. In some areas these would be esteemed as community leaders and Lower-Upper, and especially if they devoted much time and money to the local symphony or a respected charity. Elsewhere, of course, they might be scorned as social climbers.

But, in perhaps every American city, prestige flows generously to the really top-income specialists and to widely known executives. We stand in awe, partly of their capacity to generate income, partly of the ease with which they rise to any occasion. To us they seem masterful in doing always the impressive thing. Does the Acme Company need a new government contract? Mr. Harrison will speak to the governor, or to the senator. Does the art museum need a generous contribution, and some fund-raising letters? Dr. and Mrs. Bates soon have their names listed as "sustaining members" or even "patrons." Does a U.S. Court of Appeals vacancy need filling? Let's talk to Judge Phillips. The Lower-Uppers have a great deal of influence in our society.

The most impressive act the L-U can perform, sometimes, is to construct a large, tasteful home on large, tasteful grounds. Your typical L-U lady or gentleman is a millionaire, or approaching that rank, and hence can afford very professional services to assure himself of quality in his surroundings and furnishings. The same standards often apply to his hunting or skiing lodge, and to his yacht. Also a cut above U-M standards are the private clubs he elects to join.

> *Property is theft.*
> —Pierre Joseph Proudhon

The L-U lady is much admired and envied for her Bill Blass and Valentino gowns and her Cartier jewelry. For her, the *haute couture* world of Paris periodically stages its displays of elegance: fashions by Dior, Cardin, Yves St. Laurent. The L-U lord of the manor, meanwhile, is pictured in the public mind as savoring his Chivas Regal with L-U friends before stepping out back to show them proudly his first Rolls-Royce, a $34,000 Silver Shadow. Its owner has "arrived."

(His more affluent neighbors sometimes scorn the Silver Shadow. They tend to favor some of the earlier Rolls-Royce models—the Phantom I, II, or III—all flawlessly preserved from the Twenties and Thirties. In the very top L-U brackets one may occasionally find a slender, extraordinarily expensive 1914 Silver Ghost touring car. There is clearly a powerful snob appeal in ownership of such an admired antique automobile or "motor car.")

The thing that should fill one with real wonder and respect, though, is the Lower-Upper's management of the nation's language. To be sure, the Upper-Uppers retain effective control through the veto power of their great wealth; but, as a practical matter, the day-to-day decisions about acceptable language content and form are made by highly paid executives in business, industry, and their foundations, and by some rather-well-paid executives in government. Serving the commercial barons a daily diet of ideas are high-income officers of advertising and public relations firms, most or all of them L-U themselves.

I refer, of course, to the people who decide what books, articles, news stories, poems, songs, and short stories are published; what films are created; which television programs are born, and which die; what kind of publicity is given to Incumbent X and what to Candidate Y, and in what amounts; which plays will open on Broadway; which brand of shaver or bathroom cleaner will be advertised during which TV show; which entertainers are bathed in acclaim and which are sentenced to obscurity; what research will be honored and what ignored and starved; what "angle" will be featured in a cigarette company's billboards; whether or not statistics will be used in a government pamphlet, and whether its language will have this tone or that tone; whom to quote in a foundation's annual report, and so on and on, until all major language decisions are made in the councils of the nation.

Against those who rise to object that many of these choices are made by The People through their cash purchases, and that all these executives are merely public servants, I must file a countercharge of naiveté. It is of course true that occasionally executives guess wrong, and that no amount of puffery seems to make the public accept Show X or Cereal Y or Government Policy Z. But most of the time the people are quite passive; they accept what they are given; they want what they are supposed to want, even if this desire didn't even exist a few days before.

No, let no one underestimate the skill and sophistication of the Lower-Upper language executives. In decisions about rhetoric, and about what the lower classes will accept, *usually the L-U's guess right*. That's why they're being paid so well.[3] That's why they are so powerful in our society.

In his own affairs the L-U executive often has much higher standards than those he helps set for the classes below. He is always fashionably dressed, according to fashions he himself dictates, and always jets to the most "in" leisure spots. And in his own use of language he is frequently the most circumspect of men.

L-U GRAMMAR

We are running out of strictly grammatical problems to deal with; they are ordinarily lower- and middle-class. But we might take note again of a pair of upper-class conjunctions: *for* and *yet*.

For is used as a highbrow "since" or "because"—but it is often regarded as an honorary *coordinating* conjunction.

> They gave her a splendid eulogy, *for* she had always provided comfort and aid to the area's artists.

Yet is sometimes used to mean "but" and hence can also be regarded as a coordinating conjunction.

> She knew her duty, *yet* could not tear herself away.

L-U STYLE

The nation's top editors and publishers are Lower-Upper. As arbiters of writing style, they help to give American English its almost incredible richness. Indeed, the models of "educated" writing are all approved first in the editorial rooms of *The New Yorker, Harper's, Atlantic Monthly,* and a few other magazines; of the major book publishing houses; and of a few university publication offices. Let us listen to counsel given there.

Frequently, we find, what these language moguls seem to be saying is that the Principles of Composition—unity, coherence, and effective development—apply not only to the essay and its paragraphs but also to their basic elements, the sentences. Though the lower classes at times regard upper-class writing as ornate and overblown (which no doubt it is at times), the best of it is as beautifully clear and efficient as you could ask. The best of it is informed by high standards of purity and grace.

LU-S1 *Parallelism*

Parallel ideas, say the L-U stylists, should be expressed in parallel grammatical structure, so that *form clarifies content.*

LU-S1a
Create parallel structure for sentence parts meant to be coordinate.

Make an adverb parallel to another, an active verb with another, a prepositional phrase with another, and so forth, whenever you wish to stress their *equal* significance.

> State your case   quietly,
>   politely, and
>   briefly.
> We should   talk to her and
>   reason with her.
> Democracy, said Theodore Parket in 1850, is "a government
>   of all the people,
>   by all the people,
>   for all the people."

Avoid such careless middle-class constructions as the following:

> The cell was only eight feet wide and twelve feet *in length.*
>
> The prisoner was told that he'd been recommended for parole and *to report* to the warden immediately.
>
> Her job was the scheduling of the therapy and *to supervise* the nurses.

For practice, try recasting each of the above in parallel form.

LU-S1b
When it's needed for grace or clarity, repeat a part of an initial construction.

(1) Article:
   The club must elect a vice-president and (a) treasurer.
(2) Preposition:
   We all respect the chairman for his skill but not (for) his ideas.
(3) The sign of the infinitive:
   She was resolved to work hard, to stay at it, and (to) finish the job.
(4) Conjunction:
   She reported that the foundation's cash reserves were growing, that its assets remained firm, and (that) the favorable trend would apparently continue.

LU-S1c

After *correlatives*, make the construction parallel.

MIDDLE CLASS	He was *either* lucky *or* he was very shrewd.
UPPER CLASS	He was *either* lucky *or* very shrewd.
OR	*Either* he was lucky *or* he was very shrewd.
MIDDLE CLASS	They *not only* argued about money *but also* about trivial things.
UPPER CLASS	They argued *not only* about money *but also* about trivial things.

Observe the same principle with the correlatives *neither... nor* and *both... and*. Sometimes *whether... or* formations are similarly parallel, but often the *or* is followed simply by *not*.

I haven't decided *whether* I am going *or* not.

And sometimes, in somewhat less formal usage, the *or not* is dropped entirely.

I haven't decided whether I am going.

This is, in fact, the standard form of many indirect questions: "She asked whether he were all right."

LU-S2 *Subordination*

Frequently a sentence will have two main ideas, or even more; they will therefore be given coordinate rank. But when a sentence has only *one* main idea, the principles of composition all require that it be placed in a main clause, and that all other ideas be demoted to subordinate clauses, phrases, or single words.

LU-S2a

Except in very informal situations, do not join *unequal* ideas with coordinating conjunctions.

IMPRECISE	We had only a little gas *and* we decided to take the bus.
BETTER	*Because* we had only a little gas, we decided to take the bus.

LU-S2b   Avoid *immature* sentence constructions, except for certain special effects.

>We did finger-painting. Then we had cookies and milk. Then we made some paper things. . . .

These are the short bursts we often hear from a child. Or he may string the ideas like a paper chain.

>We did finger-painting, *and* then we had cookies and milk, *and* then we made . . .

A more mature speaker or writer will choose the ideas he wants to emphasize and will subordinate or omit the others.

Occasionally unusual forms like these may have some utility. Staccato bursts, say, can help create a certain mood—for example nervousness.

>The man crouched in the bleak alley, the wind whipping at him. He tried to light a cigarette. Several times he tried. He cursed softly, again and again. Finally he . . .

LU-S2c   Don't coordinate *unrelated* ideas in the same sentence.

NOT CLEARLY   My brother is an excellent gardener *and* is
RELATED   taking night-school botany classes.

Instead, make one idea subordinate to the other.

EITHER   My brother, an excellent gardener, is taking night-school botany classes.
OR   My brother, who's taking night-school botany classes, is an excellent gardener.

(The next sentence, presumably, would establish the relationship of the two ideas.)

LU-S2d   Choose subordinating conjunctions *carefully*.

L-U stylists want connectives to relate one idea to another with great precision. We saw earlier that subordinating conjunctions can set up conditions, concessions, comparisons, and several other adverbial relationships. But they must be used with some caution; fuzzy writing will not meet with L-U approval. Here are some trouble spots:

(1) *While* shouldn't be used if there is danger of ambiguity.

POOR   *While* he was in jail, they were able to talk frequently. (Time intended? or concession?)
BETTER   *When* he . . . (Time)
OR   *Although* he . . . (Concession)

(2) Nor is *while* accepted as a substitute for *and* or *but* or *whereas*.

MIDDLE CLASS   I take cream and sugar, *while* she likes her coffee black. (Use *and* or *but* instead?)
MIDDLE CLASS   The first model had defective parts *while* the second was almost perfect. (Use *but*?)

(3) *As* and *since* also at times create a problem of ambiguity.
    POOR   *As* the hay wagon was starting to roll downhill, everyone jumped off. (Cause meant? or time?)
    BETTER   *Because* the...(Cause)
    OR   *When* the...(Time)

(4) *As* is not accepted as a substitute for *that* or *whether*.
    LOWER CLASS   I don't know *as* I could answer that.

LU-S2e   Avoid *"upside-down" subordination.*

Putting a main idea in a subordinate construction usually creates a mediocre sentence.
    FAULTY   He rowed out there just in time, saving the swimmer's life.
    BETTER   Rowing out there just in time, he saved the swimmer's life.
    FAULTY   I jerked the pole back too vigorously, losing a huge trout.
    BETTER   Because I jerked the pole back too vigorously, I lost a huge trout.

Occasionally, though, such a sentence is idiomatic.
    I had hardly said it when I realized how wrong I was.

LU-S2f   Avoid excessive subordination.

Two problems come to mind here:

(1) Don't *pack* a sentence with subordinate detail; it can reduce the sentence's effectiveness.
    OVERLOADED   The realtors voted at the Thursday meeting, *their regular November luncheon session,* to oppose once again the creation *during the next legislative term* of a state land-use planning board, *an agency proposed often in recent years, each time meeting with the realtors' disapproval.*

(2) Don't create "boxes within boxes."
    AVOID   The voters re-elected Senator Jones, who had written the land-use bill which contained the agency proposal, which angered the realtors, who had organized a campaign to defeat him.

LU-S3 *Variety*

Variation adds spice to life, as an adage says, and the observation applies also to rhetoric. Gracefully varied sentences create paragraphs that are obviously more readable than those with built-in monotony. How to achieve such sentences? There are lots of ways. We've already looked at the choices among conjunctive adverbs and sentence modifiers, for instance, and at the possibility of switching now and then from active-voice verbs to the passive. We should certainly remind the writer to keep varying the length and complexity of his sentences. And here are some more suggestions:

(a) *Vary the sentence openings*. There's no reason why all sentences have to start Subject-Verb. Try some like these, noting subtle differences in meaning or emphasis:
- (1) Participial phrase
  Sitting stiffly on the park bench, an old man fed a flock of pigeons.
- (2) Prepositional phrase
  On the park bench an old man sat stiffly, feeding a flock of pigeons.
- (3) Subordinate clause
  As he sat, stiffly, on the park bench, an old man fed a flock of pigeons.
- (4) Expletive
  There was an old man sitting stiffly on the park bench, feeding a flock of pigeons.
- (5) Coordinating conjunction
  And an old man, feeding a flock of pigeons, sat stiffly on the park bench.
- (6) Adverb
  Stiffly sitting on the park bench, an old man fed a flock of pigeons.
- (7) Inversion
  Feeding a flock of pigeons *was* an old man, sitting stiffly on a park bench.

(b) *Insert parenthetical material*, for instance between subject and verb.
   An old man, *sitting stiffly on the park bench*, fed a flock of pigeons.

Be careful, though, not to move subject and verb too far apart.

See also the discussion of "periodic" sentences in the next section; they too help to provide diversity. Variety, please remember, is not just frosting on the cake but is a basic element of what's earlier been called The Principle of Effective Development. Another basic element is discussed below.

LU-S4 *Emphasis*

L-U stylists urge writers to be sensitive to the various ways that a sentence's important ideas can be stressed. This must be done judiciously, of course, so that no violence is done to a desired naturalness of the expression. We have already discussed some of the ways:

(a) The subordination of lesser ideas;

(b) The use of vivid words, specific and concrete;

(c) Repetition of words and phrases, and

(d) The use of signals (transitional devices) such as *similarly, furthermore,* and *nevertheless*.

But we must go into this matter still further.

(e) *Be economical;* try to avoid smothering the basic thought with an excessive number of words.
> Be economical; don't smother the thought with wordiness.
> Be economical; avoid wordiness.
> Avoid wordiness.

(f) *Create some periodic sentences.*
The so-called "natural" points of emphasis in a thing (a football game, a love affair, an English essay) are ordinarily the beginning and the end. It is often argued that we shouldn't waste these ready-made focus areas by putting trivia there. Now, a "periodic" sentence is one in which the main clause is either at the end of the sentence or is *completed* there. The "loose" sentence has most of its meaning up front, by contrast, and is probably the more common type. But a periodic sentence (like this one), by keeping the reader in suspense until the very end, is often a good bit more emphatic.

> LOOSE   Come see me whenever you're in town!
> PERIODIC Whenever you're in town, come see me!
>
> LOOSE   He should see a doctor tomorrow morning if those pains continue.
> PERIODIC If those pains continue, he should see a doctor tomorrow morning.

(g) When possible, put important words *near the beginning or the end* of the sentence.
The natural points of emphasis, discussed above, should often be reserved for an important idea, and not given over to a mere qualifying phrase or transitional expression. The *end*, especially, should be emphatic. Consider these three structures:

> WEAK   The Indians had been robbed of their fishing rights, *in his opinion*.
> MORE EMPHATIC *In his opinion*, the Indians had been robbed of their fishing rights.
> MOST EMPHATIC The Indians, *in his opinion*, had been robbed of their fishing rights.

It's usually a good idea to follow the third example and put subordinate elements—conjunctive adverbs, sentence modifiers, weak modifying phrases, and so on—somewhere inside the sentence. I say *usually;* don't hesitate to break this rule for variety's sake; but ordinarily keep them away from the *end* of the sentence.

(h) Try using a *climactic order*. Except for comic effects, it's best to avoid anticlimax.

> ANTICLIMACTIC We must decide what to do immediately; the contract's penalty date is the end of next month.
>
> BETTER   The contract's penalty date is the end of next month; we must decide what to do immediately.

ANTICLIMACTIC	His application for club membership was turned down because he had two felony convictions, a somewhat shady business, and a careless appearance.
BETTER	His application was turned down because he had a careless appearance, a somewhat shady business, and two felony convictions.

(i) Try putting an expression *out of its natural order*.
>*Never* did I guess he was married.
>*A more conceited man* I've never seen.

(j) Achieve emphasis with *"balanced" constructions*.

A "balanced" sentence is a distinctly formal, upper-class locution. Used with moderation, it can give emphasis to a restated or, more often, a contrasted element in a sentence. It ordinarily consists of two or more clauses, equal in length and similar or identical in structure.

>It is easy to flatter; it is harder to praise.—Jean Paul Richter
>Chance makes our parents, but choice makes our friends.—Jacques Delille
>I came, I saw, I conquered.—Julius Caesar
>Make all you can, save all you can, give all you can.—John Wesley
>The poor useth entreaties; but the rich answereth roughly.—Proverbs 18:23

A vulgar, ordinary way of thinking, acting, or speaking, implies a low education and a habit of low company.
—Lord Chesterfield
Letters to His Son, 1774

L-U USAGE

Every society has some expressions which, to aliens, are illogical or at least very puzzling. What is the literal sense of *look after, look to, look up* (a friend)? How did we ever develop *set about* or *set in*?

In America, the L-U in the mass media regards himself as guardian of the nation's idioms. He watches continuously the flux of our slang. He passes judgment regularly on new expressions and, being naturally conservative, allows only relatively few to swell the more-or-less permanent ranks. We have noted idioms in each class level's Usage section. And here are more, many with the L-U stamp of approval:

Accompany by, with. She (a person) was *accompanied by* a friend. The offer was *accompanied with* some terms.

Agree in, on, to, with. We *agreed in* principle. We *agreed on* the terms. She *agreed to* the plan. He *agreed with* her.

Angry at, with. She was *angry at* the way I had treated her; she was *angry with* me.

As (So) . . . as. In negative comparisons the upper class often insists upon *so . . . as,* rather than *as . . . as.* See also *So,* p. 178.

LOWER CLASS	He is not *as* tall as me.
MIDDLE CLASS	He is not *as* tall as I am.
UPPER CLASS	He is not *so* tall as I (am).
BUT	He is *as* tall as I.

Blame. The upper classes think "Don't blame it on me" is colloquial. They prefer "Don't blame me for it."

Compare to, with. He compared A *to* X (a dissimilar thing); we compared A *with* B (a similar thing).

Differ about, from, with. We *differ about* political matters. My views *differ from* yours. I *differ with* your opinion.

Different from, than. My tastes are *different from* yours. The room is *different from* what I'd remembered. (Much to the L-U's regret, the middle class sometimes allows *than* when the preposition's object is a clause: "The room is *different than* I'd remembered it.")

Disinterested, Uninterested. Two very different words: the first means "unbiased"; *uninterested* means "indifferent."

Frightened. Approved locutions are *frightened by* and *afraid of.* The form *scared of* is L-M and lower-class.

Handy. The upper class observes that the root here is "hand." A *handy* thing is "easy to handle" or "near at hand" (within a few feet). Don't say "His home is *handy* to his work," and especially if it's really a mile away.

Has got, Have got. The redundant *got* brings a reproach from L-U's.

| LOWER CLASSES | She *has got* a bad cold. |
| HIGHER CLASSES | She *has* a bad cold. |

Identical with, to. With is upper-class; *to* is middle-class. Say "Your coat is almost *identical with* mine."

Last, Latest. Both can mean "most recent." When they can use it gracefully, though, the upper classes prefer *latest,* since *last* often implies "final."

| LOWER CLASSES | The *last* issue of *Newsweek* was interesting. |
| HIGHER CLASSES | The *latest* issue was interesting. |

Literature. Don't use to mean *any* printed matter. If it's a "circular" or a "brochure" or a "handbill," say so.

Lot, Lots. Regarded as colloquial for "many" or "much."

| INFORMAL | *Lots* of us are overweight. |
| | I have *a lot* more free time now. |

Oblivious of, to. Of is upper-class: "He was oblivious of his promises to her." *To* is upper-middle and is used in the general sense of "unaware"—of almost anything. Classes below don't use *oblivious.*

Raise, Bring up, Rear. *Raise* or *bring up*, when used to mean "care for (a child)," is colloquial, say the L-U's. The formal term is *rear*, as in "They *reared* two children," but only the upper classes seem to use it regularly.

So. *So* is very common in middle-class speech, but the upper classes have certain reservations. It is not sanctioned, for instance, as a coordinating conjunction.

    LOWER CLASSES   The earthquake damaged the building, *so* the tenants had to move out.

    HIGHER CLASSES   ... *and so* the tenants had to move out.

    OR   *Because* the earthquake...

In "purpose" clauses *so* is thought a bit too informal.

    LOWER CLASSES   We locked the door *so* we wouldn't be disturbed.

    HIGHER CLASSES   ... *so that* we wouldn't be disturbed.

L-U style-setters also object to the so-called *"feminine" so,* used in the middle class as an intensive.

    MIDDLE CLASS   I was *so* excited.

    L-U CLASS   I was *very* excited.

    U-U CLASS   I was *very much* excited.

Start in to. Thought colloquial for "start to" or "begin to".

The same as. An unapproved substitute for "just as" or "in the same way as."

    L-U CLASS   She handled it *just as* she did all such offers.

        The new boss treats employees *in the same way as* the old one did.

That. Informal when used as an adverb.

    LOWER CLASS   No woman is *that* pretty in the morning.

    HIGHER CLASS   No woman is *so* pretty as that in the morning.

    LOWER CLASS   Who is *that* good?

    HIGHER CLASS   Who is *as* good *as* that?

(See also *All that* in L-M Usage.)

Up. The Lower-Uppers think it beneath them to attach this to certain verbs:

    She *ended* (not *ended up*) the contest in the lead.

    He *settled* (not *settled up*) with the room clerk.

    They then took a vacation to *rest* (not *rest up*).

Up until. Another "lower-class" colloquialism.

    She was healthy *until* (not *up until*) this month.

A final word: In the American idiom certain words are used with gerunds, others with infinitives—*enjoy going* but *like to go, capable of going* but *able to go,* and so forth. These usually cause trouble only for foreigners. Aliens wish we had fewer idioms.

L-U SPELLING

Lower-Uppers are good spellers, generally. This quiz provides some tougher words, just to challenge them a bit.

1. apocalypse
2. apocryphal
3. baroque
4. bouillon
5. boutonniere
6. catechism
7. chlorophyll
8. cinnamon
9. crescendo
10. demagogue
11. demigod
12. fortuitous
13. heterogeneous
14. hieroglyphic
15. larynx
16. moccasin
17. rhinoceros
18. saccharin
19. sapphire
20. schizophrenia
21. scythe
22. thyme
23. vaccination
24. vitiate
25. zephyr

L-U MECHANICS

Lower-Upper book publishers are also the style leaders and authorities in matters pertaining to documented writing.

Documenting the research paper

In the last chapter a few paragraphs were devoted to informal documentation, in the review of a single book. But that, as we said, wasn't real research; the word *research* is reserved for more extensive and more scholarly analyses. *Webster's New World Dictionary* defines it this way: "careful, systematic, patient study and investigation in some field of knowledge, undertaken to establish facts or principles." The results are typically presented in a rather long paper, often laced throughout with bibliographic data.

In your early college years, to be sure, you aren't likely to overturn many established facts or principles. But in collecting and judging and organizing bits of information, you will be serving an important apprenticeship. You will occasionally reach some sound conclusions, and thereby gain confidence as you gain experience. You will come to do "scholarly" work, which the dictionary says shows "much knowledge, accuracy, and critical ability."

An important thing about a research paper is that, aside from common knowledge, you must indicate the exact sources of your information. You have a moral obligation to credit a previous writer for his ground-breaking. Failure to recognize this responsibility results in a serious offense called plagiarism.

LU-M1 *Plagiarism*

You have several obligations, actually, in any college work. You must be scholarly, which implies objectivity and thoroughness, and you must be fair with any sources you borrow from. Many students try a little plagiarism, for various reasons, and often get away with it. But the benefits are not very satisfying. The writer knows that he is a fraud, and he knows, too, that he hasn't gained the rich experience in research which the assignment was supposed to provide. Not only that, but there is great risk. The student planning to plagiarize should be aware that if he is found out he may fail the course, and may even have a grave notation made in his academic records.

If you find you're overwhelmed by an assignment, getting panicky, and considering plagiarism, use your head. See the instructor and tell him the problem; in ten minutes he may be able to start you off, with a lighter heart, on a better path.

LU-M2 *The library's resources*

Your library, with its thousands of volumes, will be a treasure to you almost beyond imagining. Indeed, if it doesn't have the book or pamphlet or magazine you want, a librarian will sometimes go to real effort to get it for you from some other library. (It often pays, incidentally, to be on friendly terms with a librarian or two; they can make helpful suggestions when you're stumped.)

Any library worthy of the name will have available for you a map of the floor plan, showing the location of the card catalog, the reference area and all other departments, and any often-used special resources, such as foreign language tapes or rental typewriters. It will also provide informational pamphlets, telling you about its Dewey decimal (or other) book-classification system, and explaining how to use the all-important card catalog and general periodical indexes, such as the *Readers' Guide to Periodical Literature*. If it's a large library, you will be told how to borrow books from the closed stacks. Finally, there should be access to lists of readily available reference works: both general and specialized periodical indexes, dictionaries, and encyclopedias; atlases and gazetteers; books of quotations; yearbooks of current events; and specialized reference works in biography, mythology, literature, history, music and art, philosophy and religion, science and technology, and the social sciences. There may even be some indexes to bulletins and pamphlets.

Since, as I say, all that information is available to you simply for the asking, I see no purpose in taking up time here in exploring these various resources. Again, get friendly with a librarian.

LU-M3 *Formal documentation*

As you start to plan and collect information for a research paper, you should be aware that you are on a sacred mission—the search for Truth. Now, perhaps that sounds a bit pretentious. Yet research is certainly one of the finest of man's activities, and deserves to be exalted some. It is no task to be taken lightly.

At the same time, there is no sense in being grim about it, either. The search for holy truth has many more delights than most people are aware of. Most of these, strange to tell, are not in the "truth" (which may never be found) but in the *search*. That is to say, there are subtle joys in an active mind as it contemplates its own activity. The construction of a research paper is a *technique* in that search. It is an enforcement of self-discipline, a push along the path. Writing one can be a painful experience, or it can be challenging and entertaining—or both. Ideally, the finished product will be challenging and entertaining to your reader.

You begin the way you begin any essay—by choosing a topic and then narrowing it to something you can handle properly (see L-M Composition). This sharpening of the focus is especially important in research writing, where data and quoted passages can pile up in heaps of alarming size.

Next, you might phrase a very *tentative* thesis statement and make a *preliminary* outline, one which consists chiefly of directions to yourself:
 I. Define my key terms.
 II. Give the historical background.
 III. Sketch out the process of creating a . . .

And so on. Then you set to work in the library. At the end of a book, say, or an encyclopedia article, you find a bibliography—a list of suggested further readings. Or the *Readers' Guide* has a half dozen articles for you. Or the subject cards in the card catalog send you eight ways. And this just scratches the surface. Some of these sources may be *primary* materials (short stories, letters, public-opinion polls, poems, diaries, drawings, etc.). Others will be *secondary* materials—things written *about* what others have done. (As you gain seniority in college, you will probably work more and more with primary sources.)

Unless you happen to enjoy chaos, you'd better start making the collection process as systematic as possible. Here are some suggestions:

a. *For every source you plan to use, make out a bibliography card.*

Suppose you found this entry in the card catalog:

```
917.3      Curti, Merle Eugene, 1897-
C978g      Growth of American thought.    Harper 1943
           xx, 848p illus

              Contents: American adaptation of the European heritage;
           Growth of Americanism; Patrician leadership; Democratic up-
           heaval; Triumph of nationalism in social and political thought;
           Assertion of individualism in a corporate age of applied science;
           Optimism encounters diversion, criticism, and contraction
              Bibliographical note: p755-816


           1 U.S.—Civilization   2 U.S.—Intellectual life   1 Title.      917.3
```

Noting the call number, you locate the book and find that its title needs a couple of alterations. (The book also doesn't use Curti's middle name.) After some reading, you decide to set matters straight on a 3-by-5-inch "bib" card.

SAMPLE BIBLIOGRAPHY CARD

Author's name	Curti, Merle
Title	The Growth of American Thought
Place of publication, publisher's name, date of publication	New York: Harper, 1943
Call number	917.3 C978g

(Be very accurate, please; all but the call number will presumably appear later in your paper's bibliography.)

b. *Take notes on note cards.*

Before you begin your borrowings, you might want to buy some more cards—perhaps 4-by-6 inches to distinguish note cards from bibliography cards, and to allow a bit more space for writing.

Now, picture yourself in the library at 8:30 on a Wednesday night. You've checked the Curti book out again, but let's say you can use it only until 10 p.m., when the library closes. You've already read the book (rather quickly), so you know pretty well what's in it. Perhaps you've narrowed your search area down to one particular chapter. Now your job is to extract as many *useful* bits and pieces as you can in an hour and a half—perhaps all you'll need, so you won't have to consult this book again tomorrow night. As you begin, you should try to guess how each bit will be used.

(1) Occasionally you want not just a writer's facts or opinions; you want his actual words. He's made a controversial statement, say, or maybe he has a certain flair. Therefore, you copy down a *direct* quotation and *put quotation marks around it* so you won't forget, later, that it's exact language. (Omissions, remember, are indicated with ellipsis dots.) Incidentally, direct quotation should ordinarily be used sparingly.

SAMPLE NOTE CARD

"Slug" or topic heading	Mid-century reform movements
Brief identification of source	Curti
Page number	p. 368
Quotation	" 'What is a man born for,' asked Emerson, 'but to be a Reformer . . . ?' "

(2) Much of the time you'll prefer an *indirect* quotation, with many of the words changed (but of course not the meaning). In this case *do not use quotation marks*.

(3) Much of the time you'll settle for even less—just a *paraphrase* of an idea or set of facts. Suppose the original passage went something like this:

> "What is a man born for," asked Emerson, "but to be a Reformer...?" In these words the popular lyceum lecturer from Concord expressed a central tenet in the reform philosophy which inspired men and women in their efforts to reform dress and diet in the interest of universal health, to uproot capital punishment and imprisonment for debt, slavery, intemperance, war, and prostitution, and to agitate for the full rights of women, the humane treatment of the insane and the criminal, and even for the overthrow of such venerable institutions as the family, private property, and the state itself....

This might be your note card:

SAMPLE NOTE CARD

"Slug" — Mid-century reform movements

Source — Curti

Page number — p. 368

Paraphrase — Reforms were sought in diet and dress, and in the treatment of the insane and criminal. There was agitation for women's rights and against capital punishment, debtors' imprisonment, slavery, intemperance, war, prostitution, the family, private property, and even the state itself.

If you're carefully selective, the paraphrase will always be much shorter than the original.

(4) A very common practice is the *combining* of paraphrase with direct or indirect quotation:

SAMPLE NOTE CARD

Mid-century reform movements

Curti

p. 368

There was agitation for reforms of all kinds, "and even for the overthrow of such venerable institutions as the family, private property and the state itself."

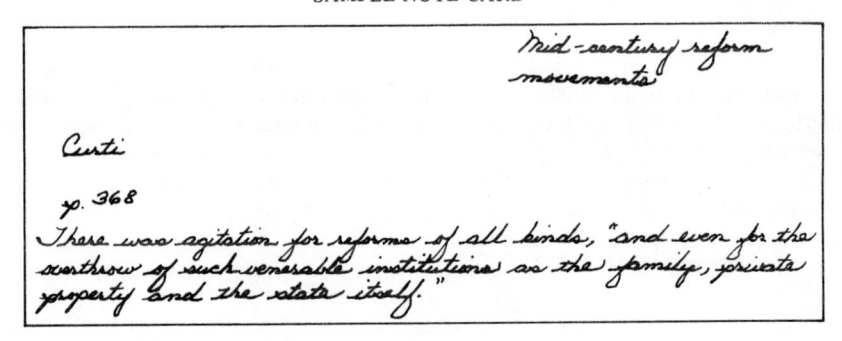

Now, all of these are just raw material, you understand; there's no assurance that any will appear in the paper in just these forms—or at all. But certainly some might, and then we would begin creating our documentation.

c. *Try to decide on your footnotes as you contruct your first draft.*

As soon as you have collected all your material, you should refine your outline and then begin on your first draft. A great advantage of 4-by-6 note cards (over, say, large notebook pages) is that you've been forced to limit yourself to one sub-topic per card. Now, you see, you can shuffle those cards various ways until you have the piles arranged just right on your desk or table.

Think ahead to each footnote as you work with each note card. You have choices, evaluations, to make:

(1) Some of the material will be thrown away; a slight change of your thesis makes it no longer relevant.

(2) Some will be too good to throw out entirely but not quite good enough for the paper's text. You might create a *"See also" footnote*—one in which you merely suggest that the reader can get additional information or corroborating evidence in such-and-such source.

(3) Some material will be good enough as a brief footnote but, again, not good enough for the text of the paper. This kind of note is called an *informational footnote*.

(4) Some will be just right for your paper. Here, as you assign the bibliographic data to a note, you are creating a *source footnote*, by far the most common type.

(5) You can create combinations of these three types of notes. In any variety, remember always to acknowledge all debts, even if you're only paraphrasing.

d. *When constructing a source footnote, follow conventional form and format.*

Your instructor will tell you whether your footnotes should be at the bottom of the pages where the passages occur, or in a list at the end of the paper, and whether they should be single-spaced or double-spaced. (See p. 192 on this matter.) The notes should be numbered consecutively throughout your essay. Study, in various sources, how the reference figure in the text and the corresponding footnote figure are handled. The reference figure is raised above the line; the footnote number usually is also, although some writers place it on the line with a period following it.

The MLA Style Sheet of the Modern Language Association of America is a very popular style guide. Its 1970 second edition recommends use of English substitutes for most of the centuries-old Latin abbreviations, but, since there are also some counter-arguments, your instructor is free to be either modernist or traditional. If he has no preference, *you* have to decide.

Before we look at some footnote models, I have one more last-minute observation. *If* your instructor allows it, you can dispense with a bibliography and, instead, put the publisher's name in the first-use footnotes:

[1]Merle Curti, *The Growth of American Thought* (New York: Harper, 1943), p. 368.

But the following are formed upon the assumption that your paper *will* have a bibliography. The models make various kinds of references. Distinguish each carefully; observe every typographical device, including white space.

FOOTNOTE STYLE

A book, one author:
> [1]Merle Curti, *The Growth of American Thought* (New York, 1943), p. 368.

A book, two or three authors:
> [2]W. Ward Fearnside and William B. Holther, *Fallacy: The Counterfeit of Argument* (Englewood Cliffs, N.J., 1959), p. 131.

A book, four or more authors:
> [3]Wilfred L. Guerin et al., *A Handbook of Critical Approaches to Literature* (New York, 1966), p. 33.

> [*The MLA Style Sheet* inconsistently prefers *et al.* to "and others."]

An edited book:
> [4]Arlin Turner, ed., *Hawthorne as Editor: Selections from His Writings in "The American Magazine of Useful and Entertaining Knowledge"* (University, La., 1941), p. 13.

> [Here Turner is being quoted. If it had been Hawthorne, *his* name would come first and then, following the title, would come the editor, as in the following example. Incidentally, *The MLA Style Sheet* says you may sometimes omit a long subtitle here—if you promise to put it in the bibliography entry.]

A section of a book, with both an author and an editor:
> [5]Walter Blair, "Hawthorne," in *Eight American Authors*, ed. Floyd Stovall (New York, 1963), pp. 121-22.

A volume from a set:
> [6]Vernon Louis Parrington, *Main Currents in American Thought* (New York, 1927), II, 450.

> [The convention is to drop the abbreviation p. (page) whenever a volume number is present.]

A book that's part of a series:
> [7]Mark Van Doren, *Nathaniel Hawthorne*, The American Men of Letters Series (New York, 1949), p. 51.

A revised or later edition of a book:
> [8]Hyatt H. Waggoner, *Hawthorne*, rev. ed. (Cambridge, 1963), pp. 188-89.

An author quoted in another's book:
> [9]Thorstein Veblen, *The Theory of the Leisure Class*, pp. 237-38, quoted by Henry Steele Commager, *The American Mind* (New Haven, 1950), p. 241.

An introduction to a book:
> [10]Leon Howard, intro. to Herman Melville, *Moby Dick: or, The Whale* (New York, 1950), p. vii.

A translated book:
> [11]Alexander Solzhenitsyn, *Cancer Ward*, trans. Nicholas Bethell and David Burg (New York, 1969), p. 25.

A signed encyclopedia article:

        ¹²Joseph Berkson, "Life Expectancy," *Encyclopaedia Britannica*, 1968.
        [Because of the alphabetical arrangement of topics here, you may omit volume and page number.]
An unsigned encyclopedia article:
        ¹³"Natural History," *Encyclopedia Americana*, 1973.
An article in a learned journal or similar periodical, with (Arabic) volume number:
        ¹⁴Neil F. Doubleday, "Hawthorne's Criticism of New England Life," *College English*, 2 (1941), 653.
        [If each issue is paginated separately (or for other good reason), add the number, date, or season.]
An unsigned magazine article:
        ¹⁵"The Ex-Con's Unhappy Lot," *Newsweek*, 25 Feb. 1974, p. 84.
        [Here we omit the volume number, and hence the p. is given.]
An unsigned newspaper article:
        ¹⁶"End to Oil Boycott Expected in a Week," *Seattle Post-Intelligencer*, 5 March 1974, Sec. A, p. 1.
        [Some newspapers paginate by sections, as here.]
The Bible:
        ¹⁷I Chron. 21:8.
        [Other popular styles are 21.8, xxi:8, and xxi.8. Incidentally, don't underscore books of the Bible.]
Also: (1) Use of a play presents a special problem, since you should always follow the citation (William Shakespeare, *Othello*, III.ii.21, the figures indicating act, scene, and line) with reference to the edition you're using. (2) Bulletins, pamphlets, and dissertations generally follow either magazine or book form. (3) Whenever an author's name appears in the text, it can be omitted from the note. In footnoting the emphasis is always on efficiency and streamlining.

    Hawthorne wrote a novel based on his experiences at Brook Farm,¹³ in which he . . .

        ¹³*The Blithedale Romance* (Boston, 1883).

    For examples of various combined footnote forms, see this book's Notes, *passim*. For a translation of *passim*, see the list below.

e. *Learn the shorthand of documenting:*
    Despite efforts to junk the ancient Latin forms, you will still encounter them (sometimes italicized, sometimes not) in older works of scholarship. It's wise for you to know them, along with other signals.

    passim   throughout; in various parts
    [*sic*]   thus (used after textual errors; see UM-P4b)

Some common abbreviations:
    anon.   anonymous
    c.   copyright; *circa*

ca.	*circa* (approximately)
cf.	confer (compare)
ch., chs.	chapter, chapters
ed.	edition; editor, edited by
eds.	editors
e.g.	*exempli gratia* (for example)
esp.	especially
et al.	*et alii* (and others)
f., ff.	the following page(s)
ibid.	*ibidem* (in the same place)
i.e.	*id est* (that is)
l., ll.	line, lines (of a play or poem)
loc. cit.	*loco citato* (in the specific passage cited) (Note: Use of this term is rare.)
ms.	manuscript
n.	note
N.B.	*nota bene* (note well)
n.d.	no date given
n.p.	no place given
op. cit.	*opere citato* (in the work cited)
p., pp.	page, pages
rev.	revised
trans.	translated by, translation, translator
v.	*vide* (see)
vol., vols.	volume, volumes.

Some random remarks: Whenever you use a Latin abbreviation, remember the period, and, if you're not convinced it's Anglicized, underscore it as a foreign term. Capitalize any abbreviation that begins an entry. Be sure, also, to distinguish between *ibid,* and *op. cit. Ibid.* should refer to the immediately preceding footnote. If the second note refers to the same *page,* say just *Ibid.*; otherwise add the new page number.

[1]Merle Curti, *The Growth of American Thought* (New York, 1943), p. 368.
[2]*Ibid.*
[3]*Ibid.,* p. 379.

Curti, *op. cit.,* would be used if some other work intervened.

But, as mentioned earlier, some modern practice is different. Although it has ambiguities, *The MLA Style Sheet* seems to be suggesting that the author's surname (or a shortened title) can be used in either situation.

[4]*Annual Report of the Acme Company* (Lutown, Nev., 1974), p. 15.
[5]*Report.*
[6]*Report,* p. 17.
[7]Richard Harter Fogle, *Hawthorne's Fiction: The Light and the Dark* (Norman, Okla., 1952), p. 192.
[8]*Report,* p. 17.
[9]Curti, p. 379.

If a second work by Professor Curti had been mentioned somewhere, an abbreviated title would be necessary here.
      [9]Curti, *Growth*, p. 379.
f. *Construct a bibliography* (but don't call it that).

You noted, probably, that the typographical style of the note card differed from that of the "bib" card, and that footnote style differed from both. We come now, finally, to the last documenting style you must learn.

First, however, a word about the heading above. Unless you are writing a dissertation, it is probably misleading to call your list of sources a "bibliography." That word carries the suggestion of completeness, exhaustiveness; it implies that you have surveyed the field and have touched nearly all the sources available. Since such an effort would be inappropriate in most undergraduate papers, call your list something like "References Selected" or "Sources Consulted."

Now we shall take those earlier footnotes, alphabetize them by author's surname, and transform each into a "bib entry." Notice some things: (1) This fourth style is strong on periods and white space. (2) Indent five spaces for "hanging indention." (3) In the case of a whole book, we drop off the page numbers. (4) We give a publisher's name (short form) after book titles; note the punctuation.

SAMPLE BIBLIOGRAPHY ENTRIES

Berkson, Joseph. "Life Expectancy." *Encyclopaedia Britannica*, 1968.

Blair, Walter. "Hawthorne," in *Eight American Authors*. Ed. Floyd Stovall. New York: Norton, 1963, pp. 100-52.

Commager, Henry Steele. *The American Mind*. New Haven: Yale Univ. Press, 1950.

Curti, Merle. *The Growth of American Thought*. New York: Harper, 1943.

Doubleday, Neil F. "Hawthorne's Criticism of New England Life." *College English*, 2 (1941), 639-53.

"End to Oil Boycott Expected in a Week." *Seattle Post-Intelligencer*, 5 March 1974, Sec. A, p. 1.

"The Ex-Con's Unhappy Lot." *Newsweek*, 25 Feb. 1974, pp. 84-88.
[Ignore *A*, *An*, and *The* in alphabetizing titles.]

Fearnside, W. Ward, and William B. Holther. *Fallacy: The Counterfeit of Argument*. Englewood Cliffs, N.J.: Prentice-Hall, 1959.

Guerin, Wilfred L., *et al*. *A Handbook of Critical Approaches to Literature*. New York: Harper and Row, 1966.

Howard, Leon. Intro. to Herman Melville, *Moby Dick: or, The Whale*. Modern Library College Editions. New York: Random House, 1950.

"Natural History." *Encyclopedia Americana*, 1973.

Parrington, Vernon Louis. *Main Currents in American Thought*. 3 vols. New York: Harcourt, Brace, 1927.

Solzhenitsyn, Alexander. *Cancer Ward*, trans. Nicholas Bethell and David Burg. New York: Farrar, Strauss and Giroux, 1969.

Turner, Arlin, ed. *Hawthorne as Editor: Selections from His Writings in "The American Magazine of Useful and Entertaining Knowledge."* University, La.: Louisiana State Univ. Press, 1941.

Van Doren, Mark. *Nathaniel Hawthorne*. The American Men of Letters Series. New York: Sloane, 1949.

Waggoner, Hyatt H. *Hawthorne*. Rev. ed. Cambridge: Harvard Univ. Press, 1963.

It's time now to look at a few pages of a specimen paper, along with some comments. First, the title page.

The effect to achieve here is one of dignified balance and symmetry. Type the title in capitals in the upper third of the page.

A variant form sometimes may begin:
        Submitted in partial fulfillment of the requirements of
                           English 410

(The instructor's name is also occasionally found on this page.)

HAWTHORNE AND REFORMERS

by
John Q. Student

English 410
Section B

Blank College
Dec. 15, 1974

If this were a doctoral dissertation, the title page would be followed by a preface and a table of contents.

The topic outline seems orderly. The thesis, a generalization, is to be supported by examples and illustrations.

Before we turn to the text itself, we should reach an understanding about two related format matters: the placement of the footnotes and their spacing. *The MLA Style Sheet* argues for single-spacing at the bottom of the several pages for very long theses and dissertations, but for *double*-spacing in a list *at the end* for most undergraduate term papers (and materials for publication). Now, I suspect this is a matter in which your instructor's preference is likely to be controlling. (My own is to have students footnote page by page in one paper, but all-in-a-heap in another. In *both* cases I prefer single-spacing.) This excerpt from a specimen paper shows the page-by-page technique.

Spacing in the bibliography, incidentally, will also follow your instructor's dictates. *(The MLA Style Sheet* again chooses double-spaced entries.)

A couple of reminders to all typists: leave ample margins on all four sides, and leave two spaces after periods, one after commas.

Outline

Thesis: Nathaniel Hawthorne had some mild sympathy with the spirit of 19th C. reformism, but none whatsoever with its more militant practitioners.

I. Response to farm cooperative movement
    A. Worked several months at Brook Farm
    B. Left because of "errors" there

II. Reaction to women's rights agitation
    A. Respected the principle
        1. Admired his characters Hester and Zenobia
        2. Favored a "moderate" feminist position
    B. Rejected militancy

III. Views of other causes
    A. Honored "genuine benefactors"
    B. Scorned various kinds of extremists

Don't number the first page.

With a title page, a title here is optional—but seems unnecessary.

Remember that all insertions of direct quotation into your own sentence must be grammatically smooth.

Raise the reference figure by half a space.

Credit the source of a paraphrased passage.

The introduction is drawing to a close. Here comes the outline's thesis statement, almost verbatim.

Separate the text from the notes by *triple*-spacing or more. (Never *crowd* a page.) Some people like a line, long or short, separating the two areas.

Footnote 1 refers to material being quoted by the author of a magazine article. Remember that when a volume number is present the *p.* (page) isn't.
Footnote 2 shows the style for the first reference ("first use") to a book.

HAWTHORNE AND REFORMERS

In the middle of the last century, the United States was swept by a fever for uplift and moral improvement. Some of the age's activists displayed almost unbridled zeal. In 1840, for example, an observer described a disorderly Convention of Friends of Universal Reform as "madmen, madwomen, men with beards, Dunkers, Muggletonians, Come-outers, Groaners, Agrarians, Seventh-Day Baptists, Quakers, Abolitionists, Calvinists, Unitarians, and Philosophers."[1] Throughout much of the nation, these worthies excitedly sought reforms in diet and dress, and in the treatment of the insane and criminal; there was agitation for women's rights and against capital punishment, debtors' imprisonment, slavery, intemperance, war, prostitution, the family, private property, and even the state itself.[2]

Against the backdrop of this frenetic activity, it is interesting to watch the reaction of some noted contemporaries. One of these, the writer Nathaniel Hawthorne, developed a complex set of attitudes that warrants some attention. It becomes clear that Hawthorne had some mild sympathy with the spirit of 19th Century reformism, but none whatsoever with its more militant practitioners.

[1] Ralph Waldo Emerson, quoted by Neil F. Doubleday, "Hawthorne's Satirical Allegory," *College English*, 3 (1942), 333.

[2] Merle Curti, *The Growth of American Thought* (New York, 1943), p. 368.

You begin numbering on this page. Put the Arabic number 2 either in the center or in the right corner.

The paper's "body" is off to a fast start in this paragraph; its first sentence purports to summarize a whole book!

Some of this doesn't really require documenting. It's "common knowledge" that his Brook Farm stay was brief and that the older Hawthorne was politically rather conservative.

This is a rather long passage to be quoted verbatim. Mr. Student apparently felt it was very important. See again "blocked" quotations, UM-P5c.

The quotation of the "protagonist" clearly takes us into the novel itself.

Footnote 3 shows the style used in documenting the comments of a book's editor. The *passim* reference here is not very helpful.

In Footnote 4, Editor Turner suddenly becomes Author Turner. Use just his surname, since the rule is to repeat as little as possible.

Footnote 5 is another citation of a periodical.

Footnote 6 doesn't need the author's name, since it's in the text above.

As early as 1836, while editing a popular magazine, Hawthorne found reasons to speak kindly of the reformist mood of the intelligentsia.[3] That mood was to affect him, too, and send him in 1841 to the utopian cooperative Brook Farm with at least "an open mind, if not indeed with enthusiasm..."[4] Within a few months, however, he backed away from all such experiments. Ten years later he wrote a novel stemming from his farm experience—*The Blithedale Romance*—and in it, says a critic, he focused upon four "characteristic errors" of socialistic reformers:

> (1) Excessive reliance upon changing the external pattern of society as a means of securing greater justice and happiness to men.
>
> (2) Visionary and impractical theories about what is possible and desirable in human association, theories not based upon the reality and variety of human nature and human events.
>
> (3) Exaggerated notions of human wisdom and force, with too little submission to the slow workings of Providence.
>
> (4) Destructive irreverence for old institutions and traditions accommodated to mankind through long ages.[5]

Hawthorne's complicated protagonist, Coverdale, says, "I feel that we had struck upon what ought to be a truth."[6] But soon comes a line of complete and heartbroken disillusionment: "As regards human progress... let them believe in it who can."[7]

[3]Arlin Turner, ed., *Hawthorne as Editor: Selections from His Writings in "The American Magazine of Useful and Entertaining Knowledge"* (University, La., 1941), *passim*.

[4]Turner, "Hawthorne and Reform," *New England Quarterly*, 15 (Dec. 1942), 703.

[5]Darrell Abel, "Hawthorne's Skepticism about Social Reform: With Special Reference to *The Blithedale Romance*," *University of Kansas City Review*, 19 (Spring, 1953), 181.

[6]*The Blithedale Romance* (Boston, 1883), p. 597.

This paragraph begins by promising a somewhat deeper examination of *Blithedale*. The blocked quotation is in quotation marks because Hawthorne is quoting his own character.

Footnote 7 is the modern way of saying *Ibid.*, and it's useful when the parent footnote is not on the same page. Or you might say *Blithedale*.

Footnote 8 is a variant form of the source footnote. It moves slightly in the direction of the "informational" note, examples of which are to be found at the book's end.

Footnote 8 has intervened between two outbursts from Coverdale. In the older tradition Footnote 9 would read:

[9]Hawthorne, *op. cit.*, p. 332.

Another critic, Hyatt Waggoner, argues persuasively that *Blithedale* is an underrated book,[8] and perhaps we should spend some time with it. There are parts which almost certainly illustrate the novelist's own tangled emotions and, no doubt, his attitudes toward the reform movements of his day. For example, this impassioned statement by Coverdale:

> "Whatever else I may repent of... let it be reckoned neither among my sins nor follies that I once had faith and force enough to form generous hopes of the world's destiny,—yes!—and to do what in me lay for their accomplishment..."[9]

And in another spot Coverdale...

---

[7]Hawthorne.

[8]Hyatt H. Waggoner, *Hawthorne*, rev. ed. (Cambridge, 1963). See Ch. 7 and esp. pp. 188-89 and 206-08.

[9]Hawthorne, p. 332.

But these, and the Notes at the back of this book, give us perhaps enough footnoting illustrations. Let's call a halt here and skip to the paper's bibliographic entries.

This bibliography page illustrates the format known as "hanging" indention.

In the Abel entry, Vol. 19's inclusion tells us to exclude the *pp.* (pages). The page-span of the article is given.

In the Blair entry the word "in" is not mandatory—but use it whenever the writer might be construed as author of the *whole* book. Usage differs in regard to the inclusion of page numbers here; when the entry focuses on the book itself, they are always dropped.

In the second Doubleday entry and elsewhere, the lines serve in place of ditto marks.

REFERENCES CONSULTED

Abel, Darrel. "Hawthorne's Skepticism about Social Reform: With Special Reference to *The Blithedale Romance.*" *Univ. of Kansas City Review,* 19 (Spring 1953), 181-88.

Blair, Walter. "Hawthorne," in *Eight American Authors.* Ed. Floyd Stovall. New York: Norton, 1963, pp. 100-52.

Cargill, Oscar. "Nemesis and Nathaniel Hawthorne." *PMLA,* 52 (Sept. 1937), 848-62.

Curti, Merle. *The Growth of American Thought.* New York: Harper, 1943.

Doubleday, Neil F. "Hawthorne's Criticism of New England Life." *College English,* 2 (1941), 639-53.

────── "Hawthorne's Satirical Allegory." *College English,* 3 (1942), 325-37.

Fogle, Richard Harter. *Hawthorne's Fiction: The Light and the Dark.* Norman, Okla.: Univ. of Oklahoma Press, 1952.

Hawthorne, Nathaniel. *The Blithedale Romance.* This and the following Hawthorne references are to the Riverside Edition. Boston: Houghton, Mifflin, 1883.

────── *Mosses from an Old Manse.*

────── *Passages from the American Note-Books.*

────── *Tales, Sketches, and Other Papers.*

────── *Twice-Told Tales.*

Matthiessen, F. O. *American Renaissance.* New York: Oxford Univ. Press, 1941.

Parrington, Vernon Louis. *Main Currents in American Thought.* 3 vols. New York: Harcourt, Brace, 1927.

Turner, Arlin. "Hawthorne and Reform." *New England Quarterly,* 15 (Dec. 1942), 700-14.

──────, ed. *Hawthorne as Editor: Selections from His Writings in "The American Magazine of Useful and Entertaining Knowledge."* University, La.: Louisiana State Univ. Press, 1941.

Van Doren, Mark. *Nathaniel Hawthorne.* The American Men of Letters Series. New York: Sloane, 1949.

Waggoner, Hyatt H. *Hawthorne.* Rev. ed. Cambridge: Harvard Univ. Press, 1963.

L-U PROPAGANDA ANALYSIS

The heads of the top advertising agencies and public-relations firms, of radio and television networks, daily newspapers, magazines, and many other mass-communication enterprises—all or most of these are Lower-Uppers. All are in business to influence us in one way or another. All are word-manipulators.

The old church-Latin word *propaganda*, which used to refer simply to the indoctrination of the masses, in this century has taken on a derogatory sense, one which suggests deception or distortion. But let's be fair; sometimes L-U (or other) propaganda is not deliberately deceptive. Occasionally it's not deceptive at all; occasionally we approve of both its aims and its methods, as in the case of cool, low-key efforts at fund-raising for the Girl Scouts, say, or the local art museum. The Lower-Uppers are prime movers in many such drives.

We should probably regard propaganda as a neutral term, and then qualify it as "good" or "bad"—not on the basis of its effectiveness, please, but rather on a moral scale. Let us call it "good" propaganda when (1) its message is truth *and* (2) its means are commendable *(i.e.,* its appeal is primarily to the intellect). Let's call it "bad" propaganda when its means are emotional and misleading, despite the truth of its statement—*or*, whatever the means may be, when the message is clearly false or dishonorable. Again, "good" propaganda must have truth *and* "good" means.

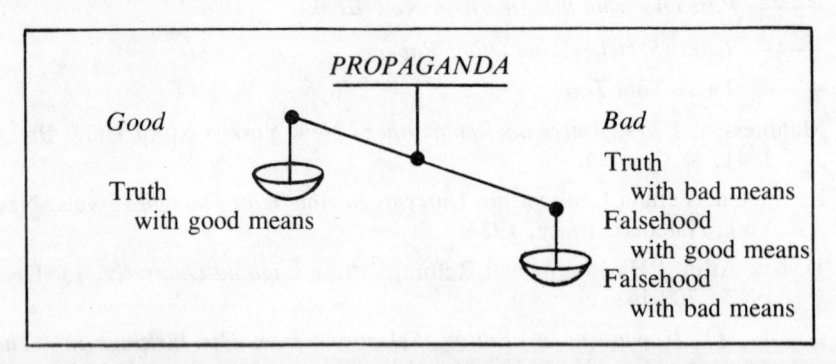

```
                    PROPAGANDA
      Good                              Bad
                                        Truth
      Truth                             with bad means
      with good means                   Falsehood
                                        with good means
                                        Falsehood
                                        with bad means
```

Now, that cuts good propaganda down to a small fraction of the total, as almost anyone can testify. But why should there be such an imbalance? Why are we bombarded with so much bad propaganda? Well, one answer is that gullible masses present a fine market. Another part of the reason is that our *means* can go wrong easily, quickly, and sometimes imperceptibly. The easiest thing in our lives, perhaps, is to fall into a fallacy.

The terms "fallacy" and *non sequitur* ("it does not follow") can be used to identify almost any mistaken idea or faulty reasoning. Often, however, they refer specifically to errors in inductive or deductive logic. Back in UM-C1, perhaps you recall, we illustrated four kinds of statements—inductive, deductive, analytic, and synthetic. We should briefly review some of that material, noting how effortlessly we stumble.

LU-PA1   *Inductive errors*

a. *Faulty classification*

Suppose you are classifying sorority houses (by size? by number of attractive members?), or cars (by price? by their gas-consumption rate?), or aircraft (by function? by number of engines? by type of engines?), or some other cluster of items. Your classifying of your materials may go wrong if you fail to observe some time-tested rules:

(1) Be sure your classes and sub-classes are clearly defined; we want no slippery, shadowy, borderline cases.

(2) Be exhaustive; account for all possible bits of the materials you're studying before getting deep into an action program, such as propaganda.

(3) Be "exclusive"; don't allow any careless overlapping of your classes. Don't group together housewives *and* mothers.

b. *Faulty causal hypotheses*

One error under this heading has a fancy Latin title: *post hoc ergo propter hoc* ("After this, therefore *because* of this"). The *post hoc* fallacy occurs whenever we assume that A was the cause of B simply because A came first. People used to believe that *because* a black cat crossed their path yesterday their bad luck came today. But even sophisticated people blunder into exactly this same kind of mistake. Ask yourself: Is there really a *necessary* causal relation?

Other related cause-and-effect fallacies were hinted at back in UM-C1: any unwillingness to wait for slow, painstaking testing procedures, or perhaps the simplistic thinking that attributes an effect, or set of effects, to just one cause. Back in the depression of the Thirties, a small native fascist group called the Silver Shirts went around telling everyone they met that "the cause" of the crisis was that "Jewish bankers" had got control of Wall Street. The facts were that non-Jewish bankers were as powerful as ever—but powerless, nonetheless, to halt the financial catastrophe. The depression proved not simple but complex, in both its causes and its resistance to ameliorative efforts.

c. *Faulty generalizations*

We might set up two categories here: (1) errors due to *haste* and (2) those due to *blindness*. The first kind, the hasty generalizations, consist of jumping from a very few particulars to a general conclusion. Statistical savants know a few things about the sufficiency of the "sample"; expert pollsters know the proper ratio of sample to "population." But if you poll a few friends and then announce a sweeping generalization—well, you may be proved quite wrong.

Those of the second type usually take longer to construct but are just as shaky; their foundations are flawed because they, too, are unrepresentative of the whole group. A classic example of distorted generalization occurred in 1936 when the magazine *Literary Digest* conducted a telephone poll and, at its completion, predicted the election of Alfred Landon over Franklin Roosevelt. Can you tell already what went wrong? Well, here's some help. In 1936, as we just said, the nation was deep in an economic depression. In a slump, of course, everyone but the Upper-Upper begins to lose the little luxuries he's held dear. If we're L-U, perhaps we buy a less expensive fur coat than we'd planned. If we're down some, U-L or even L-M, we do without telephone service; buying groceries is more important. What the poll revealed, therefore, was that U-M and upper-class telephone owners were predominantly Republican. Roosevelt, the Democrat, won a landslide victory. The poll hadn't reckoned with *suppressed* negative evidence. It had had a blind spot.

Another pernicious kind of blindness, and hence distortion, is *stereotyping*, an illogical process in which all kinds of people are yoked together and thought of as a unit. (The word was originally only a printer's term, referring to the casting of many different metal characters in a single mold.) Somehow the negative evidence of individual differences gets suppressed; then, on the silly basis of only a few particular cases, a generalization is made that *all* in the group have such-and-such a characteristic. Usually the generalization is unflattering—but any thoughtful person knows that we can't speak very sensibly about the whole class of Frenchmen, or blacks, or Jews, or Republicans. The stereotyper, once again, has a blind spot.

LU-PA2   *Deductive errors*

a. *Trouble with categorical syllogisms*

As we said in the last chapter, you get into a heap o' trouble whenever you violate any of six rules for running these little logic machines. (Please review if you've forgotten them.) Or perhaps trouble happens because one hasn't tried to express exactly the full formal syllogism. Suppose someone says, "Why, of course he's guilty. The grand jury indicted him, didn't it?" What is meant here is something like this:

(All indicted persons are guilty.)
"Mr. X is indicted . . .
"Therefore Mr. X is guilty."

The problem clearly lies in the suppressed major premise. An indictment is a *charge*, not a finding of guilt. Obviously not every indicted person will be found guilty—which, if he'd thought for a moment, our friend would have realized. Our experience is full of such abbreviated syllogisms, called "enthymemes." Very often, expressing the full syllogism is a useful technique in propaganda analysis. (See also "Circular Reasoning," below.)

b. *Trouble with disjunctive syllogisms*

The so-called "either-or" fallacy consists of seeing only polar opposites, instead of a more realistic and more common spectrum of intermediate possibilities.

EXAMPLE:	Either we merge with the XYZ Company or we might as well fold up.
COMMENT:	Maybe coexistence is possible.
EXAMPLE:	Either he votes with the party's executive committee or he's a pawn of the opposition.
COMMENT:	And all good guys wear white hats?

LU-PA3 *Analytic errors*

Various possibilities for error in analysis were touched upon in the last chapter. But, since a primary purpose of analytic work is to *clarify* something, let's add a few comments here about unnecessary vagueness.

In either classifying things into species and larger classes, or in dividing them back down again into species, it is of the utmost importance that our categories be crisp and neat. Scientists take great pains in this, but there is a significant effort showing, too, in commercial contracts and in many laws. Often contracts and penal codes will stipulate precisely the *sufficient* and *necessary conditions* for the valid use of a word; they will say that an X is a Y *if and only if* such-and-such is the case. ("Sufficient" condition A will cause B, but C might also; but *only* with "necessary" condition X will Y perform. Only when it has gasoline will my car run—although the presence of gas is not a *sufficient* condition, since the car also needs spark plugs, a battery, and so on. *Absence* of gas would be a sufficient condition for the engine to sputter into silence.)

Sometimes the law is beautifully clear about its conditions, but occasionally it is not. Let's look at two cases. Suppose a man is charged with burglary in a state where "burglary" requires the prosecution to prove that "the accused did in fact:

1. break and enter
2. the dwelling of another
3. in the nighttime
4. with intent to commit a felony ..."[4]

The law also defines carefully each of those phrases. The result is maximum clarity.

But consider this example, based on the 1921 case of *United States vs. L. Cohen Grocery Co.:*

> A grocery company was indicted under a statute making it unlawful to charge "unjust or unreasonable" prices. The attorneys for the defendant argued that the statute violated the constitutional provision, "In all criminal prosecutions, the accused shall ... be informed of the nature and cause of the accusation." The court upheld the defendant's contention since the term "unjust and unreasonable" did not reduce to clearcut acts so that an individual would know in every case whether or not his contemplated act would be a violation of the law....[5]

Similar findings have been handed down in recent years in vagrancy, obscenity, and flag-desecration cases. One of our civil liberties is the right to protection against vague descriptions of crime. But of course we also need protection against vagueness in other corners of our daily lives.

LU-PA4 *Synthetic errors*

a. *Faulty analogy*

In the last chapter we noted that, since an analogy compares two *unlike* things, it's bound to break down rather quickly. Occasionally an inspired analogy can perform a service by illuminating something hitherto very murky. But faulty analogy consists in pushing the comparison too far, and in suppressing the differences between the two items or events. It therefore must be deemed a disservice.

In courts of law, arguments frequently develop over whether a matter falls under a "precedent"; that is, whether it's analogous to some previously decided matter. Sometimes it is; sometimes it only seems so. Courts also often decide a statute's meaning by determining whether a current situation is analogous to the situation with which the statute was dealing.[6] Again, sometimes yes, sometimes no. Be very wary.

Be especially careful about strained figurative analogies, which can be especially deceptive. Consider all the political cartoons you've seen; how many of them have been based on really sound analogies? Don't most of them make rather shabby appeals, based on our feelings about horses, bears, knights, and dozens of other bits of largely irrelevant imagery?

b. *Spurious reasons*

We humans seem to love *rationalizations*, which a dictionary defines as the devising of "superficially rational, or plausible, explanations or excuses for (one's acts, beliefs, desires, etc.), usually without being aware that these are not the real motives."[7] In other words, they aren't efforts to deceive others so much as to deceive *ourselves*. We don't like to think of ourselves as capable of weak, petty, dishonest motives, so we paint over the ugliness with bright new colors. That protects the psyche against possibly dangerous shock.

We are also much given to quick, emotional, subjective reactions to our experience. The following diagram says some things about our gullibility, our wishful thinking, our prejudices (pre-judgings):

THE LADDER OF EVIDENCE

Fourth-hand account	"Have you heard? Jones and Mrs. Simpson are having an affair."
Third-hand account	"Jones was seen having a drink with Mrs. Simpson the other day."
Second-hand account	"Jones was seen with Mrs. Simpson yesterday."
First-hand account	"I saw Jones talking to Mrs. Simpson today."
Direct experience	("There's Jones over there talking to Mrs. Simpson.")

What inferences can we draw from such experience with evidence and language? Well, we can say that it is easy indeed for evidence to become polluted, and that there seems to be more pollution the farther we are removed from direct, immediate experience.

Let us set up, therefore, some criteria for truly sound testimony. Ideally it should be:

—— Objective, or as nearly so as possible
—— First-hand
—— Up-to-date (recent; not stale or superseded)
—— Authoritative

As to that fourth requirement, let us say that we would like our source to be (1) personally reliable (not careless or morally weak, or physically incapable of being a good witness) and (2) qualified as expert in the situation. In the case of technical testimony, he or she should be fully identified, not just a ghostly "leading scientist" or whatever. He should ordinarily have clear professional standing; if he does not, he should have a helluva fine case. An example might be that of the impartial eye-witness.

If we could all insist upon these criteria being met, and could somehow curb our tendency to rationalize, we could avoid many of our potentially perilous illusions.

But if we human beings, L-L to U-U, are capable of gross self-deception, we are also capable of the deception of others. Witness these kinds of attempts to bolster arguments with "reasons," all of them more or less fraudulent.

(1) *Non-authoritative testimonials*

Consider the ads and television commercials critically. Does the ballplayer know about nutritious elements in breakfast food? Does the stunning actress understand a toothpaste's chemical analysis? Really?

(2) *Faulty appeals to authority*

An example in this category might be the quotation of an out-of-date expert—such as the allusions to President Washington's famous 18th C. "farewell" speech urging that we stay clear of "entangling foreign alliances." George's admonition seems irrelevant, or perhaps even dangerously anarchistic, in an interdependent world.

(3) *The appeal to tradition*

Often a long-standing practice is cited as a *reason* for its continuance. There should be better reasons than mere longevity.

(4) *The "bandwagon" appeal*

Our junk mail entreats us to do something partly because large numbers of our fellow citizens, and especially those in the upper ranks, are doing it. We are impressed by the roster of dignitaries adding their prestige to a form letter. In subtle ways we are invited to "get on the bandwagon." Now, evidence of a program's acceptance by *experts* may in fact be good propaganda, but we should have lots of such evidence.

(5) *Emotional attacks on groups*

The so-called *ad populum* ("to the people") propaganda devices are efforts to arouse our group prejudices—our racial, political, religious, class, and other hatreds. Among the most skilled in employment of these techniques are the "super-patriots" on the far right; their shabby counterparts on the far left, by contrast, have little access to the mass media and seem weak, ineffectual, and frustrated. The anti-capitalist arguments on the left, of course, are often as emotional as the massive pro-capitalist counter-attack.

(A classic illustration of an *ad populum* appeal is Mark Antony's funeral oration in Shakespeare's tragedy *Julius Caesar*. If you haven't read a good bit of Shakespeare by now, including *Caesar*, you're not quite civilized yet and your link with the higher classes is tenuous. Please see to this matter immediately.)

A variant of this technique is sometimes called "damning the source." Suppose an obviously biased group proposes a change in public policy: the milk industry suggests new dairy price supports, a giant conglomerate like I.T.T. wants changes in our antitrust policies, the lumbermen want to cut more federal forest logs, and so forth. Or suppose the suggestion comes from someone whose politics we generally oppose. Now, if we automatically reject such a proposal as too tainted to be considered, we may deprive ourselves of a good idea. At least it's possible.

(6) *Emotional attacks on an individual*

Personal abuse is referred to as a "smear" attack. More elegantly it is called an *ad hominem* appeal—literally "to the man," but designating an attack on one's opponent instead of on the *subject* under discussion.

Consider a school-board election in which leaflets were distributed pointing out that one David Sprague was a member of the American Civil Liberties Union, a group which has defended the constitutional rights of murderers, atheists, Communists, U.S. Nazis, Teamsters, Republicans, and many others. The ACLU is the target of perennial abuse from the Far Right because some of its defendants have been Marxists—which of course is a stupid argument, as a (conservative) newspaper once pointed out.

> Last September ... we reserved our contempt for those who prate Americanism but are "so engrossed in monitoring the prayers and the patriotism of others as to lose track themselves of what America is all about." This policy stands.
>
> The growing habit of smearing the ACLU and besmirching the reputations of all who are associated with it is a smokescreen ... [8]

Mr. Sprague, incidentally, was beaten badly in the election. Smears are often effective political ploys. Related techniques (used against both individuals and groups) are rumor-mongering, innuendoes, whisper campaigns, and name-calling. This last kind, an emotional outburst, makes explicit what a smear usually only implies.

> Those who have attacked the loyalty-oath provisions of the federal student-loan program are a bunch of Commies!

The upper-class president of Harvard? The upper-class president of Yale? Heads of many other reputable institutions?

c. *Other propaganda techniques*

In our syntheses of bits and pieces into an argument, we are typically careless of the quality of those pieces or the soundness of the combination. At times actual dishonesty enters in, as we have seen. Many more shoddy techniques can be identified by propaganda analysts, but let's content ourselves with just a few.

(1) *The glittering generality*

Opposite all the snarls mentioned above we should put the purrs of this technique: all the press-agents' puffery of commerce, politics, the religious establishment, educational and other governmental bureaucracies, and many other areas of our American lives. The terms used, all undefined, have a sweet ring to them.

> The senator, as you know, stands for *individual freedom*.
>
> Our gasoline gives your engine more *starting power*.
>
> *Integrity* in *service* to the public has always been our aim.
>
> Our plant uses the most *modern* devices to insure *cleanliness* and *efficiency*.

(2) *The transfer device*

If Mr. Upper-Upper names his automobile line or his chain of banks "Lincoln" or "Ben Franklin," he is borrowing some of the glitter and prestige of another. An intelligent customer will not be dazzled.

(3) *Circular reasoning*

"Arguing in a circle" and "begging the question" ask an audience to stop thinking, or to assume as true something which the speaker avoids proving. If one moves fast enough, they often work.

> We love Munchies because they're our favorite cereal.

The reason for X is X?

> Should poisonous sodium fluoride be deliberately poured into our water supply? Vote *NO*!

The word "poisonous" here has poisoned the discussion.

(4) *The "red herring" device*

Here we could cite examples of issues raised principally to distract us from *other* issues. A "herring" has been drawn across the trail, to fool those who have been following a scent.

A variant of the above occurs when we "point to another wrong." When under attack, we often sweat and squirm and, finding no good defense, we lash out at our opponents for *their* faults.

To repeat: There are many more techniques of "bad" propaganda, but these are representative examples. With so many devices at their elbows, the nation's well-financed propagandists pose a constant threat to our liberties, and of course to our pocketbooks. We are exposed to a great deal of propaganda daily. It's a lucky day when some of it is good propaganda.

L-U COMPOSITION

After all that has just been related about the baneful effects of letting our emotions overcome our reason, the following discussion may at first seem like double-talk. But stick it out, please.

Persuasion

Many authorities say that there are important differences between argument and persuasion, and that both forms have legitimate roles. One distinction made is that argument is aimed at the intellect and persuasion at the emotions—but this is not precisely accurate. Persuasion may be aimed at both the emotions and the intellect, if that is thought the most effective tactic, the path to victory.

This passion for winning has had a long history, as John M. Wasson reminds us. "Just as the ancestor of argument was the deliberative oration of the Athenian Senate, so the forefather of persuasion was the forensic oration of Athenian law courts..."[9] The defense lawyer's object was to move the assembly to *action*—a vote of acquittal for his client. Today, too, the intent in argument often is simply to change or reinforce beliefs, whereas persuasion's aim is always to move us to *act* in some specific way.

Since the average person is frequently inhibited—by low income, low energy, apathy, etc.—it is often impossible to get him to move with reason alone. This is where persuasion comes in. Advertisers link logic to various kinds of almost sure-fire emotional appeals; these will involve anything desirable —health for oneself and family, personal attractiveness, sexual gratification, the enhancement of one's "image" or class rank, and so on and on. Politicians link logic to concepts of "national honor," "law and order," racial supremacy, and many other fuzzily abstract but powerful ideas. Religionists similarly link logic with "God's will" and personal "salvation." And, if the writer or speaker is sufficiently skilled in rhetoric, it may work like a charm.

"The ideal persuasion, certainly, would not be deliberately illogical," says Wasson, "but it would be much less likely than argument to encourage free and impartial discussion of the problem at hand."[10] The propagandist wants to project the image that he's sure he's right, that he's acting now on his convictions, and that he sincerely wants others to benefit, too.

Suppose you're asked to turn in such a paper. Wasson has some advice: "The student who plans to write persuasion should remember that the aim of writing ought to be honest communication." He is not free "to use dishonest means to gain honest ends."[11] Good persuasion, then, has at its center what we have called "good" propaganda—truth and reasonableness. The emotionalism that gives it its force should ideally be consonant with those high standards.

Remember all that good advice the next time you write a Letter to the Editor.

We began this chapter talking of the elegance of Paris fashions, Rolls-Royce motor cars, balanced sentences, and so on—all of which bespeaks the

L-U's attentiveness to matters of style. The best of upper-class writing generally, we said, is "as beautifully clear and efficient as one could ask. The best of it is informed by high standards of purity and grace." And this is of course true whether the writing has been coolly objective or warmly propagandistic.

Perhaps it is the L-U's *grace* that impels us to stand in awe of him (or her). We spoke of "the ease with which they rise to any occasion." One of the most impressive of all human feats is the construction of a truly graceful, mature sentence. The Lower-Uppers, by virtue of aristocratic upbringing and training, have learned some writing lessons from which we, in our more modest stations, could all profit.

> *The truth is that we are all caught in a great economic system which is heartless.*
> ——Woodrow Wilson, 1912

CHAPTER 8
UPPER-UPPER LANGUAGE

Congratulations are in order. You have reached, at least vicariously, the sixth and highest-ranked of our social classes. The Upper-Uppers, sitting in majestic ease by their swimming pools, are of course somewhat unapproachable behind their estates' guarded gates. They are therefore a bit difficult to get to know; we must make certain inferences from the scraps of information available to us. To begin, perhaps we can agree that the U-U Class includes those four thousand Americans (and their families) who, in 1969, had gross estates exceeding $10 million. (There may be a half dozen too coarse to admit, but generally speaking $10 million ought to qualify them.) The U-U's prestige is especially high if he didn't create the original fortune, but merely tended one and watched it grow. He, or his wife, then comes of "good stock"; they are "old family," which is to say that the original bundle was made some decades earlier. Many "very old" families trace their money back to New England whaling, sailing, and slave-trading, and to the production of textiles, in our nation's infancy.

"Old family" goes back to the Civil War's profiteering and to the stock-watering days of Jay Gould and Cornelius Vanderbilt. "Commodore" Vanderbilt, for example, amassed his pile by doing pretty much as he pleased ("Law? What do I care about law?") and son William Henry Vanderbilt continued the tradition ("The public be damned!"). The commodore left $90 million from shipping and railroads; his son, despite labor troubles and a depression, soon ran it up to about $200 million. There were fortunes to be made everywhere. The 1889 Senate was known as a millionaire's club; the nation was ruled by Standard Oil, various iron and steel trusts, and barons of insurance, sugar, lumber, the railroads, silver and gold, and manufacturing. By the turn of the century John D. Rockefeller's ruthless oil monopoly had made him a billion dollars. Wall Street banker J. P. Morgan organized U.S. Steel with $1.4 billion.[1] Titans like the Mellons, the Armours, the Harrimans, the Hearsts, the Fords, the Pews, the McCormicks, the Dukes, and many more business and industrial giants, established empires that thrived even when divided up among family members. One Mellon heiress, for instance, is today worth an estimated $250 million.

Some will object, perhaps, that four thousand families is too few, that this underestimates the number of Upper-Uppers in America. Very well, then, let us open the gates to a few thousand more—provided of course that, though less wealthy, these people enjoy high status in their communities, and especially by virtue of being well-born. They too should be "old family" and of "good stock." They must have gone to "correct" schools. And in order to wine and dine properly, they must of course not be paupers. Some additional honorary U-U members can be the nine Supreme Court justices, many senators and governors, and, ordinarily, the President of the United States.

Keeping track of the U-U hierarchy is difficult. For example, wealth, which is a significant but not sole criterion of U-U status, has a tendency to fluctuate badly in some *nouveau riche* families. J. Paul Getty and Howard Hughes seem stable entities, but what are we to make of Henry Ross Perot, who in 1970 was "the richest man in the world" with $1.5 billion[2] but who, four years later, had a mere $140 million?[3] Even Perot's high-ranked friends couldn't keep Electronic Data Systems riding high on the stock market forever. And Ray Kroc's estimated $500 million from McDonald's hamburgers—how long will that finance a risky hobby like buying baseball clubs?

When the term *upper class* is mentioned some people think immediately of the "beautiful people," the so-called jet set. According to these judges the highest U-U ranks should go to anyone who really enjoys international party-giving—St. Tropez one month, Costa Smeralda or a Greek island the next —people such as Cristina Ford, Gloria Guinness, Richard Burton. But this preference, it seems to me, seriously mistakes the very nature of the Upper-Upper Class. Many U-U families, of course, do entertain a good bit, but the last thing most would plan would be a showy affair with attendant newspaper and magazine publicity. Indeed, for some decades it has been an indication of genuine U-U quality if the family at least professes to despise ostentatiousness. Yes, there are some Rolls-Royces purchased at this level, but usually by antique-collectors. Ordinarily the chief family auto will be a less expensive Bentley or Mercedes-Benz, considered less pretentious.

> *Money is the blood of the poor.*
> —Leon Bloy, French novelist

Just as they eschew any displays which their peers might deem vulgar, so too do the U-U's avoid unusual social and political stances. Oh, some are Democrats, but their liberalism is kept well under control. No, the Upper-Uppers have adopted what John Kenneth Galbraith has called "the conventional wisdom," his term for accepted ideas which have great stability. These people are basically quite conservative, as might be expected, and the conservative, says Galbraith, "is led by disposition, not unmixed with pecuniary self-interest, to adhere to the familiar and the established."[4]

One of the doctrines they endorse strongly is the bourgeois "work ethic." (There is an ironic element in this, since some of its terms are quite alien to their own lives.) According to this credo:

(1) Work is to be thought of as a duty of man or, in a variant rendition, as a good in itself.

(2) Money and the things it buys are proper rewards for hard work. In the so-called materialism of our age there is nothing to be apologized for.

(3) Circumstances, however, often impose the moral obligations of thrift and the delay of pleasure. Postponed gratification is, in fact, as important as one's steady labor. "He should have put off getting a new (baby, boat, bowling ball)," people sometimes say, "until he could afford it."

(4) In the organization of private lives and an efficient society, the emphasis should be upon competition rather than cooperation. The virtues that should be fostered are self-motivation and individual responsibility; winning in life's assorted "games," in all our pyramids, signifies that one is a success in the business of living.[5]

Some economists have been induced to give professional approval to this position, and to various elaborations. Galbraith regards these as attempts to justify income maldistribution.

> The undisturbed enjoyment of income was held to be essential as an incentive. The resulting effort and ingenuity would bring greater production and greater resulting rewards for all. Inequality came to be regarded as almost equally important for capital formation. Were income widely distributed, it would be spent. But if it flowed in a concentrated stream to the rich, a part would certainly be saved and invested.[6]

Now, the rich people that we have been talking about have saved piles of money, all right, but saving and capital formation also occur in other classes. According to many economists, we need to concern ourselves chiefly with equitable distribution of spending-power; the saving-power will take care of itself.

But other capitalists advance still more defenses of the *status quo:*

> Excessive equality makes for cultural uniformity and monotony. Rich men are essential if there is to be an adequate subsidy of education and the arts. Equality smacks of communism and hence of atheism and therefore is spiritually suspect. In any case, even the Russians have abandoned egalitarianism as unworkable. Finally, it is argued that by means of the income tax we have achieved virtual or (depending on the speaker) entirely excessive equality.[7]

Few Americans of any station, of course, speak out for income and wealth redistribution. Not surprisingly, among the Upper-Uppers such agitation is almost non-existent. When one "has it made," he is loath to see it go.

There is, as we have said, a certain irony in the U-U's acceptance of the work ethic, with all these corollaries. The endorsement often seems based on romantic upper-class notions about the nature of work and thrift, rather than on any real familiarity with them. Perhaps what's really involved here is guilt. Ancestors among the Puritans and *Mayflower* Pilgrims subscribed to the Calvinist suspicion of sloth and extravagance. Their stern precepts, part of the "New England character," may still be operating in the inherited culture. (Some Calvinists also held, though, that prosperity and worldly goods were signs of God's grace, and maybe this gives the U-U some comfort.)

There are, to be sure, some U-U lairds who devote long hours to overseeing the affairs of a favorite corporation, or managing their investments, or inspecting a ranch, but these activities aren't "work" in the usual middle-class understanding of the term, and certainly not in that of the lower classes. They are part of the U-U's play; he enjoys them as much as his prodigal younger brother does women and racehorses. And when bored, he can always swing to some other activity. Most U-U's are not bound to a hard-driving foreman and a machine, and under threat of privation for even an hour's refusal.

U-U children are trained early for their adult life of relative ease. As soon as they have learned some social graces, they are sent off to a private school—very frequently an Episcopalian preparatory school in New England. There, and later at Ivy League colleges, they enjoy themselves, acquire more graces, and think now and then of their future careers.

That career is likely to be simply the management of the family property, or a large share of it. As we've been noting, a capitalistic society puts untold emphasis on personal property. The very possession of it, earned or unearned, is a basis of one's worth and standing in the community. Thorstein Veblen's famed 1899 work titled *The Theory of the Leisure Class* observed that wealth becomes "intrinsically honorable."[8] Veblen put no stock in the supposed viability of a Puritan heritage. He contended that, despite lip-service to the dignity of work and all that, the upper class is quite happy, thank you, to possess the wealth without the labor. Exemption from work "has ever been recognized by thoughtful men as a prerequisite to a worthy or beautiful, or even a blameless, human life. In itself and in its consequences the life of leisure is beautiful and ennobling in all civilized men's eyes."[9] Thus "wealth acquired passively by transmission from ancestors or other antecedents . . . becomes even more honorific than wealth acquired by the possessor's own effort . . ."[10]

However, said Veblen, if one is still building his fortune, it pays to have some understanding of sharp trading practices—and a very flexible moral code. "Freedom from scruple, from sympathy, honesty and regard for life, may, within fairly wide limits, be said to further the success of the individual in the pecuniary culture."[11] Being a good guy doesn't further one's interests at all; an impressive financial or marital *coup*, on the other hand, may serve as the climax to an L-U career and lead directly to U-U status; "the leisure class of today is recruited from those who have been successful in a pecuniary way, and who, therefore, are presumably endowed with more than an even complement of the predatory traits."[12] And every transaction should be accomplished with vigor, self-control, and style. "Masterful aggression, and the correlative massiveness, together with a ruthlessly consistent sense of status, . . . still count among the most splendid traits of the class. These have remained in our traditions as the typical 'aristocratic virtues.'"[13]

When one has acquired his wealth, a chief task in its management is what Veblen called "conspicuous consumption." Within the bounds of good taste, of course, there is a certain pleasure in displaying to friends "the consumption of food, clothing, dwelling, and furniture by the lady and the rest of the domestic establishment."[14] This display can involve a great deal of time and money, but, when one has $10 million, he and his family can live and entertain very handsomely using only the interest on their investments. They rarely need to dip into savings. Thus, painlessly and decorously, do the lady and gentleman of leisure establish their reputability.

U-U GRAMMAR

A very few Upper-Uppers are ornery old codgers who delight in shocking everyone within range with some decidedly lower-class language. Most U-U's, however, are conscious that they are looked up to by the classes below, and feel that they should set a good example in all things. This sense of responsibility—*noblesse oblige*—extends of course to the grammar of the language.

We have already observed that U-U people are a conservative lot, and that their conservatism extends to their language habits. Many Upper-Uppers, for example, would rather die than use *like* as a conjunction or *hopefully* as a sentence modifier. Another example of fussiness, one not found at the lower social levels, is a dogmatic insistence on distinctions between the relative pronouns *who*, *that*, and *which*. Back in U-L Grammar there was this passage:

> *Which* refers to animals and things. *Who* is commonly used with persons ... *That* usually refers to animals and things but (except in the upper classes) sometimes also to human beings.

Among the illustrations was this one:

A girl *that* (or *who*) can dance is always popular.

Once again we should caution readers that the upper classes will not accept the uncouth *that* in such a sentence.

But still another U-U precept should be inserted at this point. The Upper-Uppers, and almost no one else, feel that *that* should be used to introduce restrictive clauses—and, of course, *which* to introduce nonrestrictive clauses. These clauses are already distinguished by the use or absence of commas. But the U-U's would like another special flag to signal which kind of adjective clause is coming.

RESTRICTIVE	A law [*that* (not *which*) has no teeth] is no law at all.
NONRESTRICTIVE	The new law, [*which* has no teeth,] is no law at all.

Time will tell whether this U-U dictum will become general law. The Upper-Uppers have a great deal of influence in a society—they are, after all, the chairmen of its corporate boards of directors—but occasionally they are thwarted in little things.

U-U USAGE

UU-U1 *Idioms and other problems*

Alternative. The upper class insists that this refers to a choice between only *two* possibilities, not three or four. See *Option(s)*.

At about. "Deadwood," snaps the U-U. "We don't need two prepositions." Make up your mind which is more precise:

EITHER	We will be there *at* three o'clock.
OR	We will be there *about* three o'clock.

Beg to differ. This expression, heard chiefly among the Lower-Uppers, raises some U-U hackles. "You mean you beg *leave* to differ," says the Upper-Upper.

Business. Colloquial when it means "right."
    LOWER CLASS   She has no *business* coming here.
    HIGHER CLASS   She has no *right* to come here.

Else's. The U-U Class allows the possessive inflection of *else* in speech, but some purists object to it in writing.
    LOWER CLASS   Anybody else's name
    U-U CLASS   The name of anybody else

Hate. Too strong to serve as a synonym for "dislike."
    AVOID   I *hate* that color.

Human, Humans. Human is an adjective, as in "human being." Some U-U's object to its being used also as a noun synonym for "person."

In, Into. The upper classes insist upon a careful distinction here; *in* shows location, *into* direction.
    LOWER CLASS   The child fell *in* the swimming pool.
    UPPER CLASS   The child fell *into* the swimming pool.

Just. Not a substitute for "very" or "quite."
    COLLOQUIAL   She was *just* beautiful.

Leave, Lief. Some Upper-Uppers use the old-fashioned adverb *lief* ("gladly" or "willingly"). They object strongly to its corruption into *leave*.
    I would as *lief* stay as not.

Like, Love. U-U's often regard the use of *love* as vulgar when *like* is meant.
    LOWER CLASS   I *love* all kinds of pizza.
    HIGHER CLASS   I *like* all kinds of pizza very much.

Make. The U-U's don't like *make* used to mean "earn" unless it is followed by *from, of,* or *out of*.
    LOWER CLASS   He says he *makes* twenty dollars an hour.
    HIGHER CLASS   He has *made* a living *from* his painting.
    OR   Some people can *make* a fortune *out of* a bright idea.

Option(s). The word *option* used to mean chiefly "the privilege of choosing." To the dismay of purists, it has recently come to mean the choice itself or, in the plural, the various possibilities to choose among. The U-U's choose among *choice, preference,* and *selection.* (See also *Alternative*.)

Proved, Proven. Proved is the approved past participle in a verb phrase ("He has proved that he can do it"). *Proven* is the preferred adjectival form ("their proven worth").

Self-confessed. The *self* is redundant. Say instead "a confessed embezzler."

Stop. Informal when a substitute for "stay."
    MIDDLE CLASS   We *stopped* overnight in Baltimore.
    UPPER CLASS   We *stayed* overnight in Baltimore.

Such. Informal as an intensive: "*Such* a pretty dress!"

Transpire. Upper-Uppers say this may mean "become known" but not "happen."

Try. Colloquial when a noun substituting for "test," "trial," or "effort."
    INFORMAL   Give it a *try*.

Very. When it is used to modify a participle, say the U-U's, *very* should be followed by *greatly, much,* or *well*.
    INFERIOR CLASSES   I was *very* pleased.
    U-U CLASS   I was *very greatly* pleased.

Whereas the study of Latin is all but abandoned in the public schools, it still is taught in preparatory schools to scions of the upper class. A smattering of Greek here and there helps, too, to create what passes today for the classical education of earlier patricians.

Even this light contact with the classical languages, and with some ancient literature, may give the U-U youth a significant advantage over less-privileged youngsters. Veblen, to be sure, mocked the classics, whether in school or college, as "decorative" learning. Colleges continue to offer such courses, he said, because they confer status; they conform to upper-class "requirements of archaism and waste."[15] Yet this probably overstates his case. There must be some U-U students who have profited greatly through the development of vocabulary and of reading skills. Let us at least consider the case for the study of languages, both those living and those supposedly dead. That done, let us consider the advantages of a reading program of impressive scale—all of which, we argue, equips the U-U to be a superior judge of American usage.

UU-U2 *The history of the English language*

The upper class knows something of the development of the language and hence has a good "feel" of a word or phrase.

It is a useful exercise or theme assignment to have students study briefly and report on the history of their own language. Materials are readily available; home sources like *The American Heritage Dictionary* and *Webster's New World Dictionary* have outlines in their introductory pages, and some encyclopedias also have excellent discussions. The more ambitious students can go to the library for Albert C. Baugh's *History of the English Language*, Albert H. Marckwardt's *Introduction to the English Language,* and similar works. In such an exercise, students teach themselves about one, some, or all of the following topics:

a. The Indo-European family of languages and their common ancestor.

b. The earliest days of Britain and the competition on its isles of Celtic, Latin, Norse, and Anglo-Saxon languages.

c. The establishment, after the 5th Century withdrawal of Roman troops, of the highly inflected Anglo-Saxon tongue as "Old English," with four main dialects.

d. The Norman Invasion of 1066 and the subsequent universality of French as the upper-class language in Britain. The lower class retained their Anglo-Saxon words for the common things of their lives: *sheep, cow, hog*. But when these animals were properly cooked and served to the Norman nobility, with good wine and sometimes music, they were given aristocratic French names: *mouton* (mutton), *boef* (beef), *porc* (pork).

e. The "Middle English" period, from 1066 to about 1450 A.D. During this period (1) thousands of French words were Anglicized *(tax, government, religion, baptism, attorney)* and most are still in use today; (2) English finally, in 1362, replaced French in the Parliament and courts of law; (3) the great court poet Geoffrey Chaucer (c. 1340-1400) helped to establish "East Midland" as the standard dialect—illustrated by this fragment about the Prioress, from the Prologue to *The Canterbury Tales:*

> Ful weel she soong the service dyvyne,
> Entuned in hir nose ful semely;
> And Frenssh she spak ful faire and fetisly,
> After the scole of Stratford atte Bowe,
> For Frenssh of Parys was to hire unknowe.

In this period, incidentally, we see the first great surge in the development of an urban middle class.

f. The Renaissance and "Early Modern English," spread by (1) the printing press, (2) speedier transportation, and (3) the education and ambition of the new bourgeoisie. Baugh estimates that by 1600 more than a third of the population could read.[16] Thus they were ready for Shakespeare:

> JULIET:
> O Romeo, Romeo! wherefore art thou Romeo?
> Deny thy father and refuse thy name;
> Or, if thou wilt not, be but sworn my love,
> And I'll no longer be a Capulet.

And for the King James Bible:

> Now the serpent was more subtil than any beast
> of the field which the Lord God had made. And
> he said unto the woman, Yea, hath God said, Ye
> shall not eat of every tree of the garden?

g. The growth of the language through colonization and world trade; introduction of words from the Dutch, Spanish, Italian, African, Malayan, American Indian, and many other languages.

h. The importance of scholarly introductions of Latin and Greek in, say, the 17th and 18th centuries.

i. The terms coined to label each new wonder of our modern age: *railroad, telegraph, telephone, gasoline, automobile, airplane, movies, radio, television, atomic bomb, radar, wirephoto, laser,* many names for medicines, and so on.

The patricians, as we said, have already done their homework in these areas. In their reading they have learned that only about one-fourth of the dictionary's words are Germanic (Anglo-Saxon) but that these are very important words indeed. They include common household terms like *household, home, father, mother, son, daughter, go, sit, eat, meat, breakfast, sleep, tonight,* and *tomorrow.* The grammar of the language is Teutonic, too, as are most of the important structural words: most of the pronouns *(I, we, us,* etc.); the articles *(a, an,* and *the);* forms of "to be" *(be, is, are, was, were);* auxiliary verbs *(shall, should, may, might);* most of the connectives *(and, at, by, for, from, in,* etc.), and inflectional endings *(-ed, -ly, -s)* which can turn a Latin word into a hybrid. Despite the thousands of words introduced directly from Latin, or indirectly through the Romance languages, English is basically a Germanic tongue.

The upper class, being familiar with all that, has no difficulty deciphering the parts of a dictionary entry and getting, thereby, a fuller understanding of the word. An entry will often include the *etymology* of a word—its origin and history. Consider an example or two:

fol·low·er (fäl′ə wər) *n.* [ME. *folwere* < OE. *folgere*] **1.** a person or thing that follows; specif., *a)* a person who follows another's beliefs or teachings; disciple *b)* a servant or attendant **2.** a part (of a machine) that is given motion by another part
SYN.—**follower** is the general term for one who follows or believes in the teachings or theories of someone *[a follower of Freud]*; **supporter** applies to one who upholds or defends opinions or theories that are disputed or under attack *[a supporter of technocracy]*; **adherent** refers to a close, active follower of some theory, cause, etc. *[the adherents of a political party]*; **disciple** implies a personal, devoted relationship to the teacher of some doctrine or leader of some movement *[Plato was a disciple of Socrates]*; **partisan**, in this connection, refers to an unswerving, often blindly devoted, adherent of some person or cause

By permission. From *Webster's New World Dictionary of the American Language*, 2nd College Ed. Copyright © 1974 by Collins-World Publishing Co., Cleveland, Ohio.

After being told the spelling and syllabication, the pronunciation, and the part of speech (noun), we are given a brief history of the word; it came into Middle English from an Old English or Anglo-Saxon form, *folgere*. Following the definition comes a helpful synonymy.

in·fer \in-ˈfər\ *vb* **in·ferred; in·fer·ring** [MF or L; MF *inferer*, fr. L *inferre*, lit., to carry or bring into, fr. *in-* + *ferre* to carry — more at BEAR] *vt* **1 :** to derive as a conclusion from facts or premises <we see smoke and ~ fire —L. A. White> — compare IMPLY **2 :** GUESS, SURMISE <your letter ... allows me to ~ that you are as well as ever —O. W. Holmes †1935> **3 a :** to involve as a normal outcome of thought **b :** to point out **:** INDICATE <this doth ~ the zeal I had to see him —Shak.> **4 :** SUGGEST, HINT <another survey ... ~s that two-thirds of all present computer installations are not paying for themselves —H. R. Chellman> ~ *vi* **:** to draw inferences <men ... have observed, *inferred*, and reasoned ... to all kinds of results —John Dewey> — **in·fer·a·ble** *or* **in·fer·ri·ble** \in-ˈfər-ə-bəl\ *adj* — **in·fer·rer** \-ˈfər-ər\ *n*
syn INFER, DEDUCE, CONCLUDE, JUDGE, GATHER *shared meaning element* **:** to arrive at a mental conclusion

By permission. From *Webster's New Collegiate Dictionary*. © 1975 by G. & C. Merriam Co., Publishers of the Merriam-Webster Dictionaries.

This word, we're told, moved into Middle French on its way into English. Originally it was Latin: *in* plus *ferre*, "to carry."

UU-U3 *The persistence of Greek and Latin*

The upper class recognizes bits of Latin and Greek words and, through them, gets both a deeper meaning from many English words and a richer vocabulary.

The so-called "dead" languages of classical antiquity, Latin and ancient Greek, still have surprising vitality. Not only are they still occasionally taught, but millions of students are perennially told something about them in English texts. This one is no exception.

Ancient Greek was the language of the much-admired Hellenic culture on the shores of the Mediterranean Sea. Many old Greek words have come into English down through the centuries, either from the original tongue or through a Latin transliteration. The Renaissance, a "rebirth" of interest in the classical age, brought the Greek language a new life.

Latin, the language of the Roman Empire, later became the official tongue of the Roman Catholic Church, for several centuries the only church England had. Since the church operated the only schools, the importance of Latin is obvious. The aristocracy often used it as an international language, and even the lower classes knew many Anglicized words, such as *candle, mass,* and *shrine.* Latin also became the basis of several modern languages, including French.

Latin and Greek, in short, are part of the educated person's language experience. The inferior classes would also benefit from some kind of contact with these resources.

a. *Latin and Greek roots*

Here's a little quiz. Following are a few ancient roots; see how many modern English words you can fashion from them. To prime the pump of your memory, we give you one example for each root. When and if the pump seems to run dry, prime it again with the aid of the dictionary. Then review; note the etymology and definition of each of your words. (Some may surprise you.)

(1)	anthrop-	(man)	misanthrope
(2)	auto-	(self)	autocratic
(3)	carn-	(flesh)	reincarnation
(4)	chron-	(time)	synchronized
(5)	doc-	(teach)	indoctrinate
(6)	graph-	(write)	autograph
(7)	hydr-	(water)	dehydrate
(8)	man-	(hand)	manacle
(9)	phon-	(sound)	euphonious
(10)	psych-	(mind)	psychic
(11)	terr-	(land)	inter
(12)	urb-	(city)	suburb
(13)	verb-	(word)	proverb
(14)	vit-	(life)	vital
(15)	vol-	(wish)	volition

b. *Latin and Greek prefixes*

Ready for another quiz? This one is easier. Again, check all the dictionary entries when you have finished.

(1)	a- or an-	(without)	atheism
(2)	bene-	(good)	benevolent
(3)	bi-	(two)	bilateral
(4)	ex-	(out, out of)	exhale
(5)	mon-	(one)	monogamy
(6)	omni-	(all)	omnipresent
(7)	per-	(through)	perforate
(8)	pre-	(before)	prefix
(9)	poly-	(many)	polygamy
(10)	re-	(back)	recede
(11)	tele-	(far)	telepathy
(12)	trans-	(across, beyond)	transcendental

c. *Latin and Greek suffixes*

Many combining forms can be roots or prefixes or suffixes. The Greek suffix *-gamy* (marriage, sexual union), for an example, has a root form in biology, *gamete,* which in turn can be a prefix, as in *gametophore.* Use the following terms, however, only as suffixes for now. Find at least two words for each.

(1)	-cide	(killer, killing)	regicide
(2)	-logy	(science, theory of)	geology
(3)	-mania	(mental disorder)	monomania
(4)	-phobia	(fear or hatred)	claustrophobia
(5)	-sphere	(ball-shape; layer)	stratosphere

Regular drill in this sort of thing would do wonders in giving breadth and richness to one's vocabulary. (Perhaps your instructor will help you out with longer lists.) Words of Latin and Greek origin lend a dignified, formal, highbrow tone to one's diction, and this may be appropriate in many social situations involving the U-U Class.

A word of caution, though: As the ancient Greeks advise us, we should do "nothing in excess." *Generally speaking,* words derived from the Anglo-Saxon have much more vigor and directness and clarity than our polysyllabic Mediterranean forms. If we desire both loftiness *and* liveliness, therefore, we will create sentences which mix the two *(AS.)* kinds *(AS.)* in *(AS.)* various *(L.)* proportions *(L.).*

UU-U4 *The use of foreign terms*

The upper class enjoys several advantages from being multilingual.

Upper-class Americans, as you know, are the world's tourists *par excellence.* They jet to Copenhagen, they jet to Belgrade. They sail to Rio and *mañana* to Buenos Aires. Frequently they can make use of a second or even a third modern language learned in their youth. Indeed, the acquisition and use of secondary languages are common marks of the U-U education. They tend to broaden one's vision of the world, liberalize his sentiments about an alien group of human beings and, probably just as important, improve somewhat his understanding of his own language—and of the nature of "language" generally.

The introduction of an occasional foreign word or phrase at times will seem appropriate in one's speech or writing. It may flavor the paragraph, for instance, or bespeak the writer's *savoir-faire.* But—*Himmel!*—sometimes it is overdone. Sometimes, too, it is done just to impress the reader. This is not a legitimate reason.

UU-U5 *The benefits of extensive reading*

The Upper-Upper has read widely and intensively; he has a sound basis for judging the quality and appropriateness of a locution.

When we hear speech or read a newspaper, a magazine, a novel, or whatever, we are unconsciously receiving data (as for a computer) about the ways language is used "out there" beyond our skins. Some locutions we especially admire; they are stylistically pleasing and, just as important, they seem to fall within the range of choices an intelligent, educated writer might make on such-and-such an occasion. These expressions we file in the memory-bank of the mind's computer, to be imitated or even copied at the proper moment. They become a body of background from which to judge one's own writing and that of others.

The Upper-Uppers, because of their leisure, their civility, and the expectations of their schoolmasters and families, have read more than most of us. They have also read a great deal of *admired* writing. In a sense, they have lived more than most of us, because vicariously, through their reading, they have entered many lives, many kinds of experience. (Only a rare television show provides comparable richness.) They have a superior background and, hence, a superior basis for the evaluation of American usage.

These observations also explain the U-U's frequently observed sensitivity and acumen in the criticism of writing *style*—the next topic to be considered.

U-U STYLE

Most U-U's, despite all their leisure, aren't worth a damn as composers or artists or creative writers. Artistic imagination seems to be a gift bestowed chiefly on the Upper-Middles. Perhaps upper-class life is too soft; perhaps it doesn't have enough challenges, or enough pain. For whatever reason, among the U-U's the creative juices just don't seem to flow.

On the other hand, Upper-Uppers often are able critics. The explanation is simple: they have been taught the art of criticism all their lives, and some have learned; some have developed superior taste. To be sure, there have been some notable exceptions. Victorian mansions of the 1880's, for example, at times were grotesque, unbelievably hideous. But one can tour U-U America and see some of the finest homes in the world—the Huntington mansion, San Marino, Calif.; Holly Hill at Friendship, Md.; Carter's Grove, Williamsburg, Va.; The Elms at Newport, R.I.; The Shadows, New Iberia, La., and many more. Frequently there is palatial opulence, but the best is restrained and dignified.

Esthetic standards used in acquiring statuary for one's lawns, or paintings for one's gallery, may be put to use in judging the worth of a sentence or paragraph. The Principles of Composition become, at this level, almost like divine law from Mount Sinai. Several concerns of the critic of style were discussed in the last chapter; four more are the appropriateness of the diction, its precision, its economy, and its sound.

UU-S1 *Appropriateness of diction*

Given the right audience and occasion, of course, *any* writing may suddenly become Good English. A novel depicting the seamier aspects of

American life may very properly (despite various would-be censors) make use of our seamiest language. A good speech at a union meeting may be quite informal indeed. Generally speaking, though, it is altogether proper to set higher standards for "polite" or "educated" writing. U-U people are on fairly firm esthetic ground when they decry some of the habits of the classes below them: (1) the constant obscenities, profanity, vulgarisms, and localisms of the lower class; (2) the Lower-Middles' addiction to slang, trite expressions, and faulty metaphors; (3) the Upper-Middles' jargon and artificiality. We have noted some of these faults already, but it may be wise to take a second look.

a. *Obscenities and profanity*

An obscenity is something offensive to modesty or decency—reference to some of the bodily functions, for example, and especially in Anglo-Saxon terms. Profanity, by contrast, offends chiefly members of churches; their sacred objects have been treated irreverently. Both types of expressions should be handled with extreme care. They are often simply not appropriate in polite language situations.

It perhaps should be noted here that words, like individuals and families, can move up or down the social scale. One four-letter barnyard word that has risen to acceptability over the centuries is *muck*. Many, however, have been on the slide: *slut* originally had no suggestion of immorality; even *whore* could once be used in a bantering way, with an air of jocund familiarity; *suggestive* only recently has come to suggest sexiness.

b. *Vulgarisms*

This is a term (from the Latin *vulgus*, "the common people") used to cover all the double negatives, *ain'ts*, subject-verb discords, and so on, that the higher classes regard as illiteracies.

c. *Localisms*

Localisms or "provincialisms" are terms with geographically limited currency: *poke* for "sack" or "bag," *tote* for "carry," and the like. We fear that national television is slowly eliminating these interesting variations in our national speech.

d. *Slang*

The American Heritage Dictionary defines slang as a "nonstandard vocabulary" consisting chiefly of "arbitrary and often ephemeral coinages and figures of speech characterized by spontaneity and raciness." If U-U proprieties represent the Apollonian, orderly side of our society's speech, slang (together with obscenities and profanity) represents its raffish and disorderly Dionysian dynamism. At its best, it is fresh, imaginative, lusty, and vivid; at its worst it is stale and colorless. Some words start out as slang and become rather respectable—*e.g.*, clipped words like *ad, auto, exam, math,* and *phone*. Many slang terms stay slang for a long time: *gent, lousy, swell*. But many more have a brief life and are then forgotten: *twenty-three skiddoo, keen, jimjams*.

e. *Trite expressions*

Overworked, trite locutions are sometimes called "hackneyed" or "cliché." Most are attempts at vivid imagery: *burning the midnight oil, the crack of dawn.* Hundreds are similes (some not very logical): *happy as a clam, hot as hell, cold as hell, dumb as hell, dumb like a fox.* All are borrowed from someone else or from folk sayings.

Triteness has been called "a disease of the personality."[17] If you don't want your *mind* to be thought trite, avoid clichés as much as possible.

f. *Faulty figures of speech*

A simile (a very short analogy) uses *like* or *as* to establish a comparison: "He's as strong as an ox." A metaphor, by contrast, creates the comparison directly, by simply making A and B identical: "Jack is a skunk." Everyone knows it's not *literally* true; but it's *figuratively* true (at least to the speaker).

Human beings for several reasons are fond of animal metaphors. A man may be called (pleasantly) an old dog or (angrily) a dirty dog. "Of course, if a man were a frisky enough dog, he'd really be a cat, a swinging cat." Again, unattractive women are sometimes called dogs. But "the woman who calls another woman a dog is really being a cat. And when she is very catty, we call her a bitch."[18]

Some metaphors, and other closely related figures of speech, can be even more confusing.

MIXED METAPHORS
    They're always biting the hand that lays the golden egg.—Attributed to Samuel Goldwyn

    The first wave of belt-tightening sparked faculty interest in collective bargaining.—News report

    Another ingredient that needs to be plugged in here is . . .—Television program

Still other figures just seem illogical or incongruous.

    The ladies of the opera guild wanted to make the affair a financial success, so they worked like real eager beavers.

    At first she nibbled at the assigned poems, but then she sank her teeth in them and gobbled voraciously.

Figurative language is an attempt to say something in an unusual way. It is an important feature of good writing because, well used, it can contribute both clarity and vividness. (Look up in a dictionary, and copy in your notes, something about *personification, metonymy, synecdoche, overstatement,* and *understatement.* See also a cousin of figurative language, *irony.*) But the writer must try hard to use figures that are both fresh and fitting.

g. *Jargon*

Dictionaries list several meanings for this term, including the concept of *specialized language patterns* of those in a profession, trade, or other social group. Often, of course, such jargon is efficiently used among one's working companions—and almost unintelligible to outsiders. In some management strata these days we hear adjectives like *reciprocal, incremental, third-generation,* and *logistical* coupled with such nouns as *capability, programming, time-phase,* and *contingency.* The result, at least for the uninitiated, can be a thick fog.

Obfuscation is made worse if the jargon is also wordy. This combination, common in some governmental bureaucracies, is called *gobbledygook*. One federal agency, for example, is reported to have called for "action-oriented orchestration of innovative inputs generated by escalation of meaningful indigenous decision-making dialogue." One prefers to think that was only a parody.

h. *Artificiality*

Inflated writing is just as bad as vulgar writing and perhaps worse than jargon. Avoid language that sounds self-conscious, stilted, or pompous.

"FINE" WRITING As a lad of tender years, I would reflect upon the advantages of a residence of greater size.

MORE NATURAL As a boy, I wished we had a bigger house.

There are various forms of coarseness at perhaps all levels of society. The U-U's are surely justified in complaining about barbarisms in the language of the masses.

> *The closer and more intimate the communication the less need there is for explicit meaning. The greater the social distance... the greater is the need for explicit communication.*
> —J. B. Hogins,
> People and Words

UU-S2 *Precision of diction*

Under this heading we could talk about several subjects—idioms, semantics, and so on—but what it all comes down to is this: You should read as much as you can, and thereby develop a good ear and eye for exact meanings, and an understanding that perceptions often are affected by one's social level. By now you have learned, probably, that a word's *denotation* or "dictionary" meaning is just one of its senses. Surrounding that nucleus or core meaning is a cluster of vague associations people have with the word; these are its *connotations*. For instance, the denotation of a *well* might be "a hole or shaft sunk to tap underground water, gas, oil, etc." Connected closely with the concept are related images, sensations, feelings, and reflections: gauzy pictures of hot days and cool, delicious water (or of black-oil "gushers"); fading memories of cost figures; the sense of security that comes from possession of such a resource; the insecurity of knowing it's not inexhaustible, and so on.

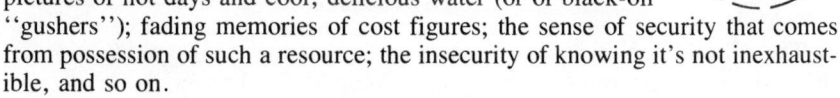

Now, whenever these filmy associations stop fluttering aimlessly about in our heads, when they take on specific form and substance, we call them *symbolic*

values; the central image is now called a *symbol.* The image of the well (or even the *word*) symbolizes the cool water, and so on, mentioned earlier; to another man specifically the difficulty he had digging it; to a pessimist, the uncertainties of life in his water-poor area; to an optimist, the benevolence of nature, and so forth. Or the image can mean *all* these things simultaneously—which of course often creates great complexity in symbol-heavy activities such as politics or religion, and especially in art and literature. A symbol can have many *layers* of meaning.

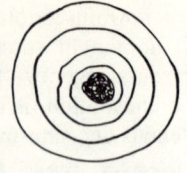

The person with a good ear for all these associations and values is sensitive to the subtleties of language. He is often of the higher classes; he has done lots of reading, much of it in respected literature. He knows he must choose with extraordinary care whenever he himself sets words down on paper. Each word is so easily mistaken!—and especially when the term is abstract, like *democracy* or *free enterprise,* or relative, like *slow* or *good.* Sometimes, in real agony, he will fret and fuss:

> In this sentence, do I mean *moral* or *ethical* or *righteous* or *virtuous?*
>
> And here—do I choose *forestall* or *preclude* or *avert,* or merely a general word like *prevent*? What about *obviate*—or is that too formal?

A practiced reader or writer knows that being close isn't good enough; he knows it is important to be exact. He knows *amiable* doesn't mean *amicable,* even though they come from the same Latin word. He knows that *practicable* is not always a synonym for *practical.* Someone has said that, close though they may be, no two words are ever perfectly synonymous—that, even if their denotations are identical, their connotations will not be.

> Should I use *amity,* from the Latin, or the Anglo-Saxon *friendship*?
>
> Which?—the Anglo-Saxon *ban* or the Latin *prohibit*?

These are often quite difficult decisions, even for a U-U. A good desk dictionary can help a great deal, and works dealing with usage also,[19] but the final decision is up to the writer—sometimes with fear and trembling, sometimes with the delight of a happy choice.

UU-S3 *Economy of diction*

We have already noted (in UL-C2) that repetition of words or ideas can often produce excellent results. Repetition helps in giving stress to a concept, or just in improving the coherence of a passage. But there is such a thing as *unnecessary* repetition, and that we should avoid. It goes almost without saying that we should also eliminate any *fat* in the sentence. Most sentences should be lean as jaguars.

a. *Redundancy*
(1) The silliest form of excess baggage is the tautology: *basic fundamentals, visible to the eye, proven facts, necessary essentials,* and so on.

> AVOID   The distant music was plainly *audible to our ears*.
> Our platoon *retreated back* to the bunkers.

Eliminate all clumsy echoes of the same idea.
- AVOID　　In the modern world *of today* . . .
　　　　　　Work will start at 9 a.m. *in the morning*.
　　　　　　That was the consensus *of opinion*.

(2) Eliminate word repetitions unless you're very sure they're effective.
- DOUBTFUL　　*Times* of stress in public *life* are *times* of excitement and *times* to remember later in *life*.

b. *Other forms of wordiness*

　　Circumlocution (literally "talking around") is one term for words that add very little, if anything, to a sentence's meaning. Another is *deadwood*, a metaphor for lifeless "branches" in a sentence that need pruning. We have already looked at that bureaucratic windiness called "gobbledygook"; now let's tend to our own sentences, preferring always the simple and direct expression to one that is needlessly complex.

- WORDY　　As soon as we'd set up camp, we started exploring the surrounding country for pyrite outcrops.
- TIGHTER　　As soon as we'd set up camp, we started exploring for pyrite outcrops.
- WORDY　　She spent most of the hours of every day in worrying about her exams.
- TIGHTER　　She spent most of her time worrying about her exams.

Another principle here is that, almost always, one economical sentence is better than two which are loosely constructed; that a phrase is often tighter (and better) than a clause; and that a single word may sometimes be best of all. Let's illustrate.

TWO SENTENCES
　　The old engine puffed noisily in its work. It pulled the train cars slowly up the snowy grade.

COMPOUND PREDICATE
　　The old engine puffed noisily *and* pulled the cars slowly up the snowy grade.

SUBORDINATE CLAUSE
　　As it puffed noisily, the old engine pulled the cars slowly up the snowy grade.

PARTICIPIAL PHRASE
　　The old engine, *puffing noisily,* pulled the cars slowly up the snowy grade.

SINGLE WORD
　　The old engine, *puffing,* pulled the cars slowly up the snowy grade.

The principle of economy applies also to single words. Some short words are in competition with longer forms. It's usually best to choose the shorter.

NOT orientate   BUT orient
NOT utilize   BUT use
NOT virtuousness BUT virtue
NOT preventative BUT preventive

UU-S4 *The sounds of words*

Many words suggest, by their sound, the things they denote: *buzz, ping pong, splash*. This effect, known as "onomatopoeia," can intensify the writer's meaning or make a scene more vivid. A related matter, musicality, was touched on by Alexander Pope in his famous *An Essay on Criticism*; read aloud, please:

'Tis not enough no harshness gives offense,
The sound must seem an Echo to the sense:
Soft is the strain when Zephyr gently blows,
And the smooth stream in smoother numbers flows;
But when the loud surges lash the sounding shore,
The hoarse, rough verse should like the torrent roar:
When Ajax strives some rock's vast weight to throw,
The line too labours, and the words move slow . . .

The rhythms of prose, and the harmonies and dissonances of its music, are topics too vast for this book. Pope's eight lines, though written about poetry, will have to suffice.

Had we but pages enough, and time, there are still more elements of style we could discuss—the density and quality of imagery and figurative language, for example. Or we could talk about the subtle distinctions between various functional types of style: the intimate; the casual; the "consultative," in which we open a conversation with a stranger; the formal style of some exposition and argument, and the "frozen" style of past literature.[20] But perhaps the material in Chapters 7 and 8 has explored this complex topic enough for most people's purposes.

If you *really* want to impress someone in your climb up the social mountains, develop a few stock terms for discussing an author's style. A new novelist arrives on the scene; what do we say, at the next cocktail party, about his book? Well, something about the plot and characters, certainly, and then something about the writing itself. Here are a few useful labels:

Fresh, original   OR Conventional, trite
Emphatic, muscular   OR Flat, flabby
Heavily figurative   OR Literal, colorless
Monotonous   OR Varied, flexible
Mannered   OR Relaxed
Simple   OR Complex
Abstract   OR Specific, concrete

Each term chosen will require two or three illustrations, remember, but this should present no problem. Who knows?—you may turn out to be the party's authority on this author. If you handle all this attention with proper modesty, you will have moved several small notches up the social ladder.

"Great purity of speech," says Veblen, "is presumptive evidence of several successive lives spent in other than vulgarly useful occupations..."[21] The evidence, however, may not be completely conclusive without corroborating data on U-U spelling ability, our next topic.

U-U SPELLING

The orthography of the English language gives trouble to all Americans, apparently, with the exception of the tiny upper class. Veblen has this explanation:

> As felicitous an instance of futile classicism as can well be found, outside of the Far East, is the conventional spelling of the English language. A breach of the proprieties in spelling is extremely annoying and will discredit any writer in the eyes of all persons who are possessed of a developed sense of the true and beautiful. English orthography satisfies all the requirements of the canons of reputability under the law of conspicuous waste. It is archaic, cumbrous, and ineffective; its acquisition consumes much time and effort; failure to acquire it is easy of detection. Therefore it is the first and readiest test of reputability in learning, and conformity to its ritual is indispensable to a blameless scholastic life.[23]

The Upper-Uppers, in and out of scholastic life, take considerable pride in being very good spellers. To permit them to show off a bit (should you meet any this evening), ask them to give you both the American and British spelling of a few words, such as:

United States	Great Britain
apologize	apologise
flavor	flavour
center	centre
connection	connexion

Then give them a real test; ask them for the *plurals* of some nouns borrowed from foreign languages. Some of these retain the spelling of the original language.

SINGULAR	PLURAL
alumna (feminine)	alumnae
alumnus (masculine)	alumni
datum	data
hypothesis	hypotheses

But the trend is toward Anglicized plurals. Many foreign borrowings, in the interim, have *two* plurals, both of which the U-U should be able to spell. The foreign plural is considered somewhat more elegant and formal.

SINGULAR	PLURALS	
	Foreign	*Anglicized*
appendix	appendices	appendixes
beau	beaux	beaus
gymnasium	gymnasia	gymnasiums

SINGULAR	PLURALS	
	Foreign	*Anglicized*
index	indices	indexes
memorandum	memoranda	memorandums
radius	radii	radiuses

U-U COMPOSITION

We began talking seriously about composition with a chapter on the Lower-Lowers' trouble in composing an acceptable written sentence. We've come a long way from the subject, predicate, and parts of speech:

UL-C   The paragraph
LM-C   "Natural order" themes: narration and description
UM-C   "Logical order" themes: exposition and argument
LU-C   Persuasion (LU-M: the documented paper)

Both the production of written work and its consumption were very low at the L-L and U-L levels, we found, but both rose dramatically in the middle social strata. An American U-M family, for instance, might receive regularly two newspapers and a dozen periodicals, great and small, all written by other Upper-Middles. When we reached the Lower-Upper Class, consumption held steady, but production fell off sharply. And here, on the sun-blessed hilltops of U-U country, this upper-class pattern is repeated. The U-U, in fact, has the reputation of being the world's best consumer of many things, while producing almost nothing.

What sort of writing commands the attention of the upper class? A difficult question to answer, that. Many L-U's are as much afflicted with humbuggery as the middle class, and put upon their coffee tables all sorts of intellectual and elegant magazines, sometimes just for show. The *Upper*-Uppers don't really have to impress anyone, yet they too subscribe to fancy or learned journals, perhaps partly because they feel an obligation to play out the highbrow role expected of them. You will find, occasionally, a U-U dowager struggling dutifully with beautifully illustrated folios on modern art even though her tastes may lie in, say, the 18th Century. Or a U-U family will be discovered vigorously discussing an obscure British drama review which has been passed among them. The males also seem committed to the *Wall Street Journal* and other business publications.

Since the U-U's have a wide range of interests—yachting, gourmet restaurants, investments, polo, fine wines, and so on—it would be hard to list all their reading. We might take brief note of a few types of articles which we have not yet discussed in these upward travels, and which are regularly perused by many U-U's.

UU-C1   *The literary analysis and critique*

Over the course of your college career, you may be asked to write several essays (or essay answers) on literary subjects. These may take various forms, the only unifying elements being a search for truth and the necessity of severely restricting your topic to manageable size. A specific assignment, or the nature of the material to be discussed, may suggest a basic pattern of organization, such as one of those in UM-C: *classification* of a short poem into the lyric or dramatic genre, a *causal hypothesis* involving an author's sources for a story, a formal *analysis by partition* of a play's chief scene, a *division* of its set of characters, *examples* of the thematic statements in a short story, *illustration* of how a novelist uses a repeated image, *comparison* of two works by the same author, or *reasons* why you think such-and-such sonnet is or isn't successful.

The instructor may give you some leeway in this kind of assignment. Unless your procedures are strictly ordained, you are free to lean toward evaluation or criticism, on the one hand, or mere analysis, on the other. The line between them is often not rigidly honored in such an essay. We use the terms only to designate, very approximately, where we are on a continuum. In the analytical essay, we are trying to stay somewhat objective. In criticism, our effort to judge the material tends to dominate the analytic work we've done. Yet that work must be shown as a substructure, a foundation, for our bias.

In either form, to be frank, the pretense of complete impartiality would not really be desirable, because it would not be quite honest. In analysis, even the weariest, least sensitive, or most objective observer is able to note a particularly effective technique, say, or a leaden, didactic style. He is not barred from slipping in an occasional verbal smile or frown: "the poet convincingly describes the battle line," or "The fusion of these images, unfortunately, creates not clarity but confusion," or "here the novelist, appropriately, shifts the scene to underscore the irony..."

The analysis sometimes takes a form known as *explication,* a very detailed effort—sometimes line by line.

> In the opening phrase, the poet begins to develop a complex image which, as we soon realize, is central in his first three stanzas. His narrator sees the "latticework" of a bridge, which...

Explication is useful in studying some sample paragraphs of a writer's style, or in the comprehensive study of very short works, such as one-page poems.

With longer works, a standard practice is to choose an aspect which seems specially relevant to the chief ideas, or to the sentiment, or to an artistic method employed. In dealing with fiction, for example, we can sometimes narrow our focus to one of these six basic narrative elements:

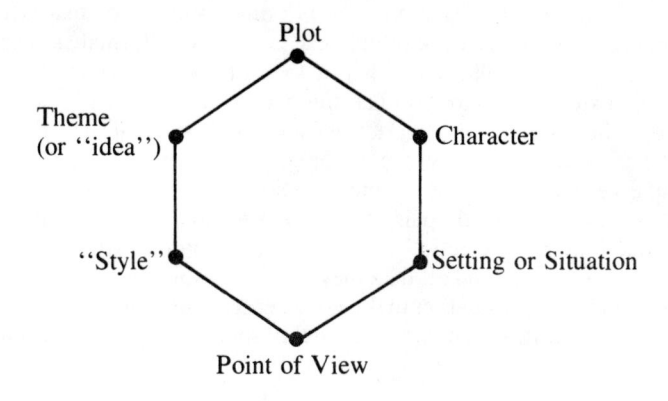

```
                    Plot
                     •
       Theme       /   \
      (or "idea") •     • Character
                  |     |
         "Style" •     • Setting or Situation
                   \   /
                     •
               Point of View
```

None of the elements, of course, is independent; all are tightly interrelated. One way to firm up our topic a bit is to select one of the links in this spider web. To illustrate: We can choose to write on the importance of the setting in the plot's action, or the setting's contribution to the themes.

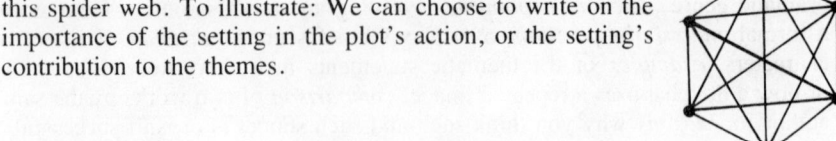

Another way to sharpen the focus is simply to sharpen the focus. Consider such topics as these:

PLOT	"The Carefully Wrought Climax of *Death in Venice*"
CHARACTER	"A Basic Weakness in *Moby Dick's* Starbuck"
SETTING	"The Role of the Setting in the Opening of Hardy's *The Return of the Native*"
POINT OF VIEW	"The Obtuse Narrator of Ring Lardner's 'Haircut'"
STYLE	"Heat-of-Battle Dialog in *The Red Badge of Courage*"
THEME	"Freudian Views of *The Turn of the Screw*"

(Still other essays, incidentally, might be written about a work's use of foreshadowing, or of irony, unless these are regarded as topics subsumed under "plot" or "style.")

This same narrowing effort is of course required in dealing with drama and poetry. Before wading in too deep there, however, you should familiarize yourself with the technical vocabulary of each of those genres. There are many helpful guides in the library.[23]

In some cases your problems may baffle you, overpower you. All right; admit you need expert assistance from works of criticism. What are the critics for, if not to help us see clearly and understand? But remember that, once you get aid from *one* such "outside" source, you will need to get some *more* views—and then to treat your paper as an assignment in research, with all your sources scrupulously credited. Remember also that your instructor will want to see your *own* thought controlling this paper; don't borrow too much from these sources.

As you gain experience in such projects, you may notice that the experts occasionally fall into "schools" of criticism. Some will use a psychological approach, often Freudian, to study the author or his characters. Others may employ a "sociological" bias, studying the times and places that affected the author, in order to see his work more clearly. A third ("formalist") group will argue that criticism is valid only when it focuses upon the craftsmanship—not upon these "external" factors. Other approaches are "moral," "archetypal," and so on. The question of a work's meaning will suddenly seem even more complex than you'd first thought. Five or six skilled critics, you find, can read a poem and get five or six varied interpretations.

If that leaves you in despair, cheer up. Probably the best criticism to be found is that done by "eclectic" types—people who don't fit into any of these categories, who use any and all data they can find, who are concerned only that a particular theory or evaluation make good sense. Amateurs, too, are welcome to try their hands at it. Often they can quickly spot a scene flawed by sentimentality, or overblown rhetoric, or imitativeness, or phoniness, or shallowness, or heavy didacticism. Instructors give assignments in criticism because they feel each will help develop your reasoning powers, your values, your sensibilities, and your judgment. It's a prime instance of the intellectual extension that higher education is supposed to produce. Give it the best you can.

UU-C2 *Other essay types*

No good purposes are served, probably, by giving more than quick mention to other essay forms which have been isolated and identified. These include:

a. *Reporting,* which is an attempt to answer our natural questions—*who? what? when? where? why? how?*—about a 3 a.m. warehouse fire, or a noontime bank robbery, or a successful philanthropic effort, or a Presidential campaign tour, or any other event with human significance. It commonly begins with a "lead," a summary paragraph or two, and then presents details in order of dwindling importance or interest. A variant type emphasizes a narrative pattern.

b. *Reflective and philosophical essays,* which are distant cousins of the personal-experience theme you may have done early in your college career. In the earlier situation your soul perhaps bled copiously, but you got the paper finished, and you survived. Now suppose, strange to say, you actually enjoyed the experience of peering into your own heart and mind. Later, as a more sophisticated, "educated" person, perhaps once again you will get the urge to reflect upon the curious ways of this old world, and upon your attitudes toward them. Or maybe this reflection will be disciplined to a degree by one of the various philosophic positions. Neither of these situations is quite comprehended by a label like "exposition" or "argument."

c. *Miscellaneous types* are usually subspecies of exposition or argument, or are mixed breeds.

The Upper-Uppers, as we said, are often capable critics of others' writing. Whether it's because of their upbringing, or their posh schools, or the foreign languages they learn there, isn't very clear—and it may be some other factor—but for some reason the U-U's know good writing when they see it. They applaud language that is appropriate to its context, precise, and economical. They admire sentences that have varied structure and, hence, inherent interest. They respect clarity, honesty and sincerity, logicality, energy, naturalness, and grace—all the qualities we have been discussing. But their highest praise goes to the writer who is able to create, out of all these other factors, a certain *sparkle.* This brilliance sometimes is seen in a special insight the writer has when dealing with what's called "human nature"; he can show human strengths realistically and our weaknesses satirically, or with just the right touch of compassion. At other times the sparkle results from a flexible style, or from inventiveness in playing with language—experimenting with alliteration, puns, and other sources of humor, and inventing fresh phrases, analogies, metaphors, allusions.

And we must agree with the Upper-Uppers; such a writer deserves many honors.

> ... the sum of all private decisions in the market is greater than its individual parts: this sum is a social system, in which disparities in wealth reinforce the position of the powerful and the privileged in a cumulative and dynamic way.
> —Joseph Featherstone, 1974

CHAPTER 9
SOME RECOMMENDATIONS

Now, perhaps it goes without saying that no American, probably, fits perfectly into one of the six sociolinguistic categories discussed here. (My own writing, with its inconsistencies and all its swings between formal and informal, illustrates our desire for verbal elbow-room.) Yet the categories can serve us, I think, as useful generalizations. In the closing years of the 20th Century we have been witness, as usual, to the extraordinary variety and richness of American English—before it expands still more and evolves into new forms for the next century.

We have seen that the six great American social classes differ, sometimes rather sharply, in their use of our national language. In view of their contrasted circumstances, it could hardly be otherwise; each class uses the few dialects it has learned—one set of them for speech, another for writing, with the refinement level determined by one's status. Moreover, once particular dialects become established in a given class, complex forces of social control tend to keep them there as unofficial standards of good taste. In the slums it is "fairy" talk or "putting on airs" to bow to the standards of the school. Or, in another mood, such an effort is merely regarded as useless or hopeless. "Why bust your ass," a lower-class girl asks somewhat coarsely, "when they ain't gonna accept you anyhow?" By "they" she means the middle class generally. Some L-L parents do not encourage their children; they think of ambition and drive as luxuries. "They require a minimum *physical* security; only when one knows where his next week's or next month's food and shelter will come from can he and his children afford to go in for long term education and training."[1] The L-L youth soon learns to be resigned and, often, to confine his attention to getting whatever rude pleasures he can.

In the Upper-Lower Class, though, there is some reason to hope for social mobility, and hence some willing conformity to middle-class speech (and other) standards. We all can cite examples of the underprivileged who, by marrying well, or by working days and going to night school, have pulled themselves up to middle-class status and relative security or even comfort.

There is frequently some pain in this for the U-L striver, and for his or her counterparts in other classes, too. Often there is a long transition period in which the upwardly mobile person is not accepted by either the class he's leaving or the one he's moving into. He has temporarily become what sociologist Ralph Turner calls "the marginal man," a person unable to resolve fully the conflicts "between value systems and between organized-group ties." These "choices are necessary because the strata have imcompatible value systems and because it is difficult to maintain ties across stratum boundaries."[2]

People born middle-class, though, have a much easier time of it than the lower-class climbers. Lower-Middles have easy access to reliable career information and aptitude testing; Upper-Middles have, in addition, a great deal of parental prodding. Before long both have mastered various kinds of specialized skills—skills necessary these days in scaling the steep slopes of occupational pyramids. Dr. Keller thinks that privileged groups no longer control all top positions. "At the highest pinnacles," she says, "the boy of privilege, no less than the 'poor boy who made good,' must achieve and maintain his elite position by hard work [and] competitive merit...This trend weakens and may eventually break the age-old link between elite status and upper-class status."[3]

The "elites" or top-level positions in most business and professional pyramids are nonetheless dominated, as we have seen, by the Lower-Upper Class. What's more, a tight kinship of mutual esteem and "class identity" has grown up among these moguls, so that a New York airlines titan can relate easily to a king of Chicago rental housing or a rich Portland cement supplier. They talk the same lingo and, of course, share the same business-oriented political persuasion. Dr. Keller has this to say about L-U cohesion: "Most members of most elites approve of ambition, self-discipline and hard work...The sheer fact of elite membership entails certain similar experiences: the necessity to supervise subordinates, the responsibilities of power and influence, the temptation to self-indulgence, the enjoyment of similar privileges."[4]

There are common denominators among the Upper-Uppers also, the chief ones perhaps being their high educational levels, their great wealth, and their power. Someone has said that the purpose of education is not to teach us how to make money, but rather how to spend it wisely. U-U spending patterns vary substantially, however, and thus it is difficult to assess U-U wisdom. Some multi-millionaires are great savers, others aren't.[5] Some spend carefully; others gamble away more in an hour than a Lower-Lower makes in a year.

But their education has certainly taught them how to *make* money. According to *Big Business Leaders in America:* "Education has become the royal road to positions of power and privilege in American business and industry."[6] That the combination of education and money leads almost inexorably to power, and to prestige, has been amply demonstrated in many texts. One final sliver of testimony on the extent of that authority, from sociologist C. Wright Mills:

> The power elite is composed of men whose positions enable them to transcend the ordinary environments of ordinary men and women; they are in positions to make decisions having major consequences.... For they are in command of the major hierarchies and organizations of modern society.... They occupy the strategic command posts of the social structure...[7]

This re-view of the American class structure leads us to this question: Are there arguments for preserving the *status quo*? The answer is, of course, yes. All institutions have an apologia; otherwise they wouldn't exist at all. Some of the defense's points were covered in Chapter 8. Here are a few more:

1. "Stratification is necessary in order to get difficult tasks performed. A man who undergoes years of arduous training necessary to become an accountant will be motivated . . . only if there is a reward at the end."[8]

2. Large segments of the masses (and of course the higher classes, too) are happy with the "stability" and "serenity" of a class hierarchy.

3. "The culture found in a stratified society. . . is more satisfying, interesting, and stimulating than that found in a homogenized society."[9]

4. And, anyhow, classless societies are impossible to create. "Since inequalities of reward are part and parcel of complex societies, equality is in principle unattainable . . ."[10]

These arguments seem rather persuasive, at least at first glance, but crumble badly when we reflect what a good (non-Communist) leftist debater might do to them. Not only that, but they run counter to some American folklore—that we already *have* essentially a classless society, and that's why the United States of America is so stable, serene, interesting, etc.

Well, then, since in actuality the United States is very sharply class-structured, and since sharp gradients are difficult to defend, we come to another question. Is there any reason to hope for more equality in the near future? Can U.S. capitalism evolve into something a bit more humane?

John Kenneth Galbraith is very optimistic; indeed, he thinks we are "well on the way" to the elimination of poverty. He thinks, too, that "the leisure class has been replaced" by something he calls the New Class, and that the United States is already a meritocracy. The New Class enjoys exemption "from manual toil; escape from boredom and confining and severe routine; the chance to spend one's life in clean and physically comfortable surroundings; and some opportunity for applying one's thoughts to the day's work . . ." Now we should enlarge this white-collar caste, through greater investments in education; "the further and rapid expansion of this class should be a major, and perhaps next to peaceful survival itself, *the* major social goal of the society." Galbraith seems hopeful that this may soon come to pass. And what about all the old manual-labor jobs? Well, he says, blue-collar workers would be so scarce (and costly to hire) that business and industry would have strong incentive to introduce more automation.[11]

For her part, Professor Keller accepts the necessity of some inequality, but she wants a social order in which "men are content with their lot." She hopes that our occupational pyramids will continue to foster equality of *opportunity*.

> If strategic elites are to lead, innovate, and inspire men to the attainment of social goals, they must accept their superiority—however temporary. Consequently, leaders of democracies must develop an ideology of superiority without its degeneration into moral arrogance or status snobbishness. This ideology, to be well founded, need not be rooted in untenable beliefs about racial or genetic superiority. . . . Elites

and the mass of men must accept the principle of inequality in talents and responsibilities without succumbing to a servile dependency or indifference.[12]

Though she sees various problems, she remains sanguine: "Saint-Simon's dream of a society governed not by force but by ability, with people submitting not out of fear but out of respect for skill and knowledge, is gradually being realized."[13]

Finally, Vance Packard reminds us of a few tendencies toward a more "open" society, including new kinds of jobs, new communities, easy access to college classes, and the ever-present advertising of the delights of ownership, which continues to be a powerful set of stimuli for the lower classes.[14]

There is something unsatisfying, though, about all these hopeful projections and predictions. Despite Professor Galbraith, both poverty and the leisure class seem to have remarkable staying-power. Despite Professor Keller and Mr. Packard, we seem no closer to Saint-Simon's Eden than we were, say, a half-century ago. The top fifth still gets 40 per cent of our personal income, whereas the bottom fifth gets about 6 per cent—and of course nothing much is being done about wealth redistribution, either.

Moreover, as Packard tells us on other pages, there are many tendencies toward an even more rigid "closed" society, including the creation of more impersonal bureaucratic structures, "the growing isolation of rank-and-file employees from management," and the "role of big unions in freezing men and women to their jobs, and discouraging initiative."[15] Seniority, he says, now decides questions about promotions, which practice customarily rewards some middle-class segments at the expense of the lower class.

Now, a third reasonable question in this closing chapter is this: Why haven't the three huge lower classes (or the Lower-Middles alone) used the ballot-box to establish equity, or to further their own interests? Marx and Engels, you recall, preached even in the first half of the 19th Century that the bourgeoisie was cheating the proletariat, was exploiting it at every turn. Somehow, though, the masses became almost fully enfranchised, despite the deep misgivings of many propertied capitalists. Marx and these nervous gentlemen noted alike that the electoral system had given the working classes a chance of victory. Yet the conservatives' fears proved completely groundless, as Ferdinand Lundberg reminds us in *The Rich and the Super-Rich:*

> these lower classes, both in the United States and Europe, have never shown the slightest inclination to use their franchise to replace existing institutions with institutions more favorable to their own comfort, convenience and necessity. They cannot even obtain an equitable tax system, do not even realize that they live under a grossly inequitable tax system that ridiculously favors "the bourgeoisie." The missing ingredient in the lower classes is knowledge, understanding and, above all, *determination* to work at all times to secure their own interests. They childishly expect some political good fairy to do this for them, and thus they stand forth as *dependents*.[16]

This is savage criticism, and yet I think it is largely justified. Of course there are other factors and other explanations. A counter-theory is that, far from being child-like and naive, the proletariat has very carefully noted that it is completely powerless to mount any kind of effective political campaign, much less an expensive one. Furthermore, the workers know how easily the higher classes can arrange the fragmentation of their voting bloc. They are, therefore, simply being realistic in their despairing cynicism.

Another theory for Mr. Blue Collar's political inaction is that he has been hoodwinked; he has swallowed the "myth of upward mobility." One version of this idea puts all the blame on the crafty tycoons of advertising. Television commercials and magazine ads seem to make the good life available to all, just around some sponsored corner, while others beckon toward seductive "doorways to success." Half-consciously Mr. Blue Collar has thus discarded his working-class identity and cast his lot with the *petit bourgeoisie*.

A variant of this is that he has limitless faith in his union—that he is unaware that the union is nothing but "a tool of the capitalists," and that it has become a *petit bourgeois* institution designed to keep wages rising at just the rate determined safe (for maximum profits) by the upper class.

Still more explanations, touched on in this book, tend to support Lundberg's "dependency" thesis. Throughout the lower classes and well into the Lower-Middle Class, we can chart the diseases of semi-literacy, low motivation, and ignorance, resulting in deep apathy in some cases and, in others, susceptibility to all kinds of propaganda, much of it debilitating. For example, the lower classes are badly afflicted with xenophobia—a fear and hatred of foreigners and their "alien philosophies." They also often display steel-hard intolerance of "non-Christian" ideas, imported or not. The result has been, for one thing, a fanatic hatred of communism—or, indeed, anything which might be thought related to it in any sense.

For these reasons, and others, surely, the great bulk of the American people have never befriended radical organizations. As we said early in the book, Americans are basically conservative, and we should probably expect the persistence of various capitalistic institutions. This will entail, of course, a great deal of continued social waste. For one thing, as experts have been warning, many impecunious young people will not be able to afford a complete college education. For another, our very costly crime rate will remain shockingly high. The U.S. Chamber of Commerce says cost estimates range from $4.19 to $6 billion annually,[17] and there would be no reason to hope for any substantial decrease.

(There *is* reason, however, to hope for increased understanding of American criminality. One of the best analyses of this complicated topic is Edwin M. Schur's *Our Criminal Society*. Schur deplores the dearth of reliable data about the dimensions of the problem. For instance, there are some problems with the FBI's reporting procedures in its annual *Uniform Crime Reports* that limit its usefulness as a statistical tool.[18] But crimes make constant headlines and seem to bother many Americans, so perhaps Schur is entitled to his book's title. Well, then, *why* is the United States so lawless? Among his answers: "America is a criminal society because it is an unequal society," with "profound frustration, hopelessness, and despair" in its lower strata.[19] And "America is a criminal society because of certain emphases in our cultural values that help generate crime... dynamism, individualism, competition and personal success," with "success" defined chiefly in pecuniary terms.[20])

So Americans rush to buy guns to protect themselves, thereby ironically increasing their own danger and that of their neighbors and friends. Many middle-class whites see the threat of crime in terms of their racial stereotypes. Once again, they are usually wrong. "Negroes are most likely to assault Negroes, whites most likely to assault whites," says a Presidential crime commission.[21] Black neighborhoods often have a high crime rate, to be sure—*if* they happen to be lower-class areas. (There are many middle-class black neighborhoods now, and these new bourgeois Negroes regard the "housing-project trash" as a criminal element.)

A good bit of social waste, as we said. But the people's acceptance of steep social-class gradients "must be taken as a central fact of American life."

In all of these observations about the rigidity of the class structure, we can see two sets of implications—one for society and one for the individual and/or his family.

For society there is, for example, the ever-more-pressing moral obligation to educate fully every child of the realm—to take him in, nurture him, adapt teaching techniques to his needs, and then monitor his performance to insure success up to his limits. Despite difficulties caused by the heterogeneity of these students, schools from kindergarten to graduate school must redouble efforts to make adequate provision for all races and social classes. This responsibility will almost certainly involve bussing to create an appropriate ethnic "mix" at many schools—or at large, well-equipped educational "centers." It will also demand multiple teaching and learning methods in perhaps every field of study.

This required flexibility is clearly necessary in the teaching of English composition. At every level there should be greatly expanded opportunities for individualized work, despite the cost. I have tried to suggest a few appropriate activities for students from all six classes. Perhaps I should say again, though, that individuals often can outdistance their class-mates and should be allowed to move at their own speed—and thus the emphasis here, not only upon tailoring the material to the student in a particular curriculum, but also upon independent study. I've suggested that, once a student has advanced appreciably, he or she could be asked to do some work in the history of the English language (see UU-U1). Beyond that, I've left a great amount to the imagination of the instructor and his student. I would hope most would select some literary topics, because developing sensitivity to poetry and other literature is developing one's very humanity. A central observation in this book has been that our language has its delights. Perhaps, too, some students might choose to discuss a few social or economic problems mentioned in these chapters, either to affirm my broad generalizations about America or to disprove them.

Continuation of the economic and social *status quo* in the American culture has implications also for the individual and his family. It may be that the optimistic social forecasts of Professors Galbraith and Keller will be borne out eventually. I remain skeptically "realistic" but can't deny the possibility. In any event, though, there will be a long wait. In the meantime, in the revered American tradition of independence, it's every household for itself. Of course there are families unfamiliar with the middle-class work ethic. In such cases the responsibility for self-starting and self-discipline will fall squarely on the individual. Indeed, a rugged individualism wins praise at many social levels. Allow me, please, to repeat an earlier passage:

> But what about the robust person who is unwilling to accept his or her lot? If he can expect little help from society—the electorate—can he still make it on his own? Can he jump the class barriers and find a better life?
>
> The answer—indeed, the cheery message of this book—is that *of course* he can! What it takes is pluck, determination, good old American get-up-and-go!

Lots of luck.

APPENDIX A
Business letters—
including the job-application letter

There is room for a few slight changes in the form of the business letter, but the models on the next pages are fairly typical. There are six parts:

1. The heading, including your full address and the date.
2. The inside address, identical with that on the envelope.
3. The salutation. (If you don't know the person's name, it's conventional to say "Sir" or "Dear Sir." If you're writing to no particular individual, make it "Gentlemen" or "Dear Sirs.")
4. The body. (In the case of a job application, be as brief as possible, but try to indicate how you learned of the opening, why you'd like the job, and why you'd be an asset to the firm. Your final paragraph should be much like that in the model.)
5. The complimentary close. (In writing to strangers, say "Yours," "Yours truly," or maybe "Yours very truly." Save cordiality for later.)
6. The signature. (Always sign in blue or black ink. If you've been typing, type your name under your signature.)

123 Voltaire Ave.,
College Town, ED 11111,
27 May 1974

Mr. John Doe,
Personnel Manager,
XYZ Insurance Corp.,
1802 Sixth St.,
Industrial City, WC 98203

Dear Mr. Doe:

     In the Industrial City <u>News</u> (I read my home-town paper regularly) you advertised this week for a claims adjustor. If the position is still open, I would like to apply.

     I understand the job requires almost daily travel throughout West Carolina. I have lived there most of my life and know the state's roads well. Such a job would let me further develop my experience in insurance work. I have not dealt specifically with motor homes and trailers before, but I have had summer employment in two insurance agencies.

     This has been my second year at East Dakota University, where I have been taking business, data-processing, and other courses. My financial situation, however, requires me to move home. I may be able to take some night classes at West Carolina State College.

     I enclose a personal data form. I shall be home after June 10 and would appreciate an interview at your convenience.

                               Very truly yours,

                               Alicia M. Donovan

                               Alicia M. Donovan

122 Main St.,
Smalltown, WA 98105
1 Sept. 1975

Apex Electronics,
6821-12th St.,
Gofar, WD 54321

Sirs:

      Your 1975 catalog lists only two models of electronic calculators; we would like more information on both. We also understood your sales representative to say, several months ago, that you plan to introduce a third model this year. If so, please advise.

      Specifically, as to Model 1718, along with the basic arithmetic and exponential functions, does it also do square roots? (One line of type is blurred.) The $25.80 list price to dealers seems a reasonable figure for an 8-digit model. Do you expect this price to be stable through the year?

      As to Model No. 1725, your "Mini-Calculator" (six digits, four math functions): does it come equipped with battery? Your catalog isn't explicit on that point. Here again, the $12.05 dealer list price seems agreeable.

      Finally, will you please specify your shipping options?

      We would appreciate hearing from you at your earliest convenience.

                                   Yours truly,

                                   R. D. Hansworthy

                                   R. D. Hansworthy
                                   Manager
                                   Smalltown General Store

RDH:aj

2402 University Drive,
College Town, ED 11111,
12 May 1975

Apex Electronics,
6821-12th St.,
Gofar, WD 54321

Dear Sirs:

    This letter is in response to your May 11 advertisement in the College Town <u>Chronicle</u>, in which you solicit job inquiries from electrical engineers.

    I am ending my college work early next month. I expect to be graduated from East Dakota University with a Bachelor of Science degree in electrical engineering. My grade-point average as of last semester is 3.18, which is the equivalent of a B-plus. My average in engineering courses is about 3.5.

    I hope to secure a position in the Gofar area because of the abundance of wildlife nearby. My chief pastimes are hunting and fishing. I have often hunted in West Dakota, and sometimes in your vicinity.

    Enclosed is a personal data sheet. Should you wish to interview me, I shall be glad to drive over to Gofar whenever you say. Until June 30 I can be reached at (209) 782-1321.

                                              Yours,

                                             Stuart Grant

APPENDIX B
The personal data form

The form that follows, often called a résumé, is largely self-explanatory, but a few introductory remarks are warranted. (1) Under *Personal information* you might want to indicate that you're a Vietnam veteran, or a Turkish citizen, or some other important detail. (2) The *Education* material should be arranged backwards chronologically, with any gaps explained. (3) The third section is a "miscellaneous" category, really; here you could cite any writing or other important work you've done. You might then wish to change the heading some. (4) Your employment record, like your education, should be related in reverse order. Indicate who your supervisors were. Don't be afraid to include even yard work or babysitting; these show an early aptitude for personal effort. (5) Include at least three references. (Don't forget to first get their permission.)

Personal information
    Name: Alicia M. Donovan
    Home address: 2322 Cotton Ave., Industrial City, WC 98201
    Home phone: 259-1967
    Age: 20 (born 2 May 1954, Savannah, Ga.)
    Marital status: Unmarried

Education

East Dakota University College Town, E.D.	1972-74
Robert E. Lee High School Industrial City, W.C.	1968-72
Stonewall Jackson Primary School Industrial City, W.C.	1960-68

Awards, honors
    Scholastic Honor Society, high school, 1970-72
    Girls' swim team, high school, 1969-71
    Secretarial scholarship (to college of my choice), 1972

Work experience

Hanson Insurance Agency,
1201-8th St.,
Industrial City
    (Duties included general office work:
    writing of policies, claims reports, etc.
    I was supervised by Mr. Clyde H. Hanson,
    the firm's owner.)
	Summer 1973

Donovan Insurance Agency,
1815-86th St.,
Industrial City
    (Duties included clerical work, some
    general office work—for my father)
	Summer 1971, 1972

Babysitting (several employers)	1968-71

References

Prof. Richard Douglas,   Mr. Clyde H. Hanson,
School of Business Administration,   Hanson Insurance Agency,
East Dakota University,   1201-8th St.,
College Town, ED 11111   Industrial City, WC 98203

Mrs. Charles Donnelly,
2517 Cotton Ave.,
Industrial City, WC 98201

NOTES

CHAPTER 1

[1]See, *e.g.*, references to a group of such servants in Gov. William Bradford's *Of Plymouth Plantation*, in Sculley Bradley, Richmond Croom Beatty, and E. Hudson Long, eds., *The American Tradition in Literature*, 3rd ed. (New York: Norton, 1967), I, 28-29. See also Louis M. Hacker, *The Triumph of American Capitalism* (New York: Columbia Univ. Press, 1947) and esp. Ch. IX, "The Building of a Class Society."

[2]St. Jean de Crèvecoeur, "What Is an American?" *Letters from an American Farmer* (1782), in *The American Tradition in Literature*, I, 192.

[3]*The Federalist*, No. 10 (1787), in *The Enduring Federalist*, ed. Charles A. Beard (Garden City, N.Y.: Doubleday, 1948), p. 70.

[4]Reported by Peter Barnes, "How Wealth Is Distributed: The GNP Machine," *The New Republic*, 167 (Sept. 30, 1972), 19.

[5]U.S. Commission on Industrial Relations, quoted by Barnes.

[6]James D. Smith of Pennsylvania State Univ., quoted by Barnes. Smith's figure of 25 per cent may be too conservative; see the studies reported by Ferdinand Lundberg, *The Rich and the Super-Rich* (New York: Lyle Stuart, 1968), Ch. 1, *passim*.

[7]From a 1972 report by the Sabre Foundation (using 1962 figures), quoted by Barnes. Similar data were derived by Prof. Robert J. Lampman, Univ. of Wisconsin, for the National Bureau of Economic Research, reported in *The Rich and the Super-Rich*, pp. 16-19.

[8]Reported by Barnes, p. 18. The study was made by Professors Lester C. Thurow and Robert Lucas, Massachusetts Institute of Technology.

[9]"Household Money Income in 1972 and Selected Social and Economic Characteristics of Households," *Consumer Income*, Bureau of the Census, July 1973, p. 3. Using 1972 and 1973 census data, Fabian Linden painted a similarly dismal picutre in "The Characteristics of Class," *The Conference Board Record*, Oct. 1973, p. 63.

[10]Barnes, p. 19.

[11]Voters in the State of Washington in late 1973 rejected overwhelmingly a mildly progressive income tax.

[12]Joel B. Montague, Jr., *Class and Nationality: English and American Studies* (New Haven, Conn.: College and University Press, 1963), p. 88.

[13]*Ibid.*, p. 90.

[14]*Ibid.*, p. 91.

[15]Russell Lynes, *A Surfeit of Honey* (New York: Harper, 1957), p. 14.

[16]*Ibid.*, pp. 15-16.

[17]Suzanne Keller, *Beyond the Ruling Class* (New York: Random House, 1963), p. 20.

[18]*Ibid.*, p. 124.

[19]The "temporary supremacy of one elite is the rule rather than the exception" (Keller, p. 125). She thinks changing societal problems continuously create new prestige values; sometimes military men are top dogs, sometimes businessmen (p. 126).

[20]Lynes, p. 12. First he admits there is a group of "intellectual floaters" (lawyers, architects, university people) who fit into perhaps several pyramids—and are therefore, I argue, more intimately and reasonably associated with a particular *class*. Second, he says there is a lot of "flirtation" between pyramids, and ambitious people often "try to score points by talking each others' language. . . .David Riesman has also called attention to this 'homogenization' of our society, with corporations cuddling up to colleges, engineers cuddling up to philosophers. . ." (pp. 26-27). This, I maintain, is frequently class-oriented or class-centered activity.

[21]Keller, p. 206. Explicitly: "The spirit of cooperation among the various strategic elites depends largely upon a common social heritage, a heritage which must be rooted in some subsection of society if it is to be more than a vague set of principles. Until recently it was generally rooted in the interests and outlook of a single social class." That, she argues, is slowly changing (p. 191).

[22]For instance, a doctrine of socio-economic classes can clarify the elites' processes of recruitment and selection; *e.g.*, we might see just how much difficulty an impecunious person would have entering Career A as opposed to Career B. Or we could understand better why some people are not given upper-class status even though their wealth and income would seem adequate. And we would come to know much more about a class stratum if we could see more clearly the occupational structures of which it is composed.

All we're doing here, really, is giving "occupation and position" more emphasis than is common. All status studies include occupation as a prestige factor. Here, by giving it distinct focus and attention, we are sharply increasing the factor's weight.

[23]W. Lloyd Warner, Marchia Meeker, and Kenneth Eells, *Social Class in America* (New York: Harper and Row, 1960); originally published in a slightly different form in 1949. (In much of his work, it should be noted, Warner used a five-class model, not six.) An earlier book with a six-class set was Allison Davis, Burleigh G. Gardner, and Mary R. Gardner, *Deep South* (Chicago: Univ. of Chicago Press, 1941).

[24]Warner, p. 88.
[25]*Ibid.*, p. 90.
[26]*Ibid.*, p. 92.
[27]*Ibid.*, p. 96.
[28]Karl Marx, *Capital* (Chicago: Charles H. Kerr, 1912), I, 708-09.
[29]Merle Curti, *The Growth of American Thought* (New York: Harper, 1943), pp. 640-41.
[30]John Kenneth Galbraith, *The Affluent Society* (Boston: Houghton Mifflin, 1958), p. 56.
[31]Lynes, p. 11.
[32]*Ibid.*, pp. 9-10.
[33]Richard A. Lester, *Economics of Labor* (New York: Macmillan, 1947), p. 250.
[34]Quoted by Charles A. and Mary R. Beard, *A Basic History of the United States* (New York: New Home Library, 1944), p. 378.

CHAPTER 2

[1]Vance Packard, *The Status Seekers: An Exploration of Class Behavior in America and the Hidden Barriers That Affect You, Your Community, Your Future* (New York: David McKay, 1959), p. 5.
[2]Pierre Martineau, director, Research Division, *Chicago Tribune*, quoted by Packard, p. 12.
[3]Lundberg, p. 56.
[4]"The Fifty-Million-Dollar Man," *Fortune* (Nov. 1957), quoted by Lundberg, p. 42 (but modified; see p. 50).
[5]Quoted by Lundberg, p. 59.
[6]Warner, p. 23.
[7]*Ibid.*, p. 21.
[8]Packard, p. 222.
[9]Warner, p. 24.
[10]Warner, quoting a 1948 source, reported: "It has been estimated that, whereas 80 per cent of the upper- and upper-middle-class children actually go to college, only 20 per cent of the lower-middle and five per cent of the lower-class children get there" (p. 25). By now (1975) all these figures are low, but the United States still has a long way to go before the disparities are eliminated. A 1973 Census Bureau study indicated that in homes with less than $5,000 annual income, 13 per cent of the household heads had had some exposure to college. At the $5,000-to-$10,000 level the percentage jumped to 20.6 and in the $10,000-to-$15,000 class, it was 28.3 per cent. Reported by Fabian Linden, "The Characteristics of Class," *The Conference Board Record*, Oct. 1973, p. 63. These data, of course, do not express the current rate of college attendance by *all* individuals in the respective classes.

[11]Warner, p. 28.

[12]*Ibid.*, p. 26; see also August B. Hollingshead, *Elmtown's Youth* (New York: John Wiley, 1949), p. 173.
[13]"Social Class and Friendship among School Children," *American Journal of Sociology*, 51 (1946), 305-13; reported in Warner, p. 28.
[14]Hollingshead, p. 168.
[15]*Ibid.*, p. 222.
[16]Packard, p. 229.
[17]Warner, p. 24. Similar views are to be found in Robert S. Lynd and Helen Merrell Lynd, *Middletown* (New York: Harcourt, Brace, 1929), Ch. XIII, "Who Go to School?" See also the Lynds' *Middletown in Transition* (New York: Harcourt, Brace, 1937), Ch. VI, "Training the Young."
[18]Christopher Jencks et al., *Inequality: A Reassessment of the Effect of Family and Schooling in America* (New York: Basic Books, 1972), pp. 209-46. In an appendix on "Estimating the Heritability of IQ Scores," the authors state: "Our best guess is that genotype explains about 45 percent of the variance in IQ scores, that environment explains about 35 percent, and that the correlation between genotype and environment explains the remaining 20 percent" (p. 315). But "neither men's genes nor the quality of their schooling explains much of the variation in their incomes. Family background explains a bit more, as does overall cognitive skill. Educational credentials also have a modest effect" (p. 209). One further possible explanation advanced in the book is that some people simply value money more than others do and make "unusual sacrifices" to get it—which seems a reasonable hypothesis.

The team, incidentally, opted for a form of socialism. The best way to end economic inequality, they said, is to do it directly: simply put on incomes both a ceiling and a floor, a maximum and a minimum (p. 220).

On the social effects of education, See also Ralph H. Turner, *The Social Context of Ambition* (San Francisco: Chandler, 1964), p. 225, and Bernard Barber, *Social Stratification* (New York: Harcourt, Brace, 1957), p. 395.
[19]Keller, p. 206.
[20]*Ibid.*
[21]Thorstein Veblen observed in 1899: "The constituency of the leisure class is kept up by a continuous selective process...In order to reach the upper levels the aspirant must have, not only a fair average complement of the pecuniary aptitudes, but he must have these gifts in such an eminent degree as to overcome very material difficulties that stand in the way of his ascent." *The Theory of the Leisure Class* (Boston: Houghton Mifflin, 1973), pp. 158-59.
[22]This assumes, of course, that you bathe frequently and are otherwise fastidious about the details of personal attractiveness. A suit or dress that is slightly out of style may sometimes be forgiven, however, if you smell good.

CHAPTER 3

[1]There are many canards abroad about public assistance—that hordes prefer it to working, that families can live comfortably on the dole, that welfare mothers bear illegitimate children to boost their income, and so on. In 1967, a prosperous year, a White House study revealed that only one out of 146 on welfare was actually employable. A reporter quoted Joseph Califano, a Presidential special assistant:

> of a total of 7.3 million Americans on relief, he said, 2.1 million are over 65; 700,000 are blind or severely handicapped; 3.5 million are children; 900,000 are their mothers and 150,000 are their fathers. Of all these fathers, fully two-thirds are incapable of being given job skills and training that will make them self-sufficient." That, says Califano, leaves only 50,000 relief receivers in the whole country who can leave the rolls and go back to work.

—"The Unemployable," *Newsweek*, May 1, 1967, p. 30.
[2]Bureau of the Census, *Statistical Abstract of the United States: 1973*, 94th ed. (Washington, D.C., 1973), p. 328.
[3]*Stat. Abstract: 1972*, 93rd ed., p. 324.
[4]*Ibid.*, p. 328.

⁵"13 Million Ill-Housed, Study Reveals," *Seattle Post-Intelligencer*, Dec. 12, 1973, Sec. A, p. 6.

⁶Galbraith, *The Affluent Society*, p. 323. Galbraith sees basically two kinds of destitution: (1) *Case* poverty—"'some quality peculiar to the individual or family involved—mental deficiency, bad health, inability to adapt to the discipline of modern economic life, excessive procreation, alcohol, insufficient education, or perhaps a combination of several of these handicaps—have kept these individuals from participating in the general well-being" (p. 325). (2) *Insular* poverty—*e.g.* in Appalachia—"the poverty of the community insures that educational opportunities will be limited, that health services will be poor, and that subsequent generations will be ill prepared either for mastering the environment into which they are born or for migration to areas of higher income outside" (p. 326).

⁷*Stat. Abstract: 1973*, p. 334.

⁸Charles Merrill Smith, *Instant Status, or How To Become a Pillar of the Upper Middle Class* (Garden City, N.Y.: Doubleday, 1972), p. 26.

⁹The instructor should be especially sympathetic and knowledgeable about the frustrations of non-whites in his classroom. For example, although more than a million poor Americans moved up to Upper-Lower Class status in 1972, the number of blacks left behind *increased* slightly. The Census Bureau reported that about 1.1 million new persons exceeded the official "poverty line" income ($4,275 for a city family of four) and the number of poor whites decreased. *The New Republic* commented that

> the relative position of blacks has worsened slightly. In 1959, 56 percent of all blacks and other nonwhites were below the poverty line; by last year that percentage had been cut to 33 percent. In 1959 only 18 percent of all whites were in the poverty category. By last year that number had been halved to nine percent. Whites are still being promoted faster, and the economic gap between whites and blacks is widening. Although the absolute number of poor people has been reduced by 15 million since 1959, the economy is still biased to favor white wage-earners. Nonwhites make up about 12 percent of the population, but last year they were 34 percent of the poor. This isn't underscored in the census report, nor is the fact that the percentage has increased since 1959, when only 28 percent of the poor were nonwhite.

—"Rich and Poor," *The New Republic*, Aug. 11, 1973, p. 8.

¹⁰William Labov, "The Logic of Nonstandard English," *Report of the Twentieth Annual Round Table Meeting on Linguistics and Language Studies*, ed. James E. Alatis (Washington: Georgetown Univ. Press 1970); reprinted with minor changes in Richard W. Bailey and Jay L. Robinson, eds., *Varieties of Present-Day English* (New York: Macmillan, 1973), p. 345. See also Labov's essay "Some Features of the English of Black Americans," *Varieties*, pp. 236-57.

¹¹Roger W. Shuy, "Language and Success: Who Are the Judges?" in Bailey and Robinson, eds., *Varieties*, p. 304.

¹²Labov, in his *The Social Stratification of English in New York City* (Washington: Center for Applied Linguistics, 1966), reports that the cultural norms of masculinity also support working-class (U-L) speech patterns. One immigrant from Massachusetts was mocked by his New York co-workers ("You speak like a fairy") until he deliberately coarsened his language. Reprinted in *Varieties*, p. 285.

¹³*Varieties*, p. 285.

¹⁴I have heard these black labels for a *woman*: chicken, deal, fish, fox, mink, side, snag. These may designate *money:* blood, bread, cake, jack, pound.

¹⁵Shuy, in *Varieties*, p. 313. See also Walt Wolfram, "Sociological Implications for Educational Sequencing," in *Teaching Standard English in the Inner City*, eds. Ralph W. Fasold and Roger W. Shuy (Washington: Center for Applied Linguistics, 1970), pp. 105-19.

¹⁶Transformationalist (sometimes called transformational-generative) grammarians are admirers of a 1957 work, *Syntactic Structures*, by linguist Noam Chomsky of the Massachusetts Institute of Technology, and of the scholarship of many others with the same general outlook. All these people work with a somewhat elaborate set of formulae in an effort to describe the English sentence in all its variety and patterned changeableness—rather than simply to prescribe rules of "proper " use. (In their theory, sentences are "generated" from certain kinds of structures and "transformed," according to strong conventions, into related patterns of various kinds.) They hope thus to get students more

aware of the stylistic possibilities of sentences, and hence able to choose more skillfully among many available forms.

Structuralists (sometimes called descriptivists) have objected to the lack of clarity and precision in traditional definitions of grammatical units (especially "parts of speech") and have created new definitions. These emphasize the "inflections" or form changes of a particular type of word, and its position and function in the sentence. A result is that, instead of eight traditional, often fuzzy parts of speech, the structuralists list twice as many but have them all meticulously defined.

Those interested in exploring these areas are directed to Noam Chomsky (see above): Winthrop Nelson Francis, *The Structure of American English* (New York: Ronald Press, 1958), Chs. 5-7; Charles Carpenter Fries, *The Structure of English* (New York: Harcourt, Brace, 1952), Chs. 4-7; H. A. Gleason Jr., *Linguistics and English Grammar* (New York: Holt, Rinehart and Winston, 1965); Paul Roberts, *English Sentences* (New York: Harcourt, Brace and World, 1962), and Donald J. Lloyd and Harry R. Warfel, *American English in Its Cultural Setting* (New York: Knopf, 1956). One of the most interesting and informative books in this area is Gleason's *An Introduction to Descriptive Linguistics*, rev. ed. (New York: Holt, Rinehart and Winston, 1961). A good general survey is Albert H. Marckwardt, *Introduction to the English Language* (New York: Oxford Univ. Press, 1942). Also relevant, although parts are too technical for the average reader, is Sheldon Rosenburg, ed., *Directions in Psycholinguistics* (New York: Macmillan, 1965).

[17]A system of eight categories has an English heritage that stretches back at least to the 15th Century. Only children of the higher classes went to school; they were required to memorize the "partyse of speche."

CHAPTER 4

[1]Linden, p. 63.
[2]*Ibid.*
[3]Edgar Z. Friedenberg, *The Dignity of Youth and Other Atavisms* (Boston: Beacon Press, 1965), p. 95.
[4]Thomas Gladwin, *Poverty U.S.A.* (Boston: Little, Brown, 1967), p. 77.
[5]August B. Hollingshead and F. C. Redlich, *Social Class and Mental Illness* (1958), quoted by Michael Harrington, *The Other America* (New York: Macmillan, 1964), p. 123.
[6]Harrington, p. 159.
[7]*Ibid.*, p. 107.
[8]*Ibid.*, p. 191.
[9]Galbraith, p. 329.
[10]See, *e.g.*, Marckwardt, *op. cit.*, or Albert C. Baugh, *History of the English Language* (New York: Appleton-Century, 1935).
[11]I started to devote a passage to *awake, awaken, wake,* and *waken,* but I grew unaccountably very drowsy. For helpful discussions, see entries in *The American Heritage Dictionary of the English Language* (1969) and esp. its usage label at *wake.*
[12]Lynes, p. 15.

CHAPTER 5

[1]Linden, p. 63.
[2]*Ibid.*
[3]*Ibid.*
[4]*Ibid.*
[5]"Median Money Income of Persons with Income, by Sex and Occupation: 1950 to 1970," *Stat. Abstract: 1973*, p. 334.
[6]"Households Owning Cars and Appliances, 1960 to 1971, and Percent Distribution, by Income Level, 1970 and 1971," *Stat. Abstract: 1973*, p. 332.
[7]*The American Heritage Dictionary of the English Language* (1969), p. xxiv.
[8]James Hamilton, *A Linguistic Study of Jonathan L. Moore's "Journal,"* unpublished monograph (1967), p. 9.

CHAPTER 6

[1] Linden, p. 63.
[2] "Median Money Income of Persons...1970," *Stat. Abstract: 1973*, p. 332.
[3] *Stat. Abstract: 1973*.
[4] "Households Owning Cars and Appliances...1971," *Stat. Abstract: 1973*, p. 332.
[5] Linden, p. 63.
[6] See esp. a Chicago *Tribune* survey cited by Packard, pp. 112-13, and Warner and others, *Social Class in America*, pp. 140-41.
[7] Packard, p. 126.
[8] Don Fair, "Sonics: High Payoff, No Playoffs," *Seattle Post-Intelligencer*, Nov. 13, 1973, Sec. C, p. 1.
[9] Packard, Ch. 7, *passim*.
[10] *The Social Context of Ambition* (San Francisco: Chandler, 1964), p. 45.
[11] *Ibid.*, pp. 63-64.
[12] *Ibid.*, p. 36.
[13] "Nor is all of the work involved highly professional. Throughout much of the 'real' world, in fact, is strung a vein of exceedingly routine, unskilled chores which constitute the bulk of many a practitioner's daily performance." Jethro K. Lieberman, *The Tyranny of the Experts* (New York: Walker, 1970), p. 86.
[14] "We have had to recognize that nearly all parents are going to try to gain unfair advantages for their offspring.... As members of a particular family, they want their children to have every privilege. But at the same time they are opposed to privilege for anyone else's children." Michael Young, a British sociologist, in *The Rise of the Meritocracy* (New York: Random House, 1959), p. 25.
[15] For example, see Karen Horney, *The Neurotic Personality of Our Time* (New York: Norton, 1937), and Maragaret Mead, ed., *Cooperation and Competition among Primitive Societies* (New York: McGraw-Hill, 1937).
[16] Turner, p. 2. He had special reference to August B. Hollingshead, Robert Ellis, and E. Kirby, "Social Mobility and Mental Illness," *American Sociological Review*, 19 (Oct. 1954), 577-84.
[17] Lynes, p. 108.
[18] Smith, p. 40.
[19] *Ibid.*, p. 149.
[20] *Ibid.*, p. 157.
[21] *Ibid*.
[22] "Happiness Is a Five-Letter Word," *Psychology Today*, 6 (May 1973), 18-20.

CHAPTER 7

[1] Only 28.4 per cent of all upper-class wives are in the labor force. Figures from Linden, p. 63.
[2] "Personal Wealth—Top Wealthholders...1953...and 1969," *Stat. Abstract: 1973*, p. 342. The totals here may be underestimated. The 1962 estimate, for instance, was 71,000 possessing a gross estate of more than $1 million—but a 1962 *Survey of Financial Characteristics of Consumers*, prepared for the Board of Governors, Federal Reserve System, listed 80,000 millionaires. (See Lundberg, p. 22.)
[3] It is interesting to trace the paths taken by people who have arrived in these critical positions. W. Lloyd Warner and James Abegglen, in a study of *Big Business Leaders in America* (New York: Harper, 1955), point out that the "great industrial and business empires" are controlled by "a small group of powerful leaders" (p. 1). More than half had businessmen fathers—23 per cent of them in big-business leadership positions. The authors found, too, that big-businessmen are much more highly educated than those in a 1928 study (p. 47).

Warner and Abegglen learned in 1955 that the most popular institutions in the business community were, in order, Yale, Harvard, Princeton, Cornell, and the University of Pennsylvania (p. 51). More recently, Harvard and the University of Chicago have gained top status, and especially Harvard. According to Peter Cohen in *The Gospel According to the Harvard Business School* (New York: Doubleday, 1973), HBS boasts 3,300 board chairmen or presidents of companies among its alumni.

[4]W. Ward Fearnside and William B. Holther, *Fallacy: The Counterfeit of Argument* (Englewood Cliffs, N.J.: Prentice-Hall, 1959), p. 55.
[5]*Ibid.*, p. 62.
[6]*Ibid.*, p. 24.
[7]*Webster's New World Dictionary of the American Language*, College Edition, 1956.
[8]"The ACLU: What Are We Talking About?" Seattle *Argus*, 15 Feb. 1963, p. 1.
[9]John M. Wasson, *Subject and Structure*, 5th ed. (Boston: Little, Brown, 1975), p. 383.
[10]*Ibid.*
[11]*Ibid.*, p. 385.

CHAPTER 8

[1]Roger Butterfield, *The American Past* (New York: Simon and Schuster, 1947), p. 213 and ff.
[2]"Dollars and Sense," *Moneysworth*, 12 Nov. 1973, p. 4.
[3]"Ross Perot's Problem Child," *Newsweek*, 18 Feb. 1974, p. 71.
[4]*The Affluent Society*, p. 9.
[5]For a thorough analysis of these positions, see Max Weber, *The Protestant Ethic and the Spirit of Capitalism* (New York: Scribner's, 1930) or R. H. Tawney, *Religion and the Rise of Capitalism* (New York: Harcourt, Brace, 1926).
[6]Galbraith, p. 79.
[7]*Ibid.*, p. 80.
[8]Veblen, *The Theory of the Leisure Class* (Boston: Houghton Mifflin, 1973), p. 37.
[9]*Ibid.*, p. 42.
[10]*Ibid.*, p. 37.
[11]*Ibid.*, p. 151. The "pecuniary employments," Veblen writes, are the prime areas for the promotion of one's interests; here we find "the survival and culture of the predatory traits" (p. 156).
[12]*Ibid.*, p. 158.
[13]*Ibid.*, p. 159.
[14]*Ibid.*, p. 60.
[15]*Ibid.*, p. 256.
[16]*History of the English Language* (New York: Appleton-Century, 1935), p. 246.
[17]Glenn Leggett, C. David Mead, and William Charvat, *Handbook for Writers*, 3rd ed. (Englewood Cliffs, N.J.: Prentice-Hall, 1960), p. 361 (note).
[18]Myron Taube, "Felines and Canines," *Word Study*, 42 (Mar. 1967), 8.
[19]See, for example, Wilson Follett, *Modern American Usage: A Guide*, ed. and completed by Jacques Barzun et al. (New York: Hill and Wang, 1966); W. Nelson Francis, *The English Language: An Introduction* (New York: Norton, 1965), Ch. 6; Bergen and Cornelia Evans, *A Dictionary of Contemporary American Usage* (New York: Random House, 1957); Margaret Bryant, *Current American Usage* (New York: Funk and Wagnalls, 1962); William Strunk, Jr., and E. B. White, *The Elements of Style*, 2nd ed. (New York: Macmillan, 1972), and Clarence L. Barnhart, Sol Steinmetz, and Robert K. Barnhart, *The Barnhart Dictionary of New English Since 1963* (Bronxville, N.Y.: Barnhart/Harper and Row, 1973).
[20]Martin Joos, *The Five Clocks*, quoted by W. Nelson Francis, *The English Language*, Ch. 6, *passim*.
[21]Veblen, p. 257.
[22]*Ibid.*
[23]See, for example, an anthology such as Sylvan Barnet, Morton Berman, and William Burto, *An Introduction to Literature*, 2nd ed. (Boston: Little, Brown, 1963); a booklet, such as Leon T. Dickinson, *A Guide to Literary Study* (New York: Holt, Rinehart, and Winston, 1961); or a handbook for themes about literature, such as Barnet's *A Short Guide to Writing About Literature* (Boston: Little, Brown, 1968) or B. Bernard Cohen, *Writing About Literature* (Chicago: Scott, Foresman, 1963). Or get suggestions from your instructor or librarian.

CHAPTER 9

[1]Allison Davis, a Univ. of Chicago sociologist, quoted by Packard, *The Status Seekers*, p. 43.
[2]*The Social Context of Ambition*, p. 109.

[3]Keller, p. 217.
[4]*Ibid.*, p. 220.
[5]This is how hotel tycoon Conrad Hilton spent his $555,000 personal income in 1948:

Taxes	$352,000	Maintain two homes	$32,000
Charity	80,000	Boat expense	6,500
Family, friends	36,000	Clothing	4,000
Insurance	11,000	Club dues, etc.	12,000

The rest, about $21,000, went to savings. Osborn Elliott, *Men at the Top* (New York: Harper, 1959), p. 24.
[6]Warner and Abegglen, p. 57.
[7]*The Power Elite* (New York: Oxford Univ. Press, 1956), pp. 3-4.
[8]Packard, p. 323.
[9]*Ibid.*, p. 327.
[10]Keller, p. 269.
[11]*The Affluent Society*, p. 345.
[12]Keller, p. 270.
[13]*Ibid.*, p. 278.
[14]Packard, Ch. 20, *passim.*
[15]*Ibid.*, pp. 299-300.
[16]*The Rich and the Super-Rich* (New York: Lyle Stuart, 1968), p. 795 (note).
[17]*Marshaling Citizen Power Against Crime* (Washington: Chamber of Commerce of the United States, 1970), p. 8.
[18]Edwin M. Schur, *Our Criminal Society: The Social and Legal Sources of Crime in America* (Englewood Cliffs, N.J.: Prentice-Hall, 1969), p. 34.
[19]*Ibid.*, pp. 16, 18.
[20]*Ibid.*, p. 19.
[21]President's Commission on Law Enforcement and Administration of Justice, *Task Force Report: Crime and Its Impact—An Assessment* (Washington: U.S. Government Printing Office, 1967), quoted by Schur, p. 27.

INDEX

(A number of Usage entries from the book's central chapters aren't repeated here. Browsers are invited to check the Table of Contents for such lists.)

A

A, an, 74
Abbreviations
  bibliography entries, 186-87
  dates and numerals, 80
  days of week, 79
  footnotes, 186-87
  in formal writing, 80
  in technical writing, 80
  states, 80
  titles and names, 79
About, around, 100
Absolute phrases, 37, 98
Abstract and concrete words, 116, 159
Accept, except, 75, 111
Accusative case
  see Objective case
Acknowledging sources, 164, 179-80
  see also Footnotes, Bibliography
Active voice, 56, 62-63
Ad, 100
Address of letter, 244-45
Ad hominem appeal, 208
Adjective clauses
  illustrated, 36, 38-39, 74
  restrictive and nonrestrictive, 38-39, 106, 217
Adjectives
  adjectival pronouns, 30, 94
  after linking verbs, 91-92
  and adverbs, 90-94
  articles, 74, 145, 220
  commas with, 105-06
  comparison of, 93-94
  coordinate, cumulative, 105-06
  defined, 30, 90
  nouns as, 93
  predicate adjective, 30, 31, 34, 91-92
Ad populum appeal, 208
Adverb clauses
  illustrated, 35, 40
  types, with various subordinating conjunctions, 39-40
Adverbs
  and adjectives, 90-94
  classified, 32
  comparison of, 93-94
  conjunctive, 42, 95-96
  defined, 32, 90
  highbrow, common forms, 93
  position of, 96
  sentence modifiers, 94-95
Affect, effect, 75
Affixes
  see Prefixes, Suffixes
Aggravate, 100
Agreement, pronoun
  antecedents with *and, or*, 67
  other problems, 67-68
Agreement, subject-verb
  after *it, there*, 66
  collective nouns, 64-65
  compound subjects, 63-64

259

each, either, etc., 65
  indefinite pronouns, 65
  in relative clauses, 65
  intervening words, 65
  none, 65
  predicate noun, 66
  singular meaning, 64
  titles and words, 66
Ain't, 45
All that, 100
Allusion, illusion, 75
Almost, most, 75
Alternative, 217
Among, between, 129
Amount, number, 129
Analogy, 159, 206
Analysis
  by division, 157-59
  by partition, 156
  of literary works, 232-35
And etc.,
  see *Etc.*, 76
And/or, 129
Angry
  see *Mad*, 102
Angry at, with, 177
Antecedent
  ambiguous reference, 68-69
  in hypothetical syllogisms, 154
  pronoun agreement, 67-68
  remote, 69, 70
Any, anybody, etc.,
  see Indefinite pronouns
Anyplace, 100
Apostrophe
  in contractions, 115
  in plurals, 114, 115
  in possessives, 73, 114
  not in personal pronouns, 115
Appositives
  case of, 71-72
  punctuation of, 106, 134
  restrictive, nonrestrictive, 106
Appropriateness of diction
  to audience, 116, 224-27
  to situation, 224-27
  to subject, 224-27
Apt, liable, likely, 129
Argument, 162-64
Around, about, 100
Articles (*a, an, the*), 74, 145, 220

Artificiality, 227
As, ambiguous, 173
As, as if, as though
  see *Like*, 132
As (So) . . . as, 177
As, than, with pronouns, 71
Auxiliary verbs, 59
Awkwardness, 64, 70, 96, 97

B

Bad, badly, 91
Balanced sentences, 176
Be
  auxiliary verb form, 59
  in subjunctive mood, 60
  linking verb, 31
  without auxiliary, 45
"Begging the question," 209
Beginning the paper, 118
Beginning the sentence (structural variety), 174
Being as how, 45
Being that, 75
Between, see *Among*, 129
Bibliography
  cards, 181-82, 188
  entries, 188-89
  format, 188-89
  specimen, 200-01
Bilinguals, 24
Black-proletarian dialect, 24, 44, 45, 46
Blame, 177
Blocked quotation, 138, 196-97
Book titles
  capitalized, 145
  italicized, 140
Brackets
  inside parentheses, 136
  to indicate insertions, 137
  with *sic*, 137
Bulletins, 180, 186

Business letter
    form, 244
    specimens, 245-47
Bust, 75
But
    coordinating conjunction, 32-33
    correlative, 63
But that, but what, 100

C

Can, may, 59
Can't hardly, don't hardly, 75
Can't help but, 129
Can't seem to, 129
Capitalization
    following a colon, 143-44
    of first words, 143
    of proper nouns, etc., 144-45
    of titles, 145
    when to avoid, 145-46
Card catalog, 180, 181
Careless omissions, 99
Case
    of nouns, 70, 114
    of pronouns, 70-74
Cause-and-effect, 150, 203
Center around, 129
Characters, in fiction, 233-34
Choppy paragraphs, 86
Chronological order, 83, 117, 119
Circular reasoning, 209
Circumlocution, 229
Classification, 149-50, 157-58, 203
Class structure
    see Table of Contents
Clauses
    dangling elliptical, 97-98
    defined, 26-27, 33, 35
    dependent
        see Subordinate clauses
    diagramed, 27ff.
    elliptical, 71
    independent ("main"), 26-27, 33-34
    restrictive, nonrestrictive
        see Adjective clauses, 38-39, 106, 217
    see also Adverb and Noun clauses
Clichés, 225-26
Climactic order
    in paragraphs, themes, 162
    in sentences, 175-76
Clipped words, 225
Coherence of paragraphs
    clarity and logicality, 82-85
    consistent point of view, 84, 98
    parallelism, 85
    repetition, 85
    transitions, 84-85
    use of pronouns, 84
Coherence of sentences
    careless omissions, 99
    consistent point of view, 98
    dangling modifiers, 97-98
    misplaced elements, 96-97
    mixed constructions, 43
    pronoun reference
        see Reference of pronouns, 68-70
    "squinting" modifiers, 96
    subordination, 171-73
    see also Parallelism, Transitional expressions
Collective nouns, 29, 64-65, 68
Colloquialism, 44
Colon
    before appositives, 134
    introducing series, quotations, etc., 134
    separating clauses, 134
    various other uses, 135
    when to avoid, 135
Comma
    to separate items in series, 105-06
    to separate main clauses, 104-05
    to set off concluding elements, 105
    to set off introductory elements, 105
    to set off parenthetical elements, 106-07
    various other uses, 107-08
    when to avoid, 108-09
Comma fault, 42-43
Comma splice
    see Comma fault

261

Common nouns, 29, 145
Comparative degree, of adjectives
 and adverbs, 93-94
Compare to, compare with, 177
Comparison-and-contrast, 159-60
Comparison of adjectives and adverbs,
 93-94
Comparisons
 illogical, 99
 incomplete, 99
Complected, 100
Complements
 defined, 27
 direct object, 30, 33-34
 subjective complement
  see Predicate adjective and
   Predicate noun, pronoun
 types, 29
Complex sentences, 35-36
Composition
 defined, 82
 modes
  argument, 162-64
  description, 83-84, 117-18, 119
  exposition, 84, 146-62
  narration, 83, 117, 119
  persuasion, 210
 of paragraphs, 82-86
 of themes, 115-20
 principles of unity,
  coherence and effective
  development, 82-86
  see also these Index entries
 steps: (1) planning, (2) outlining,
  (3) first draft, (4) revising,
  115-20
Compound-complex sentences, 36
Compound predicate, 34
Compound sentences
 with conjunctions, 35
 with semicolons, 77-78
 see also Comma fault, 42-43
Compound subject
 agreement of verb, 63-64
 diagramed, 34
Compound words, 114, 141-42
Conclusion of theme, 119-20
Concrete and abstract words, 116,
 159
Condition clauses
 see Adverb clauses

Conditions
 necessary, 205
 sufficient, 205
Conjugation of verbs
 defined, 56
 of *to give*, 56-59
Conjunctions
 coordinating, 32-33, 35, 42, 104,
  171
 subordinating, 32-33, 35, 39-40,
  171-72
Conjunctive adverbs
 defined, 95
 punctuation with, 42, 43, 95-96,
  107
Connectives
 see Conjunctions and Prepositions
Connotation and denotation,
 227-28
Consistency
 see Point of view, 98
Continual, continuous, 130
Contractions, 73, 115
Coordinate elements
 in outlines, 146-47
 in sentences, 33, 77-78, 171
 see also Correlatives
Coordinating conjunctions, 32-33,
 35, 42, 104, 171
Copula
 see Linking verb
Correction of manuscript, 81, 120
Correlatives, 63-64, 67, 171
Could of, 45
Couple, 100
Critical, criticize, 130
Cross-classification, 147, 157-58

D

Dangling modifiers, 97-98
Dash
 uses, 135
 with quotation marks, 139

262

Data, 64
Dates, 80, 107
Deadwood, 229
Deal, 100
Declarative sentences, 36
Declension of pronouns, 70
Deductive logic
   defined, 151
   errors, 204-05
   syllogisms, 151-55
   validity, invalidity, 151-54
Definition
   methods, 149, 161-62
   problems, 161-62
Degree
   see Comparison of adjectives
      and adverbs, 93-94
Demonstrative adjectival pronouns,
   30, 68, 94
Denotation and connotation, 227-28
Dependent clauses
   see Subordinate clauses
Description, 83-84, 117-18, 119
Details
   informal partition, 156
   in paragraphs or themes, 156
Development, effective
   of paragraphs, 82, 86
   of themes, 82, 174-76
Diagraming, 27ff.
Dialects
   current English, 26
   see also Black-proletarian
Dialogue
   and quotation marks, 137
Diction (choice of words)
   appropriateness, 116, 224-27
   connotation, denotation, 227-28
   dictionary help, 220-21, 228
   economy, 228-30
   foreign words, 223
   precision, 227-28
   sounds, 230
   usage levels, examples
      see Levels of usage
   see also Idioms, Vocabulary
Dictionaries
   assistance, 53, 80, 228
   entries, illustrated, 220-21
   verb entries, 53
Different from, than, 177

Direct address, 29, 107
Directness and energy, 120-21
Direct object
   defined, 29, 30
   diagramed, 30
   with transitive verb, 33-34
Direct quotation
   on note cards, 182-83
   punctuation with, 137-38, 139
Discourse, shift in type of, 98
Disinterested, uninterested, 177
Dividing words, with hyphen, 142
Division, analysis by
   formal, 157-58
   informal, 158-59
Documentation
   informal, 164
   see also Research paper
"Do" forms of verbs, 59
Done it, 75
Don't never, don't have no, 45
Double negatives, examples, 45, 75
Drownded, 45
Due to, 130

E

Each and every, 101
Each, either, etc.,
   see Indefinite pronouns
Each other, one another, 68
Ecology, 101
Economy in sentences, 175, 228-30
Effect
   see Affect, 75
Effective development
   of paragraphs, 82, 86
   of themes, 82, 174-76
Either
   see Indefinite pronouns
Either . . . or correlative
   pronoun agreement, 67
   verb agreement, 63-64

Either-or fallacy, 155, 204-05
Ellipsis, 142-43
Elliptical clauses
   dangling, 97-98
   with pronoun, 71
Emigrate, immigrate, 130
Emphasis in sentence
   means of achieving, 174-76
   points of, 175
Ending a paper, 119-20
Endorsement of paper, 81
English language
   foreign words in, 110, 140, 220
   Germanic influence, 220
   history of, 219-20
   Latin and Greek in, 220, 221-23
Enthused, 101
Essay answers, 232
Essays
   see Themes
Etc., 76
Etymology, 221
Everyone, anyone, etc.,
   see Indefinite pronouns
Everyplace, 76
Evidence, sound, 206-07
Exactness
   see Precision of diction, 227-28
Exam
   see Ad, 100
Examples
   informal division, 158-59
   in paragraph development, 86
Except, accept, 45, 111
Excessive coordination, 171-72
Excessive subordination, 173
Exclamation point, 46-47
   with quotation marks, 139
Exclamatory sentences, 36
Expletives, 66
Exposition
   defined, 84
   methods of, 146-62
      see list, 148

F

Fallacies, logical
   defined, 202
   illustrated, 202-05
False analogy, 206
Farther, further, 130
Fewer, less, 130
Figurative language (figures of speech)
   metaphor, 226
   simile, 226
   symbol, 227-28
   synecdoche, etc., 226
Figures, plural of, 114, 115
"Fine writing," 227
Footnotes
   abbreviations used, 186-87
   form, style, 184-87
   illustrated in specimen paper, 194-99
   types, 184
For, as a conjunction, 41, 169
Foreign words
   when appropriate, 223
   when italicized, 140
Formal usage, 44
Former, latter, 131
Form of manuscript, 80-81
   see also Research paper
Fractions, 49
Fragment
   illustrated, 26, 35, 41
   when acceptable, 41
   when not acceptable, 41-42
Further
   see Farther, 130
Fused sentence, 43

G

Gender
   of nouns, 29-30
   of pronouns, 67

General
    and abstract (words), 116, 159
    not specific, 116, 159
Generalizations
    in induction, 150-51
    with examples, 159
Genitive case
    see Possessive case
Gentleman, lady, 131-32
Geographical names
    abbreviation of, 80
    punctuation of, 107
Gerund
    defined, 31
    diagramed, 31
    tense of, 60
    with a "subject," 72-73
Gerund phrases
    dangling, 97
    illustrated, 36, 60, 72-73
"Gobbledygook," 227
Good, as an adverb, 45
Gotta, 45
Grammar
    defined, 25-26
    parts of speech, 28-33
    references, 254-55
    sentence types, 33-36
    subject, predicate, 26-28
    see also Table of Contents and
        abbreviations list opposite
        back cover
Greek
    influence of, 220, 221-23
    roots and affixes, 222-23

H

Hackneyed phrases, 225-26
Had of, 45
Hanged, hung, 131
Hanging indention, 200
Has got, have got, 177
Hate, 218

Hierarchies, and Scales, 160
Hopefully, 94
However, punctuation with, 107
Human, humans, 218
Hyphen
    dividing a word, 142
    with affixes, 142
    with compound adjectives, 141
    with compound nouns, 141
    with compound numbers, 141

I

Ibid., 187
I could(n't) care less, 101
Idioms, 61, 66-67, 176-78, 217-18
If, whether, 101
Illogical constructions, 99-100
    see also Dangling modifiers,
        Logic, Propaganda
Illusion
    see *Allusion*, 75
Illustration, 158
Immature sentences, 172
Immigrate
    see *emigrate*, 130
Imperative mood, 56
Imperative sentences, 36
Imply, infer, 101-02
In, into, 218
Incomplete comparisons, 99
Incomplete sentence
    see Fragment, 41-42
Indefinite pronouns
    number of, 65, 67-68
    possessive of, 73, 114
Indention
    hanging, 200
    in outlines, 146ff.
    of blocked quotations, 138
    of poetry, 138
Independent (main) clauses
    and coordinating conjunctions, 33

265

defined, 33
patterns, 33-34
separated by comma, 104-05
separated by colon, 134
separated by semicolon, 77-78
Indexes to periodicals, 180
Indicative mood, 56, 57-58, 61-62
Indirect discourse, 98
Indirect object, 29, 33-34
Indirect question, 46, 137
Indo-European languages, 219
Inductive logic
causal hypothesis, 150
classification, 149-50
errors, 203-04
generalization, 150-51
scientific method, 149-50
Infer, imply, 101
Infinitive
defined, 31-32
diagramed, 31
pronoun following, 72
sign of, 31-32
split, 97
subject of, 72
tense of, 60
Infinitive phrases
dangling, 97
illustrated, 37, 60, 72, 97
Inflection, 27, 53
see also Declension of pronouns, 70
Informal usage, 44
In regards to, 102
Intensive pronouns, 30
Interjections, 33, 107
Interrogative pronouns, 30, 73
Interrogative sentences, 36
Into, in, 218
Intransitive verbs, 30, 33
Introduction of a paper, 118
Inversion, 27, 174
Irregardless, 102
Irregular verbs, 53-55
Is when, is where, 76
Italics (underlining)
for certain names, 140
for certain titles, 140
foreign words, 140
for emphasis, 141
words used as words, 138, 140

It as an expletive, 66
It being, 102
Its, it's, 115
It's me, 70-71
-ize, 131

J

Jargon
defined, 44, 226
"gobbledygook," 227
Job-application letter, 244-46
Just, 96

K

Kind of a, sort of a, 102
Kind of, sort of, 102
Kind, sort, and adjectival pronouns, 68, 94

L

Lady, gentleman, 131-32
Language
see English language
Latin
abbreviations in footnotes, 186-87

common abbreviations, 80
influence of, 220, 221-23
roots and affixes, 222-23
Latter
　see *Former*, 131
Lay, lie, 55
Learn, teach, 45
Leave, let, 45
Lend
　see *Loan*, 132
Length
　of outlines, 118
　of paragraphs, 86
　of sentences, 174
Less
　see *Fewer*, 130
Let
　see *Leave*, 45
Letters
　business, form of, 244, 247
　job-application, specimens, 245-46
　see also Personal data form
Levels of usage, examples of,
　Lower-Lower, 45-46
　Upper-Lower, 74-77
　Lower-Middle, 100-04
　Upper-Middle, 129-34
　Lower-Upper, 176-78
　Upper-Upper, 217-18
Liable, likely
　see *Apt*, 129
Library
　card catalog, 180, 181
　resources, 180, 234
Library paper
　see Research paper
Lie, lay, 55
Like, as, as if, as though, 132
Limiting the subject, 115-16
Linguistic changes, 24
Linking verbs, 31, 34, 66, 91-92
Literally, 132
Literature
　analysis, 232-35
　criticism, 232-35
　explication, 233
　flaws, 234-35
　narrative elements, 233-34
　references, 255
Loan, lend, 132

Localism, 44, 225
Logic
　in outlines, 146-48
　in paragraphs, 82-85
　in sentences, 99-100
　see also Deductive logic, Fallacies, Inductive logic, *Non sequitur*
Logical orders, 84, 85
Loose sentence, 175
Lot, lots, 177

M

Mad, angry, 102
Magazines
　cited in bibliography, 188
　cited in footnotes, 186
　italics for titles, 140
Main clauses
　see Independent clauses
Manuscript form, 80-81
　see also Research paper
Margins, 81
Math
　see *Ad*, 100
May, can, 59
May of, might of, must of, 45
Mechanics
　abbreviation, 79-80
　apostrophe, 114-15
　capitalization, 143-46
　ellipsis, 142-43
　hyphen, 141-42
　italics (underlining), 140-41
　manuscript form, 80-81
　numbers, 48-49
　of documenting
　　see Research paper
Metaphors, 226
Might of
　see *May of*, 45
Minus, 102
Misplaced elements, 96-97
Mixed constructions, 43

267

Mixed metaphors, 226
Modifiers
   dangling, 97-98
   misplaced, 96-97
   "squinting," 96
   see also Adjectives, Adverbs, Phrases, Subordinate clauses
Mood of verb
   defined, 56
   imperative, 56, 58
   indicative, 56, 57-58, 61-62
   shift of, 98
   subjunctive, 56, 58, 60-62
More, most, 93-94
Most
   see *Almost*, 75
Mr., Mrs., Ms., 79
Musicality in sentences, 230
Must of
   see *May of*, 45
Myself, herself, etc., 102

N

Narration
   in literature, 233-34
   in paragraphs and themes, 83, 117, 119
Narrative elements
   characters, 233-34
   plot, 233-34
   "point of view," 233-34
   setting, 233-34
   style, 233-34
   "theme," 233-34
"Natural" orders
   chronological
     see Narration
   spatial
     see Description
Neither . . . nor
   see Correlatives
Neologisms, 131

Newspapers
   cited in footnotes, 186
   italics for titles, 140
Nominative absolute, 29, 37
Nominative case
   see Subjective case
Nominative of address
   see Direct address, 29, 107
None, and verb agreement, 65
Nonrestrictive elements
   defined, 38-39
   punctuation of, 38-39, 106
Non sequitur, 202
Noplace, 76
Not about to, 102
Note-taking, research
   card system, 182-83
   specimen cards, 182-83
Not only . . . but also
   see Correlatives
Noun clauses, 36, 38, 74
Nouns
   abstract, 29
   case of, 29, 70, 114
   collective, 29, 64-65
   common, defined, 29
   concrete, 29
   defined, 28-29
   gender of, 29-30
   list of functions, 28-29
   number of, 29
   predicate, 29, 34, 66
   proper, defined, 29
No way, 102
Nowheres, 46
Number
   defined, 29, 63
   pronoun's agreement with antecedent, 67-68
   shift in, 98
   subject-verb agreement, 63-66
Number
   see *Amount*, 129
Numbers
   at beginning of sentence, 48
   compound, hyphenated, 48
   in dates, 49
   other uses, 48-49
   spelled out, 48

O

Object
  direct, 29, 30, 33-34
  indirect, 29, 33-34
  of a preposition, 29, 32, 71
  retained, 29
Objective case
  for all objects, 71
  for subject of gerund, 72-73
  for subject of infinitive, 72
Objective complement, 29, 34, 92
Obscenity, 225
Obsolete words, 44
Off of, 102
Oftentimes, 102
O.K., 132
Omissions
  careless, 99
  ellipsis in quotation, 142-43
  elliptical clauses, 71, 97-98
  incomplete comparisons, 99
One and the same, 102
One another, each other, 68
Only, position of, 96
Onomatopoeia, 230
Op. cit., 187
Option, options, 218
Outline
  sentence, 116-17
  topic, 117-18, 146-48
  see also Research paper for specimen outline
Outlining, 116-18, 146-48
Overloaded sentences
  see Excessive subordination, 173
Over with, 102

P

Page numbers, 81, 196
Pamphlets, 180, 186

Papers, assigned
  manuscript form, 80-81
  see also Themes, Research paper
Paradox, 151
Paragraphs
  coherence, 82-85
  concluding, 119-20
  effective development, 86
  introductory, 118
  length, 86
  logical orders, 84, 85
  "natural" orders, 83-84
  topic sentence, 82
  transitions, 84-85
  unity, 82
Parallelism, grammatical
  in outlines, 117, 146
  in paragraphs, 85
  in sentences, 170-71
  with correlatives, 171
Paraphrase, of quotations, 183
Parentheses
  and other punctuation, 136
  uses, 136
Parenthetical elements, 106-07, 135, 136-37
Participial phrases
  dangling, 97
  illustrated, 37, 60, 73
Participle
  dangling, 97
  defined, 31
  diagramed, 31
  tense of, 60
Parts of speech
  classified, 28
    adjectives, *see* main entry
    adverbs, *see* main entry
    conjunctions, *see* entry
    interjections, 33
    nouns, *see* main entry
    prepositions, 32
    pronouns, *see* main entry
    verbs, *see* main entry
  history of, 26
Passim, 186
Passive voice
  defined, 56, 62-63

269

of *to give,* 57-58
   sometimes weak, 62-63
Per, 103
Per cent, 103
Percentage, 103
Period
   uses, 47, 142-43
   with an ellipsis, 142
   with quotation marks, 139
Periodicals
   cited in bibliography, 188
   cited in footnotes, 186
   indexes to, 180
Periodic sentence, 175
Person
   shift in, 98
   see conjugation of *to give,* 57-58
   see also Agreement
Personal data form, 248-49
Personal pronouns
   case, 70-73
   declension, 70
   illustrated, 30
   no apostrophe, 73
Persuasion, 210
Phenomenon, phenomena, 132
Philosophy, 103
Phone
   see *Ad,* 100
Phrases
   absolute, 37, 98
   classified, 36-37
   dangling, 97
   defined, 36
   gerund, 36, 60, 72-73
   infinitive, 37, 60, 72
   misplaced, 96
   noun, 37
   participial, 37, 60, 73
   prepositional, 37, 97
   verb, 27, 53, 96-97
Piece, 76
Plagiarism, 179-80
Planning a paper, 115-18
   see also Research paper
Plenty, 76
Plurals
   of letters, etc., 115
   spelling, 113-14
Plus, 103
Poetry
   analysis of, 233, 234
   quotation of, 138

Point of view
   in literature, 233-34
   in sentences, paragraphs, 98
   shift of, 98
Poorly, 46
Positive degree
   see Comparison of adjectives and adverbs, 93-94
Possessive case
   apostrophe with, 73, 114
   of nouns, 29, 73, 114
   of pronouns, 70, 72-73, 114
   with gerunds, 72-73
Post hoc fallacy, 203
Practically, 132
Précis, 162
Predicate
   compound, 34
   defined, 26
Predicate adjective
   defined, 30
   diagramed, 31
   with linking verb, 34, 91-92
Predicate noun, pronoun, 29, 34, 66, 70-71
Prefixes, 112, 142, 222
Prepositional phrases
   dangling, 97
   defined, 37
   with gerunds, 97
Prepositions, 32
Principal, principle, 111
Principal parts of verbs
   defined, 53, 56
   list of, 54-55
Prior to, 132
"Process" papers
   see Narration
Profanity, 225
Progressive form of verb, 59
Pronominal apposition, 25, 45
Pronouns
   adjectival, 30, 94
   agreement with antecedent, 67-68
   case, 70-74, 114-15
   classified, 30
   defined, 30
   for coherence, 84
   reference of, 68-70
   verb agreement, 65

Pronunciation
    and spelling, 110, 111
    see also Black-proletarian dialect
Propaganda
    bad, defined, 202
        analytic errors, 205
        deductive errors, 204-05
        inductive errors, 203-04
        synthetic errors, 206-09
    good, defined, 202
Proper nouns, 29, 144-46
Proved, proven, 218
Punctuation
    brackets, 136-37
    colon, 134-35
    comma, 104-09
    dash, 135
    exclamation point, 46-47
    of footnotes, bibliography
        see Research paper
    parentheses, 136
    period, 47
    question mark, 46
    quotation marks, 137-39
    semicolon, 77-78
    see also Apostrophe, Ellipsis, Hyphen, Italics

Q

Question mark
    after direct question, 46
    with quotation marks, 139
Questions
    short, affixed, 107
    with verb phrases, 27
Quotation
    and note-taking, 182-83
    blocked (or "display"), 138, 196-97
    comma introducing, 109
    direct, 109, 137
    indirect, 109, 137

Quotation marks
    direct quotations, 137
    quoting in a quotation, 138
    quoting multiple paragraphs, 138
    quoting poetry, 138
    slang words, etc., 139
    with certain titles, 139
    with other punctuation, 139
    words with a special sense, 138-39
Quote, quote marks, 132

R

Raise, rise, 55
Rarely ever, 103
Readers' Guide, 180, 181
Real, 103
Reason is because, 103
Reasons
    set of, 160-61, 162-64
    spurious, 206-08
Reciprocal pronouns, 30, 68
Redundancy, 228-29
Reference books
    cited in this book
        grammar, 254-55
        literary analysis, 257
        usage, 257
    in library, 180
Reference of pronouns
    ambiguous, 68-69
    indefinite *it, they, you,* 69
    logical, 69
    remote, 69
    that, who, which, 70
    vague, 70
Reflective essays, 235
Reflexive pronouns, 30
Regular verbs, 53
Relatives, introducing
    adjective clauses, 39, 73-74
Relative pronouns, 30, 39, 73-74
Repetition
    for emphasis, 174

of sentence structure, 85
of words, for coherence, 85
unnecessary, 228-29
Reporting, 235
Research paper
    abbreviations used, 186-87
    bibliography cards, 181-82
    bibliography form, 188-89, 200-01
    crediting sources, 179-80
    danger of plagiarism, 179-80
    footnotes, 182-86
    format
        see specimen paper, 190-201
    library's resources, 180, 234
    note cards, 182-83
    purpose of, 179, 180
    quotations, 182-83
    specimen paper, 190-201
    title page, 190-91
Restrictive constructions
    defined, 38-39
    problems with, 39, 106, 217
Resume
    see Personal data form, 248-49
Reverend, 76
Revision of manuscript, 81, 120
Rhetoric, 82
    see also Composition, Argument, Persuasion, Propaganda
Rhythms in sentences, 230
Right, 77
Rise, raise, 55
Roman numerals, 49
Roots, Greek and Latin, 222
Run-on sentences
    see Comma fault, Fused sentence

S

Scales and hierarchies, 160
Seeing as how, 77
Seen, 77

Seldom ever, 103
Semantics, 25, 227
Semicolon
    linking main clauses, 42, 77-78, 96
    with elements in a series, 78
    with quotation marks, 139
Sentence modifiers, 94-95, 107
Sentence outlines, 116-17
Sentences
    balanced, 176
    classified by form:
        (1) simple, 26-27, 33-34
        (2) compound, 35
        (3) complex, 35-36
        (4) compound-complex, 36
    classified by function, 36
    emphatic, 174-76
    fused, 43
    immature, 172
    inverted, 27, 174
    loose and periodic, 175
    topic, 82
    unity, coherence, effective development, 170
    variety in, 173-74
Separation of clause elements
    with commas, 108
    with semicolons, 78
    with words, 96-97
Sequence of tenses, 59-60
Series
    parallelism in, 170
    punctuation of, 78, 105-06
Set of reasons, 160-61, 162-64
Set, sit, 55
Shall, will, 127-28
Shape, 133
Shift in point of view
    of metaphor
    of mood
    of person
    of physical perspective
    of style
    of subject
    of tense
    of type of discourse
    of voice
    of writer's attitude, 98
Should, would, 127-28

Should of, 46
Sic, 137, 186
Simile, 159, 226
Simple sentence, 26-27, 33-34
Sit, set, 55
Slang, 44, 225
So (As) . . . as, 177
So, as a coordinating
        conjunction, 41, 104, 178
So, "feminine," 178
So, in purpose clauses, 178
Social classes
    see Table of Contents
Some, as an adverb, 133
Someone, anyone, etc.,
    see Indefinite pronouns
Someplace, 77
Somewheres, 46
Sort
    see *Kind,* 68, 94
Sort of
    see *Kind of,* 102
Sort of a
    see *Kind of a,* 102
Sound of words
    and spelling, 110-11
    choosing for effect, 230
    onomatopoeia, 230
Sources
    crediting, 179
    see also Plagiarism, 179-80
Spatial order
    in paragraphs, 83-84
    in themes, 118, 119
Specific
    and concrete, 116, 159
    not general, 116, 159
Speech
    bilingual, 24
    informal, 65, 68, 71, 91
    overcorrectness, 23-24
    phonological variables, 24
    see also Black-proletarian
        dialect
Spelling
    adding suffixes, 112-13
    and pronunciation, 111
    British, 231
    changing *y* to *i,* 113
    compound words, 114

doubling final consonant, 112-13
dropping final *e,* 112
ei, or *ie,* 113
lists, for practice
    Lower-Lower, 47-48
    Upper-Lower, 78-79
    Lower-Middle, 111-14
    Upper-Middle, 139-40
    Lower-Upper, 179
    Upper-Upper, 231-32
plurals, 113-14, 231-32
possessives, 114-15
prefixes, 112, 222
roots, 222
rules, 111-14
similar words, 111
suffixes, 112-13, 223
    see also Apostrophe
Split infinitive, 97
"Squinting" modifiers, 96
Standards of usage, 44
    see also Levels of usage
Stereotypes, 204
Structuralist grammar, 26, 255
Style
    appropriate diction, 224-27
    "closed," "open" punctuation,
        109
    economy, 228-30
    emphasis, 174-76
    in documentation
        see Research paper
    in literary works, 233-34
    parallelism, 170-71
    precision of diction, 227-28
    Upper-Middle stylists, 134
    variety, 173-74
    word sounds, 230
Subjective case
    after *than, as,* 71
    with subjective complements, 70-
        71
    with subjects
        see Subject of clause and
            of verbals
Subjective complements, 70-71
    see also Predicate adjective and
        predicate noun, pronoun
Subject of clause
    compound, 34, 63-64

defined, 26-27
  position of, 27
  shift in, 98
  understood, 27
  verb agreement, 63-66
Subject of verbals
  gerunds, 72-73
  infinitives, 72
Subjects for papers, 115-16
Subjunctive mood
  and class levels, 60-62
  defined, 56
  in conditional clauses, 61-62
  in idioms, 60-61
  in *that* clauses, 61-62
Subordinate clauses
  as sentence fragments, 35, 41
  adjective, 36, 38-39, 73-74
  adverb, 35, 39-40
  for variety, 174
  misplaced, 96
  noun, 36, 38, 74
Subordinating conjunctions
  defined, 32-33
  examples in clauses, 35, 39-40
  precise use of, 172-73
Subordination
  excessive, 173
  faulty coordination, 171-72
  "upside-down," 173
Such, 218
Suffixes, 112-13, 114, 223
Summary writing, 162
Superlative degree
  see Comparison of adjectives and
    adverbs, 93-94
Sure, 103
Sure and, 103
Syllabication, 142
Syllogisms, 151-55
Symbol, 227-28
Symbols in marking student
  papers (opposite back cover)
Synecdoche, 226
Synonyms, 161,228
Syntax, 25, 26, 37, 96
Synthetic statements
  defined, 159
  examples of, 159-62

T

Take and, 77
Tautology, 228-29
Teach
  see Learn, 45
Tense
  conjugation of *to give,* 56-59
  principal parts, 53
  sequence of tenses, 59-60
  shift of, 98
  use of six tenses, 55-56
Term paper
  see Research paper
Than, as, with pronouns, 71
That, as colloquial adverb,
  see also All that, 100
That there, this here, 46
That, which, who, 70, 217
Themes
  defined, 115
  manuscript form, 80-81
  see also Composition
There is (are), 66
These kind, these sort, 68, 94
Thesis statement, 116-17, 118, 119
Thusly, 103
Title of paper
  capitalization of, 145
  examples, 116
  location of, 81
  not quoted or italicized, 81
  punctuation of, 47
Title page, 190-91
Titles of articles, books, etc.,
  capitalization of, 145
  when in quotation marks, 139
  when italicized, 140
Titles (names) of works of
    art, ships, etc., 140
Titles with proper names
  abbreviation of, 79
  capitalization of, 145
  punctuation of, 107
Tone, 118
Topic outline, 116-18, 146-48
Topic sentence of paragraph, 82

Topics for papers, 115-16
Transformational grammar, 26, 254-55
Transitional expressions
 for coherence, 84-85
 see also Conjunctive adverbs, Sentence modifiers
Transitive verb, 30, 33-34
Transpire, 218
Triteness, 225-26
Try, as a noun, 218
Try and, 104
Type (of), 104

U

Underscoring for italics, 138, 140-41
Undeveloped paragraphs, 86
Uninterested
 see *Disinterested*, 177
Unique, 94
Unity
 in paragraph, 82
 in sentence, 170
 in theme, 119-20
"Upside-down" subordination, 173
Usage
 defined, 25, 44
 examples at six social-class levels:
  Lower-Lower, 45-46
  Upper-Lower, 74-77
  Lower-Middle, 100-04
  Upper-Middle, 129-34
  Lower-Upper, 176-78
  Upper-Upper, 217-18
 references, 257

V

Vague pronoun reference, 70
Variety in sentences, 173-74

Verb-adverb combinations, 66-67
Verbals
 dangling, 97
 defined, diagramed, 31
 see also Gerund, Infinitive, Participial phrases
Verbal, verbally, 104
Verb phrases, 27, 53, 96-97
Verbs
 agreement with subject, 63-66
 auxiliary, 59
 conjugation of *to give*, 56-59
 defined, 27, 30
 "do" forms, 59
 diagramed, 27, 30-31, 34
 intransitive, 30, 33
 irregular, 53-55
 linking, 31, 34, 91-92
 mood
  imperative, 56
  indicative, 56, 61-62
  subjunctive, 56, 58, 60-62
 principal parts, 53-55
 progressive form, 59
 regular, 53
 sequence of tenses, 59-60
 shall and *will*, 127-28
 tenses, 55-56
 transitive, 30, 33-34
 voice, 56, 62-63, 98
Very, before a past participle, 218
Viable, 133
Vocabulary, 219, 221-24
Vocative
 see Direct address
Voice
 active, 56, 62-63
 passive, 56, 62-63
 shift of, 98
Vulgarisms, 44, 225

W

Wait on, 77
Want in, etc., 133

Way, ways, 77
Weird, 133
Where at, 77
Where to, 104
-wise, 133
Whether,
   see *If,* 101
Whether . . . or, 171
Which, who, that, 70, 217
While, ambiguous, 172
Who, whom, 73-74
Wordiness
   circumlocution, 229
   deadwood, 229
   "gobbledygook," 227
   redundancy, 228-29
   unnecessary complexity, 229
   unnecessary repetition, 229

Word choice
   see Diction, Usage,
     Vocabulary
Word order
   see Variety, Emphasis
Worst way, 134
Would of, 46

Y

Yet, as a coordinating
   conjunction, 104, 169

NOTES

NOTES

Abbreviations frequently used in marking themes, with page references:

abr	faulty abbreviation, 79-80	paral	parallelism, 170-71
adj	use correct adjective form, 90-92	par	paragraph
adv	use correct adverb form, 90-93	no par	don't indent
agr	(1) agreement of subject and verb, 63-66 (2) agreement of pronoun, 67-68	par und	paragraph undeveloped, 86
		pn	punctuation error
apos	apostrophe error, 114-15	no pn	omit punctuation
awk	awkward	quot	error in use of quotation marks, 137-39
c	case error, 70-74	ref	vague or faulty reference, 68-70
cap	capitalization error, 143-46	rep	repetition, 228-29
cf/cs	comma fault (splice), 42-43	rest	restrictive element (delete punctuation), 106
coh	transition or better organization needed for coherence, 84-85	shift	shifted construction, 98
comp	(1) comparison of two things, 99 (2) "comparison" of adj/adv, 93-94	sp	spelling error, 110-14
		sub	subordinate less important material, 171-73
d	inexact word (diction) or wrong level of usage, 224-28	syl	error in syllabication, 142
dg	dangling modifier, 97-98	t	tense error, 55-60
fig	faulty figure of speech, 226	tr/⌐⌐	transpose order of elements
frag	sentence fragment, 41-42	trite	triteness, 225-26
fused	fused sentence, 43	und	underline (italics), 140-41
id	faulty idiom, see Index	no und	don't underline
inf	too informal	vague	make clearer with details
logic	sound argument? see Index	vf	verb form, 53-55
mis	misplaced element, 96-97	w	wordy (deadwood)
mix	mixed construction, 43	ww	wrong word
ms	manuscript form, 80-81	x	obvious error
nonrest	nonrestrictive (insert commas), 106	∧	insert
		⌐⌐	transpose
num	error in use of numbers, 48-49		
o/∧	omission		

Some of these matters are complex; they may also be discussed elsewhere in the book. See the Index for additional page references.